Rights

Where do rights come from? Are they invented or discovered? What sort of rights are there and who is entitled to them? How can rights be protected? In this comprehensive and accessible introduction, Tom Campbell introduces and critically examines the key philosophical debates about rights.

The first part of the book covers historical and contemporary theories of rights, including the origin and varieties of rights and standard justifications of them. Campbell considers challenges to rights from philosophers such as Bentham, Burke and Marx. He also examines different theories of rights, such as natural law, social contract, utilitarian and communitarian theories of rights and the philosophers and political theorists associated with them, such as John Stuart Mill, John Rawls, Robert Nozick and Michael Sandel.

The second part of the book explores the role of rights-promoting institutions and critically assesses legal rights and international human rights, looking at institutions like the Supreme Court of the United States and the United Nations. The third part of the book examines how philosophies of rights can be applied to three Human Rights: freedom of speech, sustenance and self-determination. The final part of the book applies to the author's theory of 'democratic positivism', which combines a conceptual commitment to the institutional (or positivist) nature of rights with a normative commitment to democracy as the basis for determining their form and content.

Rights: A critical introduction is essential reading for anyone interested in the subject of rights and any student of political philosophy, politics and law.

Tom Campbell is Professorial Fellow at the Centre for Applied Philosophy and Public Ethics, Charles Sturt University, Canberra, Australia. He is the author of *The Left and Rights* (1983), *Seven Theories of Human Society* (1981) and *Justice* (2001).

Routledge Contemporary Political Philosophy

Edited by David Archard, Lancaster University
and Ronald Beiner, University of Toronto

Routledge Contemporary Political Philosophy is an exciting new series for students of philosophy and political theory. Designed for those who have already completed an introductory philosophy or politics course, each book in the series introduces and critically assesses a major topic in political philosophy. Long-standing topics are refreshed and more recent ones are made accessible for the first time. After introducing the topic in question, each book clearly explains the central problems involved in understanding the arguments for and against competing theories. Relevant contemporary examples are used throughout to illuminate the problems and theories concerned, making the series essential reading not only for philosophy and politics students but also those in related disciplines such as sociology and law. Each book in the series is written by an experienced author and teacher with special knowledge of the topic, providing a valuable resource for both students and teachers alike.

Also available in the series:

Theories of Democracy
Frank Cunningham

Forthcoming titles:

Equality
Melissa Williams

Public Reason and Deliberation
Simone Chambers

Toleration
Catriona McKinnon

Rights

A critical introduction

Tom Campbell

LONDON AND NEW YORK

First published 2006
by Routledge
2 Park Square, Milton Park, Abingdon, Oxon OX14 4RN

Simultaneously published in the USA and Canada
by Routledge
270 Madison Ave, New York, NY 10016

Routledge is an imprint of the Taylor & Francis Group

Typeset in Goudy by
Florence Production Ltd, Stoodleigh, Devon
Printed and bound in Great Britain by
MPG Books Ltd, Bodmin

British Library Cataloguing in Publication Data
A Catalogue record for this book is available from the British Library

Library of Congress Cataloguing in Publication Data
Campbell, Tom, 1938 –
Rights: a critical introduction/Tom Campbell
p. cm – (Routledge contemporary political philosophy)
Includes bibliographical references and index.
1. Human rights – Philosophy I. Title. II. Series
JC571.C225 2006
323–dc22 2005012397

ISBN 0–415–28114–8 (hbk)
ISBN 0–415–28115–6 (pbk)

To my delightful daughter
Emily Katherine Campbell
who knows her rights

Contents

Preface

Exploring rights[1]

This book is an exercise in critical philosophy, focusing on the concept of rights. Rights are claims to entitlements that individuals (and perhaps groups) can justifiably make on other people and organisations. Critical philosophy subjects concepts and theories to rigorous intellectual and moral scrutiny and, if necessary, rejects them as confused or harmful, or reconstructs them in a more coherent and useful form. In the case of rights this means analysing what is meant by 'rights', examining the role of rights in practical discourse, and assessing the benefits and drawbacks of a rights-based approach to morality, law and politics. It involves rejecting analyses of rights that are confused, ineffective, or morally unacceptable, and it includes recommending how rights are best understood, formulated and protected.

Critical philosophy is normative in that it makes recommendations as to what we should believe and what we should do. It is also theoretical in that it approaches its normative task in a systematic and intellectually rigorous manner. Critical philosophy asks questions and is sceptical about answers. In this book the broad and interconnected range of critical thought in relation to rights is addressed through five core questions: What are rights? Who can have rights? What rights have they got? What rights ought they to have? How can we best secure rights?

Answers that have been given to the first question (what are rights?) include 'normative controls over the behaviour of others', 'legally protected interests' and 'trumps'. This question concerns the meaning of rights. Formulating answers requires analysis of how we speak, and what we believe, about rights. However, as we will see, deciding which analysis of rights discourse to accept depends a lot on how we want to answer our other, factual and normative, questions.

Answers to the second question (who can have rights?) vary from 'living organisms' to 'all sentient beings' and 'only moral agents'. Assuming, for the moment, an answer to the first question along the lines that rights are mechanisms for the protection of significant interests, our answer to this second question will depend on what sort of beings can have interests and how important we think these interests are. A particularly divisive issue here is whether animals, as well as (all?) human beings have significant interests, and can, therefore, have rights. An extreme view is that all complex living organisms, such as trees and natural phenomena like deserts also have interests and, therefore, can have rights.

Answers to the third question (what rights have they got?) range from 'none at all', to 'those enumerated in the Universal Declaration of Human Rights'. If we take this question to be raising factual questions about what is the case in the world as it is now, then the answers we will be looking for are based on finding out about the laws, customs, political realities and experiences of people living in a particular time and place. My view is that what rights people have is a matter of social fact. However, most philosophers think that finding out about what rights exist is a matter of moral judgment, not social fact, derived, perhaps, from certain beliefs about human nature or from knowledge available to rational beings. Critical philosophers tend to be sceptical about that sort of answer to questions about whether a particular right (or set of rights) does or does not exist, although they accept that moral judgment is involved in answering the next question: what rights ought to exist?

Answers to the fourth question (what rights ought they to have?) may be, for instance, 'those that maximise human happiness' or 'those that are needed to protect them from majority oppression' or 'those that secure their status as a moral being'. We cannot settle this question until we have dealt with the first three questions. Once we are clear about what rights are, who can have them, and how we can know when a right exists, we can address what rights people ought to have. It is a matter of reasoning on the basis of our fundamental values and our knowledge of social and political life, to decide what rights ought to be established and protected. This question requires us to develop a normative social and political philosophy through which to justify one possible set of rights as being morally better than any alternative set.

Finally, answers to the fifth question (how can we best secure rights?) range from 'through democratic politics' to 'by adopting legally enforced bills of rights'. This is the most practical question of them all, particularly if we take the view that rights are mechanisms for protecting important (human) interests. The answer to the question of how best to secure rights depends on a further crucial question about rights, namely who has the duty to see that rights (or the vital interests they are established to protect) are secured. Central to the analysis of rights is the correlativity thesis that one person's right correlates with another person's duty, a duty which is, in some way, owed to the person who has the right. Talk of rights, and how to secure them, is, therefore, inextricably bound up with talk about these correlative duties, and how they should be allocated and enforced.

This, in turn, raises all sorts of empirical questions about what works best in securing the desired results. However, questions about this very practical aspect of rights all presuppose an answer to the first, analytical, question: what are rights? The illustrative answers given to the subsequent questions above all presuppose that rights are interests of sufficient importance to justify having institutionalised duties on the part of others to respect and protect these interests.

As we examine this set of questions and explore different sets of answers to them, it becomes clear that the discourse of rights in everyday life is highly flexible, variable and open ended, sometimes to the point of inconsistency and incoherence. It is possible to fall back on the technical legal discourse of rights, but this is itself diverse and often confused, and heavily dependent on moral discourse. Moreover, it is clear that competing ideologies, representing very different political outlooks, have their own favoured slant on rights. Rights discourses are inherently messy. It is, therefore, not possible to produce an account of rights, even at the most abstract level of analysis, that will meet with the approval of everyone. Yet it is possible, I believe, to arrive at a preferred analysis and theory of rights that is deeply rooted in the discourse and institutions of rights and yet enables us to express our own social and political viewpoint in a clear and coherent manner.

The approach to rights developed in this book concentrates on the distinctiveness of rights talk in political discourse generally. The aim is to distinguish the concept of rights from other normative concepts, such as right, justice and duty. This analysis takes rights as a form of legitimate political demand that requires establishing and maintaining mechanisms for the equal protection and furtherance of important interests. I develop this analysis in a theory of rights that should be acceptable to everyone who is committed to the equal worth of all human beings and the centrality of democracy in the determination of how such beings ought to live together, even if they disagree about exactly what rights they ought to have. The theory fastens analytically on what I find to be the distinctive aspects of rights discourse and, at the level of justification, emphasises the (not exclusive) connection between rights-based politics and the idea of the inherent, equal and high value of human lives.

This is an introductory book, in that it does not presuppose extensive prior knowledge of political philosophy. But it is more demanding than elementary. It is not a survey of the views of other philosophers, although these are noted and sometimes commented on as we progress. Rather it seeks to promote a vision of rights that is best suited to current domestic and global political problems. My approach to rights is part of a more general political theory I call 'democratic positivism', which is outlined in the final chapter. This theory is 'positivist' in emphasising the social, economic and political importance of having social and political rules embedded in effective institutions. It is 'democratic' in stressing the need to achieve agreement as to what these rules and institutions are to be through dialogue and democratic process. Rights are part of this picture in that they are means for securing the instantiation and sustenance of social norms that can provide the basis for securing legitimate interests.

Not all of these rules are legal rules. Rights are also constituted by interest-protecting societal rules that are enforced by community opinion and civil society. Rights are also the discourse in which political rules are articulated that establish the designated legitimating objectives of governments and other locations of political and economic power. In their fullness rights identify the defined justifying objectives of social and political life and are manifest in the rule-based legal, social and political mechanisms that turn these objectives into entitlements. This is a moral view that recommends an analysis of rights that promotes the benefits to be derived from the social and legal institutions informed and enforced by the distinctive contribution that rights can make to human wellbeing.

The underlying thesis of the book is that that the potential benefits of rights discourse is crucially dependent on combining moral affirmations about equal worth with practical means for ensuring implementation of this ideal. Rights require organised social, legal and political support, and their violation calls for effective remedies and systemic reforms. It is a mistake either to identify rights with the mechanisms for their implementation or to equate them with moral demands that are unrelated to securing institutionalised protections and remedies. Rights are, at base, best seen as morally justified demands for establishing and maintaining socially secured entitlements. As I see it, the distinctiveness of rights relates to their role in the institutionalisation of the moral commitment to equal worth, although they have lots of other useful social features.

There are many good reasons to treasure rights, so construed. Rights, as justified and secure entitlements enabling rights-holders to make effective claims on others, are valuable possessions that enable us to exercise freedom of choice and protect our own interests and those of other people. From the individual's perspective, to have rights is to be recognised as someone who counts and to have the social power to make a difference for other people as well. To have equal rights is a powerful basis for self-respect and a socially useful life.

Importantly, in the social and political sphere, rights provide a person-centred structure for thinking about right and wrong relationships in social, economic and political life. To be a rights-holder is to have an important social status. It counts for something. Moreover, rights, and their correlative duties, can provide security and stability to communal life by making clear what we can expect of each other and ensuring that these expectations are met. Additionally, from a constitutional point of view, rights play a crucial part in establishing the legitimate goals and methods of governments and other social and political institutions. At the same time, rights can secure some protection against abuses of political and economic power. In democratic systems, rights have a particular role in shielding vulnerable minority groups from the impact of the selfish, misguided or malevolent power of other more powerful minorities and from dominant majorities. No wonder we value rights.

Yet, there is much that can be said against rights. The benefits of rights are often exaggerated, especially when promulgated in abstraction from the availability of resources to implement them and in ignorance of the social consequences of giving rights to powerful minorities, rights that they can then use to protect their perhaps illegitimate interests.

There are a number of grounds for being sceptical about rights. Claiming and demanding rights often go with a narrow selfishness and egoism that emphasises the personal rather than the social aspect of our lives. In other words, rights can be seen as essentially self-centred and *egotistical*. Further, rights often lead us into litigious modes of argument that get in the way of sensible compromise and common humanity. People 'stand on' their rights, often to the detriment of others. Rights can be excessively adversarial and *legalistic*. Moreover, appeals to rights can be a way of avoiding deep moral argument and denying the relevance of the consequences of our conduct. In other words, rights can be simplistic, unrealistic and irrational, reducing moral discussion to an unenlightened exchange of irreconcilable demands that has been referred to as a 'clash of absolutes' (Tribe 1990). In other words rights can be unduly *dogmatic*. Finally, despite their egalitarian appearance, often rights contribute to injustice and inequality through the entrenchment of the power of those who are in a position to control and manipulate their content and operation to exclude and control others. In other words, rights can be in practice highly *elitist*.

Our task is to consider these criticisms of the egoism, the legalism, the dogmatism and the elitism of rights, and see if they can be countered without undermining our confidence in the prospect of a distinctive and effective rights-based approach to morality and politics. A first step in this process involves recognising that systems of rights and duties can serve many different goals, not all of which are desirable, and that even a good system of rights and duties can be abused and exploited.

It also requires us to appreciate that the importance of rights is tied in with the background justifications for having rights, in particular the way in which rights can both express and promote the moral importance of the individual person, and provide a basis for effective social cooperation. At its best, what is referred to as a rights-based approach to morality and politics is rooted in the belief that all human beings are of profound and equal significance and that their potential can be realised only in appropriate social settings. What has to be investigated is what sort of rights are the best means for giving practical, effective and secure social and political expression to this ideal of equal human worth. Indeed, these values provide the background justification for having systems of rights in the first place as well as being guides to what particular rights people ought to have.

Throughout the book, I argue that there are ways of responding to the often evident deficiencies of rights in the real world that do not involve abandoning the core conclusions as to the overriding moral significance of the individual person and the need for a social structure that recognises and secures that significance. While rejecting some versions of the idea of moral rights, according to which such rights 'exist' whether or not they are socially recognised and implemented. I contend that the concept of rights is sufficiently flexible to accommodate its critics, and can be fashioned and deployed so as to express the core value of equal human worth in ways that meld with the equally important insight that we are social creatures whose wellbeing is largely dependent on the patterns of cooperative social and political relationships that we can develop and sustain. Rights can be more than instruments to protect the individual against the collective, they can also be a means to harmonise the cooperative endeavours of social beings. Moreover, some form of rights discourse is essential to social democracy as well as to any version of liberalism that is fundamentally democratic. Rights are a common factor in most ideological disputes within democracies.

This critical exposition and revision of rights-based approaches to politics takes the reader on a journey that may be likened to a mountaineering expedition. The journey has commenced already, in this introductory preface, with a preview that suggests why it may be interesting, even exciting, to undertake such a journey. What is on offer is the chance to arrive at a broad perspective on the domain of rights, critically explore some of the complexities of rights-talk and rights-institutions, culminating in a particular outlook, the theory of democratic positivism, according to which rights are a human invention that can be formed, filled and institutionalised in law and social morality to serve the purposes that we chose together as individuals whose lives matter equally. Despite a measure of scepticism with respect to some current orthodoxies, the critical perspective thus turns out to be constructive and progressive.

My approach is inspired by the intellectual and moral programme of the critical philosopher, politician and rhetorician, Roberto Mangabeira Unger, a politically active Brazilian and professor of law at Harvard University, who seeks to engage us in what he regards as his 'primary vocation in a democratic and enlightened society: to inform us, as citizens, in the attempt to imagine our alternative futures and to argue about them' (Unger 1996: 1). Unger's philosophically liberating approach to politics invites us to articulate political conceptions appropriate to our circumstances, to fill these conceptions with a content that captures our current moral aspirations, and to take steps to enshrine this vision in the institutions and practices of our social and political systems.

I have also been influenced by the work of feminists such as Iris Marion Young and Robin West whose critical approaches to rights and justice involve not abandoning but 're-focusing' (Young 1990)[2] or 're-imagining'

(West 2003)[3] ideas of justice, rights and the rule of law that have been captured and diminished by particular undesirable ideological perspectives. These more caring and creative deployments of the discourse of rights provide a glimpse of the peaks that draw us on.

Continuing the mountaineering analogy, no significant summits can be reached without considerable preparation and some wearisome foot-slogging. The essential first stage of our expedition, undertaken in Part I of the book, analyses the discourses of rights. Understanding what has been rather disrespectfully referred to as 'rights talk' (Glendon 1991) requires us to develop a feeling for the language of rights, for the many contexts from which this discourse has emerged and in which it flourishes, and for the different uses to which it is put. This understanding cannot be had without some knowledge of the history of rights from their slender origins in the late medieval period to their pervasive centrality in our contemporary world. An historical perspective enables us to appreciate that rights as we know them are contingent historical phenomena with inherited meanings and contents, rather than cultural and historical universals, although this is what we may strive to make them for the future.

History also teaches us that, while rights have been used to found democratic states, to justify rebellions against tyrants, to punish war criminals and to arrive at peace agreements, they have also been used to justify horrendous wars, slavery, genocide, inequality and the rule of elites. With all this in mind, Chapter 1 explores the historically variable reputation of rights before going on to examine the principal arguments that have been made for and against a rights-based approach to politics in different eras.

Becoming aware of the historical and contemporary diversity of the role of rights requires us to undertake some rather strenuous analytical work as to the meaning and implications of rights discourse and the theories that purport to guide us through questions about what rights are, who can have rights, what their content is and should be, and how they are best put into practice. This work is undertaken principally in Chapter 2 ('Varieties of rights') which argues that the distinctive meaning of 'rights' is related in various ways to the concept of social rules, and in Chapter 3 ('Theories of rights'), which centres on the contrast between 'will' and 'interest' theories of rights that lead on to two competing ways of answering the five core questions addressed throughout this book. In Chapter 4, we survey the complex variety of rights and the contending theories of rights from an evaluative perspective that takes seriously the view that rights are instruments of contending and often incompatible political ideologies.

These chapters, which form Part I ('The Discourses of Rights'), take us through the foothills of the rights adventure to a base camp from which progressing further requires us to pay attention to what may be called the institutions of rights, that is, the social, political and legal mechanisms that can both embody and implement rights. Chapter 5 ('Legal rights') builds on the fact that much of the logic and power of the discourse of rights derives from legal contexts and argues that a great deal of the value of rights relates to their existence as social mechanisms for securing shared objectives through adopting agreed mandatory rules. Without endorsing the view that rights are essentially legal phenomena, this chapter takes us from an awareness of the somewhat humdrum role of legal rights in everyday life to the more dramatic terrain in which it seems that the prime mode of implementing rights is that of a constitutionally entrenched bill of rights administered by courts with powers similar to that of the Supreme Court of the United States, powers that enable legal elites to override democratically enacted legislation. This model, which is being increasingly adopted throughout the world, despite (or perhaps because of) its anti-democratic aspects, is presented as threatening rather than protecting certain fundamental human rights.

Chapter 6 ('International human rights') takes this quasi-legal perspective to the international level at which much of the activity around rights, specifically human rights, takes place. Indeed international human rights law is often treated as being synonymous with human rights, to the point where the whole idea of human rights has, for some, come to be identified with the 'International Bill of Rights' that encapsulates the core values and goals of the United Nations and large areas of international law generally. This chapter provides the occasion to deal with the problems that arise in dealing with issues of globalisation and cultural diversity as well as the dangers of identifying human rights with the compromises worked out in the process of forging international treaties and developing international enforcement mechanisms. At this point in the journey we can glimpse the ideal of a global system of universal rights capable of providing a basis for a peaceful and prosperous world and the dangers in seeking coercively to implement this model.

Concluding Part II, Chapter 7 ('Rights and civil society') considers what is omitted from the legal perspective, both national and international, and looks beyond current enthusiasms for bills of rights and international instruments, to the more basic mechanisms of civil society and public opinion, and their roles in articulating and implementing an acceptable and successful rights culture. Moving from the traditional idea that rights are primarily rights against the state and fall to be respected and implemented by states, this chapter looks at the need for protection against other sources of oppression and through mechanisms other than the state. The role of non-governmental and corporate organisations as both enemies and friends of human rights is examined in this light.

From here, using the techniques and distinctions developed along the way, we focus on particular rights as exemplars of the practical issues at stake that highlight the significance of rights for human wellbeing. This section of the journey (Part III) takes us through the stages that are generally accepted as representing the historical development of rights, from the ('first generation') political rights characteristic of the eighteenth century and more recently the International Covenant on Civil and Political Rights (ICCPR), through the ('second generation') social rights characteristic of some nineteenth century movements and the International Covenant on Social, Economic and Cultural Rights (ICSECR), to the ('third generation') group and environmental rights that are emerging as the focus of many recent global concerns. Together, the examples of free speech (first generation), subsistence (second generation) and group self-determination (third generation) bring out the variety, complexity and difficulties that emerge when we seek to identify and apply specific rights at the level of specificity at which they impact on people's lives.

Finally, in Part IV, we make a dash for the summit. A single chapter ('Democratic positivism') brings the themes of the book together to provide a particular perspective on rights. Drawing on the theory of democratic positivism, this concluding chapter combines conceptual, moral and political arguments in an approach to rights that meets the principal critiques of liberal rights and offers a framework for achieving just societies and political systems utilising the more social aspects of the discourse and institutions of rights.

The reader does not have to endorse the theory of democratic positivism to benefit from undertaking the intellectual journey. Indeed, from that particular summit it will be clear that there are other mountains worth conquering and that the principal benefit of the exercise is not to reach this particular peak but to have absorbed the knowledge and gained the experience that are required for any number of similar expeditions aimed at re-focusing, re-imagining, or simply re-assessing, rights.

At this point the analogy with mountaineering, already somewhat strained, must be abandoned altogether. In understanding rights and adopting a preferred theory of rights we are not participating in a sport, however enjoyable and rewarding that may sometimes be. Rather, in conducting a critical examination of rights we are putting ourselves in a better position to make up our minds about the most important moral and political issues of our time. It is with this in mind that we should address the core questions about rights: what are rights, who can have rights, what rights have they got, what rights should they have, and how should we go about implementing and securing those rights?

PART I

THE DISCOURSES OF RIGHTS

Chapter 1

The reputation of rights

Rights currently enjoy a highly favourable reputation. The discourse of rights is pervasive and popular in politics, law and morality. There is scarcely any position, opinion, claim, criticism or aspiration relating to social and political life that is not asserted and affirmed using the term 'rights'. Indeed, there is little chance that any cause will be taken seriously in the contemporary world that cannot be expressed as a demand for the recognition or enforcement of rights of one sort or another. It is not enough to hold that a proposal will lead to an improvement in wellbeing or a reduction in suffering, unless it can also be presented as a recognition of someone's rights, preferably their human rights. We live in 'The Age of Rights' (Bobbio 1996, Loughlin 2000: 197–214, Douzinas 2000).[1]

The pervasive popularity of rights has many sources. First, rights discourse is the language of *priority*. To have a right is to have something that overrides other considerations in both moral and legal discourse. It is a language of high normative force that demands our attention. In the words of one influential rights-theorist, Ronald Dworkin, 'rights are trumps' (Dworkin 1977: xi, 90–4, 364–8)[2] by which he means that treating people in accordance with their rights takes priority over promoting general utility or the common good. The premier political philosopher of recent decades, John Rawls, gives a similar priority to justice, and then goes on to make rights the principal ingredient in justice, ascribing a 'lexical' priority to basic rights that gives them the dominant position in his theory of justice (Rawls 1972: 43).[3]

A second, source of the popularity of rights discourse is that it is perceived as the language of *individualism*. While it is now common to speak of group rights (see Chapter 10), it is rights as the valued possessions of individuals that dominates the discourse. In their typical expression, rights are attractive because they express the great moral significance of every individual human being. A society that is based on rights is believed to manifest and affirm the dignity of each and every human life as something that is deserving of the highest respect. Rights affirm equal human worth (Vlastos 1962).

Third, rights are associated with the language of *remedies*. Rights are part of a practical discourse that not only invites but requires action to be taken in response to the claims that rights express. Rights are seen as providing protection against the abuses of the powers that be: officials, employers and, in particular, governments. Rights establish the institutional basis for achieving justice in social and economic relationships: normally, they allocate to rights-holders the capacity to control, possess or at least claim that to which they have a right. In legal contexts it is a truism that there is no right if there is no remedy. The moral discourse of rights also carries an imperative for remedial action where rights are not secured. Rights are not associated with simply aspiring to do what is good or desirable but demand restraint, redress and rectification of wrong done in violation of rights.

Fourth, rights discourse is *decisive*. Rights promise clear and relatively simple answers to difficult moral and political questions. By identifying those factors that are determinative in establishing what it is right and just to do in particular circumstances and excluding other considerations as being of lesser significance, rights promise clear answers to moral problems (Nozick 1974: 26–53). If a person has a right to do or have something then that settles the matter. Asserting rights cuts short debate and let us get on with our lives. This is both helpful for the individual and an efficient way of reducing social conflict and encouraging cooperation. It also provides a moral certainty that can be a comfort and inspiration.

Fifth, rights offer *security* through a system of social and political entitlements. Having rights enables us not only to enjoy certain benefits but to have the knowledge that they are ours 'by right' and cannot therefore be taken away at the whim of others. This is the theme that is expressed most strongly in republican theories of government which stress the importance of not being 'dominated' by those who have the power to arbitrarily deprive us of things we value (Pettit 1997). Security also features in even the most revolutionary calls to overthrow existing rights-violating régimes since the declared aim is normally to establish a new order based on a system that will provide and secure essential elements of wellbeing.

Finally, rights discourse is general in that it features the protection and furtherance of the interests of types of person rather than particular privileged individuals and, in the case of human rights, has the attraction of *universality* (Gewirth 1982, Ignatieff 2001: 3–12). Rights, particularly in the form of human rights, provide a basis for setting standards that apply to everyone in all societies and to every government, thus holding out the prospect of universal justice. Even where certain rights are ascribed to individuals of a particular type this is done on the basis of general rather than personal characteristics and no one who has such characteristics can be excluded from having the rights in question. The generality of rights offers protection to individuals against arbitrary treatment, a feature which is most evident when universal rights are ascribed to all persons irrespective of the race, religion, class or gender. Such inclusive rights are a focus for the moral critique and control of all social and political arrangements.

Drawing together these six points, we may say that rights discourse has a high reputation because it gives overriding importance to a heady combination of heightened personal worth, valuable and secure practical protections, decisive answers to disputed political issues and the hope of global justice.

Our problem is, however, that this encouraging profile of rights discourse coexists with substantial scepticism amongst those who have sought to define the nature and content of rights in practice. These sceptical critiques are explored in this chapter, first by reviewing cycles of optimism and disillusionment in the history of rights and then by taking a look at some current critiques which suggest that there are endemic problems if not with the idea then certainly with the practice of rights in their current form and content.

Historical ups and downs

There is nothing inevitable about the current dominance of rights in political discourse. The history of rights covers a comparative brief period of human civilisation (Edmundson 2004, chapter 1). Rights (as distinct from the more general ideas of right and wrong) were unknown to the Ancient Greeks and Romans, although the idea developed in the course of medieval theorising concerning Roman law (Tuck 1979: 5–31). Rights talk emerged in the medieval period with the notion of natural rights, a by-product of the idea of natural law.[4] Natural law was a fundamental concept of pre-modern western political philosophy. It represented the natural order of things, believed to be established by God as the creator of the universe, and applied in particular to the norms that govern the conduct of human life. According to natural law doctrine, human beings do not always follow the order ordained by the Creator, but they have the capacity to know and to perform that which the natural order requires of them, which is generally taken to mean living according to the nature that God has given them. This means that human beings have obligations or duties, such as to refrain from killing other human beings, telling the truth, and worshipping God, the fulfilment of which enables both the beneficiaries and those fulfilling their obligations to flourish as the social beings God made them to be (Aquinas 1979).

Conceptually it is a short step (although a major political advance) to say that those harmed by the violators of natural laws, such as the law against murder, have been personally injured or wronged. In the act of theft, for instance, not only has the violator of the natural law against theft disobeyed God, he has at the same time harmed and therefore wronged the victim of the theft. Thus, the person who did wrong, as defined by natural law, came to be seen as having also committed a wrong against the person injured.

Victims of human wrongs came to be seen as having a legitimate personal grievance against the wrongdoer and a personal claim for recompense or revenge against those who had injured them in violation of natural law. In this way the idea of natural rights emerged from the discourse of natural law (Ritchie 1895, Tuck 1979, Bagger 1989, Tierney 1997, Brett 1997).

Natural law was conceived as being God's law, and therefore of universal application. This means that natural rights can be held to exist even when the actual or 'positive' law of the land does not treat breaches of God's law as illegal. Further, everyone with the rational capacity to understand natural law has these rights and obligations for they are based on nature rather than convention or agreement. This applies also, perhaps especially, when the perpetrator of the violation is a ruler who is, by virtue of political power, immune from the constraints of positive law. Hence the emergence of the connection of natural rights with the idea of legitimate rebellion against those rulers who persistently injure their subjects contrary to natural law and thus violate their rights. Hence also the idea that it is the duty of governments to enact, adhere to and enforce positive laws that protect the natural rights of their subjects, as well as the obligation of subjects to obey such laws.

The genesis of rights in the idea of natural law may be a problem for the reputation of rights in a world that has largely lost the belief in a natural order ordained by God. Indeed, some philosophers doubt that the idea of rights (beyond positive or legal rights) makes much sense in a secular age marked by diverse cultures and detached from shared assumptions about the natural order of things (MacIntyre 1981). Yet the first major impact of rights on human history arose precisely at the time when philosophers were attempting to find a justification for natural law that does not depend on specific theological beliefs. Natural rights, derived from 'reason', 'self-evidence' or an empirical conception of 'nature' based on a study of how humans actually behave, were used to critique feudal society, justify rebellion against hereditary monarchs and establish 'republics' committed to such ideals as liberty, equality, fraternity and the pursuit of happiness, including the universal right to the ownership of property and participation on an equal footing in commerce and trade. It is the essence of this 'enlightenment' project of the seventeenth and eighteenth centuries that 'reason' not revelation, is the only defensible basis for morality and politics.

Secular forms of natural rights played a crucial role in the political discourse of eighteenth century Europe and its colonies, as manifest in the United States Declaration of Independence (1776) and the French Declaration of the Rights of Man (1789). In the American case, the prime inspiration was the work of English philosopher John Locke (1632–1704) who drew on the idea of a 'state of nature', that is society existing prior to the emergence of government, as a basis for working out what rights and duties apply once government is properly established. Locke himself, starting from a theological basis, deduced from his belief that a benevolent God is the creator of life, that human beings have the right to the life that God had given them, and the liberty to act so as to protect and sustain that life. Moreover, he deduced from the benevolent intentions of God, the implied right to such property as was necessary to support that life and those liberties (Locke 1988). On this basis, he concluded, governments are justified only in consequence of a 'social contract' or agreement between individual human beings in the state of nature to establish a sovereign authority or supreme political and legal power for the protection of these rights. An important corollary of the social contract, for Locke, is that governments retain their legitimacy only by observing and protecting natural rights they were established to protect. Citizens can justifiably disobey and overthrow such governments, as in the revolt of the American colonies against British rule, when that trust is broken through the governmental violation of natural rights.

In a very different cultural context, the emergence of rights discourse in France marked the transition from feudal social orders based on a version of natural law that included natural social hierarchies, to a bourgeois society in which, in theory at least, all have the right to participate in economic and political life within a public sphere, independently of social class or religious authority. Here the prime inspiration was provided by Jean Jacques Rousseau whose *Social Contract*, published in 1762, also drew upon the idea of the state of nature, in his view a time of noble simplicity marked above all else by spontaneous liberty but lacking the elements of economic development and moral consciousness (Rousseau 1968). In the state of nature the 'noble savage' lives a free but morally, socially and economically underdeveloped existence. Rousseau presents a vision of legitimate government as a system in which democratic participation reconciles the conflict between the restrictions of a civilised society governed by law and the need to protect the original natural liberty of individuals. This is achieved by making citizens the authors of the laws that bind them.

The revolutionary implications of Locke and Rousseau were developed and applied in the blunt and stirring rhetoric of the republican activist Thomas Paine, an Englishman who emigrated to the United States, which matched the mood of both the newly independent American colonies and the post-revolutionary régimes in France. Paine, in a series of remarkably modern political booklets attacking the monarchical-aristocratic system, that stressed social and economic rights as well as civil and political ones, captured the radical political implications of demanding that governments respect universal rights and declaring that they gain legitimacy only through obtaining the consent of the governed (Paine 1969).

The long term reputation of the rights articulated by Locke, Rousseau (although not the economic and social rights introduced by Paine) rode high on the economic and imperial successes of the emergent capitalist societies, but in the short term it suffered through what were seen as the excesses of some post-revolutionary societies, such as the domestic brutalities and subsequent military adventurism of France. A famous critic of the French Revolution, Edmund Burke, laid some of the blame for post-revolutionary barbarities on the notion of natural rights used by the revolutionaries to justify overturning the existing social order. The essence of Burke's complaint is that the abstract and ahistorical rights enunciated by the enlightenment theorists, such as 'the right to life, liberty and property', were so devoid of specific content that they could be used to undermine the social traditions and institutions on which real liberty is founded, as the descent of the French Revolution into anarchy, war and dictatorship amply demonstrated (Burke 1969).

The attractive simplicities of the rights to life, liberty and property that came to form the ideological foundations of modern market systems and legitimate the dominance of the new middle classes were overwhelmed by the miseries and inequalities of nineteenth century industrialised states in which freedom of contract and the uncontrolled private ownership of the immensely productive manufacturing processes, led, particularly in Europe, to demands by and on behalf of a suffering majority for social and economic justice. For some, like Karl Marx, this involves a repudiation of the entire panoply of natural rights on the grounds that they represent no more than the disguised interests of the bourgeoisie, that is those who own the means of production in a capitalist society. The equal right to property produced not only an inequality in what is owned by different individuals but brought about an exploitation, close to slavery, whereby one social class, the owners of the means of production, used the labour of another social class, the proletariat (those who earn wages by working for the bourgeoisie) to accumulated unmerited wealth (Marx 1977).

Marx predicted and worked for the abolition of the capitalist system of production and looked forward to a society in which human needs would be met by collective action free from the coercion of law and the exploitation made possible by private property in the means of production. In a communist society there would be no place for the abstract rights of the individual. Real, fulfilling freedom would be achieved for beings whose nature is inherently social and non-acquisitive working together in harmony. Rights have no place in a post-bourgeois society.

For other philosophers at the time, such as Jeremy Bentham (1748–1832), the widespread suffering amidst plenty that resulted from industrialisation generated political rights for everyone (or at least all men) so that the majority could exercise democratic control over an irrational system that produced such unnecessary misery. Bentham famously renounced natural rights as 'nonsense upon stilts' (Waldron 1987) on the ground that the idea of rights only makes sense in relation to an actual social and legal system rather than some imaginary natural order. However, he argued for a system of positive rights that would serve the general happiness by channelling selfish behaviour in socially useful directions. For Bentham, rights are a human creation which can play a beneficial role in any society that seeks to achieve the utilitarian moral objective of the greatest happiness of the greatest number through the enactment of laws that protect the individual and promote the general good, thus securing real benefits for all and hence serving the interests of the individual (Bentham 1982: 12–13).

Marx is the father of a certain type of socialism and Bentham of a certain type of economic liberalism, yet both endorsed the ultimate value of human happiness. This emphasis on the wellbeing of the majority had powerful appeal at a time when industrial capitalism was at its height. Indeed, until comparative recently, appeals to the 'common good' or the 'general welfare' or 'social justice' had as much if not more salience than the idea of respecting and protecting rights, which were often thought of, by Marxists and Benthamites alike, as obstacles to social and political progress which entrenched the power of property owners and established political elites.

The welfare provisions, including the social rights, that now exist in varying degrees modern democratic states emerged as a result of an emphasis on public goods, the general welfare and the common good, not as an expression of rights. In the United States of America the clash of rights and social wellbeing is epitomised in the so-called Lochner era when the Supreme Court repeatedly blocked the social legislation to protect exploited workers in the early decades of the twentieth century (*Lochner v. New York* 1905). Similarly, in the UK, traditional common law rights were used to frustrate the development of trades unions and employee protection. This led to widespread suspicion of rights, as is manifest in opposition to the European Convention of Human Rights (1950) on the grounds that it might restrict the development of the post-war welfare state and limit the traditional sovereignty of the parliamentary system that brought about such social improvements. Similarly current anti-globalisation movements point to the inequalities and suffering caused by the application of the private property rights of multinational corporations throughout the emerging global economy.

Nevertheless, rights have regained their present dominance since the Second World War, first under the auspices of the United Nations, and its Universal Declaration of Human Rights (1948)[5], which were created to avoid a recurrence of the inhumanities which characterised that war, and later through the growing international acceptance of a US legally-oriented culture and the perceived role of the Supreme Court in promoting racial integration in the 1960s. Fostered by the Cold War as an ideological battleground between West (civil and political rights) and the East (social and economic rights), the discourse of rights flourished. The idea of protecting rights through constitutional entrenchment and international organisations has blossomed further with the demise of the Soviet Union, the emergence of new states in Eastern Europe, and the development of the European Union and the European Convention on Human Rights. More recently, rights have also become crucial in the justification of the increasing readiness of the international community to intervene in the affairs of sovereign states engaged in genocide, the move to establish an international criminal court to deal with violations of certain human rights, and campaigns to eradicate widespread and severe poverty, especially in developing countries.

Despite the increasing hegemony of rights talk over its ideological rivals, it cannot be assumed that it has achieved universal acceptance. Notwithstanding the increasing similarities of form and substance of political and economic life sometimes equated with 'the end of history' and referred to as 'globalisation', rights discourse is often seen as part of a basically western and therefore parochial culture that is ill-suited to the needs and aspirations of majority of the world's population. Selective interventions in the affairs of culturally different societies on the basis of human rights violations, the imposition of particular forms of economic life associated with western freedoms that impoverish the majority of citizens in developing countries, and the capture of international human rights by governments with dubious moral standing, all serve to undermine the salience of rights talk in many parts of the world.

Even within western societies the pervasive impact of rights discourse is not always seen as a good thing. Part of this scepticism is based on an historical awareness that rights have not always served progressive purposes. It is a plausible, if contentious, account of the history of rights to say that they began as a means of expressing moral and political dissent and rebellion against existing authorities only to be appropriate by these very authorities as instruments for consolidating and justifying their powers to promote their own partial interests. By and large the doctrine of natural law has been supportive of political authorities. Rights are increasingly used to bolster a status quo that is supportive of gross economic inequality. Further, the use of human rights in the justification of constitutional provisions that permit judiciaries to override democratically enacted legislation is perceived by some to be a diminution of the capacity of the people to protect their interests against the minority who control that part of the legal process.

The authoritarian uses of rights and the sometimes dismal outcomes of rights-based régimes may be said to be aberrations, but it is clear that evil as well as good has been done under the mantle of rights. While this may sometimes be explained in terms of dishonesty, distortion and mistake, there are historical grounds for contending that rights do not always serve the high ideals that they seem to represent and may indeed contribute to the harms they purport to prevent. With this in mind, we turn to the critiques of rights that may offer some explanations for the chequered history of rights.

Four critiques of rights

Many criticisms of rights turn out to be directed at particular rights or at questionable assumptions about the nature of rights and can therefore be responded to without abandoning the discourse and institutions of rights altogether. Nevertheless the criticisms that have been and are made of the current conceptions and contents of rights are powerful and continuing. Some of these critiques are conceptual and focus on the alleged opacity, inconsistency and incoherence of the very idea of rights, while others have more to do with moral disagreements about the normative standards and values they involve. To these conceptual and moral concerns must be added other worries about the empirical theories underpinning different views of rights and their role in social life. Most critiques run together these conceptual, moral and empirical aspects, and we will often have to untangle them in order to understand and evaluate them properly.

The critiques outlined here and developed throughout the book are directed at the egoism, the legalism, the dogmatism and the elitism of rights. It will become apparent that convincing responses can be made to some aspects of these critiques provided that we are flexible in our thoughts about what constitutes a right and how they should be implemented. However, in conjunction, they present a powerful and recurring challenge to the reputation of rights that must be addressed if we wish to identify and retain what is most valuable in the rights tradition.

The egoism critique

The strong appeal of rights has something to do with their role in affirming the equal worth of all human persons. This is not true of all rights. Indeed many rights serve to foster and sustain inequality. Yet the idea that all human beings have some rights, and that some rights belong to everyone, is held to be an acknowledgement of the significance of every human life. However, this high evaluation of human life may be undermined by the selfishness or egoism of human beings which some see as underlying the very idea of rights. Rights are said to be individual possessions characteristically used to demand things from others and deny our responsibility for each other. Individuals 'stand on their rights' and thereby unfairly damage the interests of other people. Rights, it may be argued, are the treasured possessions of egoists, that is people who care only for themselves and give preference to their self-interest even when it conflicts with the welfare of others (Macpherson 1962, Wellman 1985, Glendon 1991, Hutchinson 1995: 89–95).

Moreover, however universal the form of some rights may be, historically rights have been largely confined to the public sphere, particularly the protection of the interests of citizens against the state, leaving those who live mainly within the private sphere, such as the family, largely unprotected, a circumstance that extends to employees in societies where economic production and distribution is also considered to be a private matter (Tushnet 1984: 1364–71, Horowitz 1988: 403, West 2003: 77f).

The very individualism of rights, as possessions of each particular rights-holder, can be seen as a denial of the irretrievably social nature of human existence and an invitation to a self-centred denial of social responsibility. Rights discourse fosters the false belief that what is central and worthwhile about human life relates to the qualities of the isolated person and their personal characteristics, to the detriment of a life that is embedded in social relationships and community values. Rights, it has been argued, encourage individuals to think primarily of what they can do by and for themselves, keeping others at bay, unless they can be of use to them, giving undue importance to their own choices, however self-centred these turn out to be, and encouraging a way of life that is as an ongoing and endless competition between individuals.[6]

Having rights predisposes the individual to make claims on other people, to blame other people for shortcomings that are in fact her own fault, and to deny their responsibility for each other's welfare. In consequences people in a rights-dominated society become alienated from other members of their society and end up finding little satisfaction in a world of private concerns in which they fail to engage with others in mutual responsibilities and shared goals. Looking only to their own welfare, individuals in rights-based cultures disown their past, cut themselves off from their contemporaries and ignore the wellbeing of future generations, ultimately to their own detriment.

Rights egoism also takes its toll on society as a whole. Reducing everything to individual rights ignores the significance of 'public goods', that is those benefits, such as peace, the rule of law and clean air, that can be enjoyed only by groups or communities and cannot be conceived of as simply an aggregate of individual benefits. Each individual seeking to maximise their own welfare contributes to a system in which all are worse off than they would be in a less competitive and more communally oriented society.

This catalogue of complaints about the egoism of rights can be broken down into two rather different themes, both of which go back to the work of Edmund Burke and his opposition to the French Revolution and both of which have been reaffirmed recently by 'communitarians' such as Michael Sandel (1982) in their criticisms of the liberal individualism of John Rawls's theory of liberal democracy (Rawls 1972).

The first theme of the communitarian critique is that liberal individualism is based on an unreal abstraction: the idea of the autonomous individual with an existence independent of all social relationships. The second theme of the communitarian critique is that abstract individualism encourages the values of individual autonomy over those of community wellbeing, thus endorsing selfishness and anti-social behaviour. The criticism of the abstractness of rights discourse is manifest in Burke's dislike of appeals to highly general principles, especially when taken out of concrete historical context and used to undermine established social norms, as exemplified by the revolutionary slogan 'liberty, equality, fraternity'. Burke was all in favour of liberty as he experienced it in the historically rooted practices of his own society, but not liberty as an abstract ideal (Waldron 1987).

According to Burke, abstract liberty encourages selfish conduct. He warns that liberty as a 'metaphysical right' is a form of licence in which 'everyone may do as they please', a prognosis that his readers believed to be confirmed as the French Revolution degenerated into bloody chaos. Social stability and human wellbeing generally is, in Burke's view, an inheritance to be nurtured, sustained and passed on as the cumulated wisdom of generations. Customary rights transcend the rationality of the individual and represents a partnership between generations. Denial of these social truths and enthusiasm for abstract principles of rights was, for Burke, a recipe for short-sighted partiality leading to an 'antagonistic world of madness, discord, vice, confusion, and unavailing sorrow' (Waldron 1987).

Two centuries later, Sandel is similarly concerned with the danger of metaphysical abstractions, particularly in relation to our ideas about what he calls the 'unencumbered self', the human being conceived in isolation from concrete social contexts. Sandel argues that human individuals cannot be understood, described and explained except in relation to their membership of particular social communities. He finds fault with the idea that society can be conceived of as no more than an aggregate of individuals who bring with them into society their personal attributes in the way that someone does when they join a club or subscribe to a magazine. Human beings are social creatures whose nature is constituted by their social relationships and group memberships. They do not form society, society forms them.

In dealing with this question we should note that the philosophical claim about the socially constructed nature of the human individual does not require us to take any particular view about whether that socially constructed individual nature is, in any particular community, egotistical, even in the weak sense that each person focuses predominantly on their own autonomy or wellbeing to the exclusion of others. The most that can be said to follow from the communitarian analysis of human nature is that individuals who have the self-awareness to conceive of themselves as being of independent worth and therefore as having rights achieve this consciousness as a result of a process of socialisation within a particular community. This is an important point when analysing the social preconditions of rights but it does not show that these preconditions are incompatible with a form of individualism that is not egotistical but allows for the possibility that the self-conscious individual is able to give equal weight to every person's interests and have rights-related wishes and desires that relate to the wellbeing of others as well as their own.

Sometimes community oriented critiques are little more than an attempt to turn the clock back to a more hierarchical form of society governed by tradition, as with Burke. In the case of Sandel and other contemporary communitarians, the political message is more directed at the significance of cultural identity and the importance of allowing diverse social groups to flourish in their own way. We can accept Burke's view that there is a need to embed the discourse of rights in actual social circumstances without rejecting the programme of reforming existing rights in a more egalitarian direction, as the enlightenment theorists demanded. Similarly we can accept Sandel's insight into the community grounding of most of what makes individuals while holding that this is perfectly compatible with believing in the value of each individual. However we do have to be able to demonstrate that the role we ascribe to these rights and the way we go about determining what they are, or ought to be, does not involve affirming abstract individualism or endorsing the view that human beings are in fact necessarily egotistical or that their selfish tendencies should be encouraged rather than moderated by the discourse and institutions of rights. The fact that egotistical people are selfish about how they use their rights does not mean that having and asserting rights is necessarily a selfish activity.

The legalism critique

One of the benefits of rights discourse is that it grounds moral and political debate in a pre-existing normative order of accepted rules and expectations in terms of which current issues about human relationships can be debated and resolved. If we have an agreed normative framework which tells us what our rights are then we can arrange our lives and relationships accordingly. In this way rights can bring social stability and a measure of protection to individuals against each other and against the state.

The connection of rights to an existing normative structure render them subject to the critique of law as an inefficient, unrealistic and even inhumane means of settling social disputes and furthering human welfare. Law, especially when focused on the conflicting rights of individuals, encourages an adversarial culture in which disputes are settled by an appeal to the rights and neglected duties of past conduct, without consideration of how problems and disagreements may be most beneficially resolved for all concerned. The discourse of rights is alleged to be at home in this legalistic setting and its use within moral discourse encourages adversarial and backward looking approaches to moral and political disagreements and a concern with fault finding which do little to solve the problems which beset genuine cooperative efforts to make then world a better place (Shklar 1986, Glendon 1991, Kennedy 2002: 588–603).

There is a strong analytical case for insisting that rights in their distinctive meaning should be understood primarily in legal terms, for it is in such settings that we can most evidently distinguish between questions about rights and more general questions about right and wrong generally. In law, to establish that you have a right to something is usually sufficient to win your case and obtain official backing for your claims against others. A legal finding that someone has acted within their rights is, in general, enough to end a dispute and to establish what must or may be done. There is no need to indulge in further argument and dispute about the matter. If I act in accordance with my rights I do not have to justify my conduct further before the law and therefore to anyone else. This is an important function of the discourse of rights. Rights are part of a normative system that enables us to settle disagreement definitively and to coordinate our activities without having to endlessly debate the rights and wrongs of the matter from scratch. Actual rights, especially legal rights, are a socially useful device for coordinated activity and dispute settlement.

This analysis of rights is 'positivist' in that it identifies rights with the existence of authoritative rules laying down rights and duties (Raz 1979, Hart 1961). Arguments about rights are arguments about whether there is or is not an established rule in an authoritative system of rules that entitles one person to act in a certain way or possess certain things and or requires others to permit or assist that person in such respects. It is arguable that the discourse of rights makes no sense outside such a system of social rules.

In fact, these rules need not be legal rules, for they may include the rules of customary or agreed morality within a society or social group. 'Moral rights' can be conceived analogously to legal rights as the rights that derive from the general accepted rules of a social group that are enforced by social approval and disapproval and the shared moral consciences of group members (Austin 1954). Other systems of rights relate to different sets of rules, such as those accepted by the adherents of a religious faith, or the rules set up by a voluntary association to constitute its existence and *modus operandi* as an association.

The difficulty with this positivist approach to rights is that right discourse is often used in ways that make no assumptions about pre-existing or anticipated positive rules. Thus human rights are used to criticise the actual or positive laws of particular countries. It may be, therefore, that this critique does not apply to all rights. This is a debate about the nature of rights that is taken up in the next chapter. There it is argued that we cannot distance rights in general from the characteristics of legal rights. The discourse of rights is legalistic to the extent that it is necessarily connected to some actual or contemplated system of rules, in which case the legalism critique cannot be easily dismissed.

The dogmatism critique

Rights promise clarity and definitiveness in the ordering of human relationships. The reverse side of this advantage is the charge that rights are overly dogmatic. Thus Glendon (1991: 14) criticises 'rights talk' for its absoluteness which 'promotes unrealistic expectation, heightens social conflict, and inhibits dialogue that might lead towards a consensus, accommodation, or at least the discovery of common ground'.[7]

This critique is applied at two levels. First it is used against the assumption that all moral disagreement focuses on the determination of what our rights and duties are, when in fact real moral issues are much more complicated than that, if only because it is sometimes morally right to waive our rights and decline to fulfil our duties (when, for instance, this might generate an unjust benefit to another person or unduly harm ourselves).

The dogmatism critique is also applied to the process of deciding the content of the rules that constitute the system of rights and duties to which appeal is made in moral and legal disputes. This is because rights are commonly associated with 'deontological' theories of morality, according to which moral knowledge is based on direct insights into the rightness or wrongness of different types of conduct, and morality is a matter of following a code of 'dos' and 'don'ts'. Killing and lying are wrong and ought not to be done. Kindness and honesty are right and ought to be practiced. Hence the morality of clear and strict commandments, prohibitions and rules. On the deontological approach, these rules are often taken to be self-evident or at least known without working out the consequences of their adoption. Thus, the deontologist will characteristically argue that it is not necessary to show that lying produces unhappiness in order to know that lying is wrong. This aspect of the dogmatism critique is that the rights approach to social relationships assumes that deciding what rights we ought to have is a matter of deciding what rights we do have in terms of some self-evident moral code which exists independently of the actual social or legal codes that can be observed to operate in actual societies.

Since the Enlightenment, many advocates of rights ultimately rest their case on bold claims to self-evident truths, often backed up by claims that they are universally acknowledged as such, but ultimately justified by an appeal to 'reason' or 'intuition'. This is not an inherently implausible approach to morality. All justifications have to stop somewhere and where better than in some undeniable truth such as that it is wrong to cause unnecessary suffering. We all know that it is always at least *prima facie* (that is in the absence of countervailing considerations) wrong to inflict pain. However, when it comes to drawing up rules for the complexities of everyday life, where other considerations always do play a part, simple truths are inadequate.

Moreover, many of the apparently incontrovertible self-evident truths of deontological morality are actually little more than tautologies which merely draw out the meaning of the terms involved. Aquinas, in expounding natural law, states that the good is 'what ought to be done', an incontrovertible statement that does little more than define the word 'good'. Even where there is more apparent content to the moral truth in question, as with the right to liberty, it is clear that 'liberty' here refers only to some liberties, namely those liberties to which we have a right. Many of the things we might want to do are considered to be 'licence', not liberty. 'Liberty' is therefore defined as doing those things that are not wrong to do. The substance of the right to liberty may be rendered self-evident by saying that *prima facie*, or other things being equal, freedom is a good thing, but it is far from self-evident to say that we have a right to freedom in all respects irrespective of its consequences.

And so, while a degree of self-evidence is inescapable in any 'objectivist' or 'moral realist' theory of morality, that is any theory which holds that there are indeed moral truths of some sort or another, it seems highly dogmatic to translate this into a series of rights that definitively establish the moral priorities of social and political life, especially if these are presented as 'absolutes' to which there are no exceptions. Indeed, as soon as we descend to the level of practicalities, it is inevitable that, in assessing what rights people ought to have, we must draw on the consequentialist reasoning that deontology seeks to exclude or subordinate. When it comes to defining the scope of a right to freedom of speech, for instance, it is inevitable that appeal is made to such consequences as whether or not freedom of speech, of a particular sort, will or will not lead to truth, and perhaps also whether or not that truth will enhance human wellbeing.

One response to this critique of dogmatic over-simplification is to say that we should adjust rights to bring about the best consequences. However, supporters of the rights approach protest that one of the points of rights is to limit the appeal to good consequences because this inevitably leads to the unwarranted sacrifice of the legitimate interests of some people to advantage others, usually the majority. Rights that are based on or give way to calculations of utility are not rights at all.

Thus Robert Nozick (1974: 26–53) holds that there are at least some basic rights, such as the right to do what I like with my own body provided that I do not interfere with the same right in others, that are simply immune to considerations of their good or bad consequences. There are some things, he insists, that we may never do to each other, regardless of the consequences, and from these basic rights he deduces the outline of an entire political system of extensive liberty in which taxation for the wellbeing of others is seen as theft and redistribution of wealth is a violation of fundamental rights.

More generally, the philosophical basis of the dogmatism critique is that moral epistemology (that is our capacity to gain knowledge of moral truth) does not justify claims to moral knowledge of the sort that much rights discourse seems to assume. We may agree in the abstract that we have right to life, liberty and property but this does not provide us with knowledge of how these rights are to be articulated or interpreted in practice. The further choices that are presented to us when we ask, for instance, whether the right to life is compatible with capital punishment, or requires free medical treatment for life-threatening illnesses, cannot be settled by an appeal to self-evident truths.

Of course, there may be other objective ways of determining what rights we have that are not consequentialist in nature. We can deploy Immanuel Kant's test of 'universalisability' to determine what rules we are prepared to endorse as universal rules by asking which maxims of conduct we as rational beings are willing that everyone follows (Kant 1948). Or we can deploy Rawls's method of deriving the content of rights from the hypothetical decisions of abstract individuals in an 'original position' (Rawls 1972). Or we draw on Alan Gewirth's deployment of the concept of agency to establish basic rights as the necessary prerequisites of being an agent (Gewirth 1982). However, it is highly optimistic to believe than any method will generate agreement as to the rights that we ought to have in the sort of detail that is required to articulate rights that can reasonably be used to settle actual social and political controversies in society.

The dogmatism critique holds that there is no epistemological methodology that can provide us with clearly justifiable specific answers to the issues that divide us as to the form and content of rights. Many of our most important rights are based on long experience of the unfortunate consequences that follow from certain types of conduct and the need to have clear and firm rules that do not allow exceptions that people can manipulate to avoid conforming to them. Complex and often consequentialist moral reasoning, rather than moral intuition, lie behind the adoption of many of the most important rights, including, as we shall see, human rights. Once these rights are adopted there is good reason to have them rigorously enforced without assuming that they are based on simple moral certainties. The utility of adopting clear and definitive rules should not be confused with the uncertainty that often underlies the decision as to which rules to adopt. Rights enthusiasts, the anti-dogmatist argues, ignore the facts of reasonable moral disagreement and continue to express their views about what rights we ought to have in simplistic absolutes.

The elitism critique

The claim that rights are elitist draws on the preceding critiques of the egoism, legalism and dogmatism of rights, by pointing to what happens when societies are organised on the basis of a system of interest-protecting rules that is rigidly adhered to. Inevitably, it is argued, the economically and politically more powerful members of a society can utilise these rules, however universally they may be expressed, to their own advantage.

This is evident, as we have seen, in the economic sphere, where outside a very temporary period of revolution, property rights serve to protect inegalitarian distributions of wealth. The right to own property does not mean that anyone does in fact have a right actually to possess property. Inevitably any property system tends to disproportionately benefit those who already have more than others. The elitist and inegalitarian consequences of rights applies particularly to those systems that predominantly use rules to protect the 'private' aspects of life, in which other people, particularly the state, are not permitted to interfere. Rights, it is said, serve to mark out a 'private' sphere in which individuals must be left alone to pursue their own goals in their own way. By staying out of such areas as family life, the state permits injustices and inhumanities to flourish in the so-called private or reserved areas in which children, women and dependent persons are defenceless against the superior financial and physical power of managers, husbands and carers. Rights enable the powerful to oppress the powerless. This operates in the economic sphere, where those with little money and few skills are exploited by those with superior resources and good fortune. It operates also in the family sphere where money and brute strength can dominate. All of which is exacerbated where racial differences mirror economic disadvantage and rights to equal treatment prevent legislative intervention to protect vulnerable minorities.

Other forms of elitism emerge from legalism of rights. Abstract rights in particular become, in practice, the domain of learned elites whose job it is to interpret and apply such rights. Particularly where such rights are entrenched in constitutional provisions, and judges become responsible for interpreting and enforcing some idea as to what constitutes 'the right to life' or 'the right to due process', this takes important decisions out of the hand of the elected representative of the people to the detriment of democracy through the imposition of the will of unelected officials (Bork 1990: 187–241). Similarly, in the international sphere, 'human rights' become the preserve of professional diplomats and inter-governmental elites even further removed from the lives of those whose rights they define and embody in international law.

More generally, we may consider that rights are elitist in the common emphasis they place on the significance of choice and autonomy in human life as distinct from the more mundane concerns that most people have about their material security, employment, health and personal relationships. Even where these more basic human requirements are equally recognised as rights, they tend to be justified in an elitist way by arguing that material wellbeing is important only because it provides the preconditions for autonomous living.

So it is that, while many see rights as a means for attaining a more just and democratic world, others see the same phenomena as an invitation to those with economic power to exploit their advantages or to those with political power to curb the capacity of majorities to protect their interests against entrenched elites.

Preserving the reputation of rights

The serious reservations about rights outlined above can be countered in many ways. Some of the critiques appear to be simply mistaken. For instance, it is often said that the discourse of rights ignores or plays down duties, giving rise to a culture in which people always think of themselves and seldom of others, confining their attention and concern to their own narrow circle of family and friends. This overlooks the fact that the primary use of affirming rights is to make a case for asserting that other persons have duties towards those that have or claim the rights in question. In other words, rights are characteristically correlative to duties. One person's right correlating with other person's duty, so that if person A has the right to do a type of action, it means that person B has a duty not to prevent A doing that sort of thing, and maybe to assist A in doing it.[8] The language of rights is also a language of duties.

Moreover, the most important rights are usually the rights that everyone has and often the duties are as widely spread as the rights with which they correlate.[9] And so, while affirmations of rights may take us no further than 'negative' duties (duties not to interfere in the lives of others), it is clearly wrong to say that the discourse of rights is, in general, in conflict or in competition with the discourse of duties.

Other criticisms, such as egoism, may be dealt with by extracting rights from the confines of liberal individualism insisting that the individual that is sovereign in the domain of rights may be a social individual, motivated by all sorts of altruistic and sympathetic desires and that the duties which correlate with rights are not confined to negative duties, duties not to cause harm to others, but include a panoply of positive duties, duties to render aid, assistance and cooperation. It is not necessarily the case that rights are seen in terms of my rights and your duties.

Further, many of the problems with rights may relate more to the rights we have than to the rights we might or ought to have. If certain property rights lead to unacceptable inequalities then they may be modified or even abandoned in favour of other rights. Moreover the rights we then adopt need not be of the abstract and highly general form that has been assumed to be characteristic of rights. In fact rights may be highly specific and truly determinative of what ought to be done, albeit such rights have, inevitably, more limited scope.

Also there may be no need to hand over the articulation of such rights to a small minority of rights specialists who dominate the authoritative interpretation of the rights we adopt. If, for instance, we take the right of self-determination seriously, as perhaps, 'the right of rights' then we may consider taking some control over those aspects of rights that tend to render them elitist (Waldron 1993: 211–31).

However, it is not at all clear how such proposals would turn out. Perhaps duties would not get specified and fulfilled if we did not emphasise the priority of rights over the general welfare in their abstract and highly general form. Perhaps inequality would be worse, and prosperity much reduced, if there were significantly different property rights. Indeed, these proposals may not even be consistent with each other. More precise rights, for instance, might mean less expansive duties and so less mutual benefit, and this might require more control by technocratic elites. These are just some of the challenges that confront those who wish to reconstruct rights in a way that sustains their advantages while minimising their associated drawbacks.

Whatever view we take of these debates, this brief analysis of the fluctuating reputation of rights brings out the complexity and plasticity of the terminology of rights (and their associated duties). Any attempt to philosophise about rights takes us into a minefield of shifting definitions and alternative formulations that point to the diversity of normative discourse of rights, duties, liberties and wellbeing. In order to make further progress in working out what we think about rights, we need to consider in more detail the variety of forms in which rights may present themselves, the variety of rights bearers there may be, the diversity of contents that rights may have, and the many different ways in which rights may be implemented.

Chapter 2

Varieties of rights

A principal objective of this book is to provide analyses of rights discourse that will put us in a better position to understand, criticise and utilise the language of rights in all its diversity. This requires us to attend to the variety of things that may be meant when we speak of rights and how these various meanings can be tested, deployed and interpreted. This, in turn, involves an examination of the social, political and legal contexts in which the discourse of rights is used and the different purposes to which it is put. Rights talk does not exist in a social vacuum and its meaning, implications and significance vary with the context in which it is deployed.

Further, there is no autonomous philosophical point of view, or as we might say no Archimedean point, from which we can determine the 'essential' or 'correct' concept or analysis of rights. There is no such thing as the 'intrinsic nature' of social phenomena such as rights. There is no morally neutral analysis of the concept of rights. Rights, like all political discourse and institutions, are socially constructed in diverse and dynamic ways. More particularly, social concepts, such as rights, that have a favourable reputation, tend to be expanded to take in all the positive things that the users of the discourse favour. Being aware of this puts us in a position to develop a flexible approach to rights discourse and better utilise the various methods of instantiation and implementation that different sorts of rights, and different approaches to rights, involve, some of which are better suited to pursuing some values and goals than others. Ultimately we will want to adapt and adopt those aspects of rights discourse that enable us to express our own moral and political views most clearly. I suggest that, when doing this, we should have regard, in the interests of clarity and precision, to the distinctive uses of the discourse in question.

These points relate directly to our first core question: the meaning or definition of rights. It is always important to define our terms just in order to make it clear how we are using what is often vague and ambiguous language. Yet if we are to engage in debate about rights we need to be aware how the discourse has developed and how it is deployed both in ordinary social and political contexts and in the more technical contexts of law and political philosophy. Here we should be constrained by general usage and by the power of analyses to capture what those who use the discourse mean when they say certain things. Some analyses of terms will explicate actual discourse more accurately than others. However, the empirical constraints of actual discourse are complicated by the fact that what may appear to be the same discourse is understood differently by individuals and groups within the same society, with greater variations arising as we widen our horizons to include other societies and other languages. Nevertheless, the realities of social discourse and the institutional arrangements that exist within a society provide the context in which we should work out our own philosophy of rights.

Faced with the multiplicity of social understandings that characterise the discourse of rights we could simply note the differences and what they tell us about the concepts used by the specific individuals, groups and societies in question, or we could recommend and develop a set of meanings that best promote the sort of social relationships that we would like to see established and maintained in our own society, and perhaps in others as well. At this point we move from description to prescription and become participants in an ongoing social process wherein the language with which we communicate is developed to suit our emerging values and circumstances. That is the path taken in this book.

It might be expected that a chapter on the variety of rights would first explore the differences in content between substantive economic, social, political, religious and welfare rights, such as the right to own property and the right to drive a car. That, however, comes later. At this stage we are concerned with our first question (what are rights?) in the hope that an understanding of different ideas about rights in general will make us better prepared to identify important differences between the operation of the substantive rights that feature in different spheres of social life.

In exploring the variety of rights it is important to keep in mind three logically distinct types of enterprise: the analytic or conceptual (stipulating meanings and analysing discourse), normative or evaluative (setting values and making prescriptions) and the descriptive or empirical (making and testing factual claims). The first step in any debate about rights is to determine whether we are dealing with analytical issues of meaning or terminology, or commending one thing as being more desirable or more important than another, or disputing matters to which a factual answer may be given or sought. In this chapter we are primarily concerned with conceptual questions but, in view of what I have just said about the moral and empirical context of conceptual analysis, in ways that leads on to a consideration of the normative and descriptive issues that lie behind and beyond the purely analytical distinctions that are drawn in identifying the varieties of rights.

Right and rights

The immense popularity of rights discourse encourages a tendency to enlarge the domain of rights to take in all important moral and legal values (Sumner 1987: 1–14, Thomson 1990, Wellman 1998).[1] This expansion applies not only to the multiplication of particular rights, but to the concept itself which is increasingly enlarged to the point where it swallows up associated but distinctive terms such as right, justice and equality. In order to retain the distinctiveness of rights it is important to hold onto the distinction between saying that someone has a right to do something and to say that they are right to do it. There is an important difference between saying that I have a right to do something and that I am right to do it. I may act within my rights but be morally wrong to do so. It makes perfect conceptual (and often moral) sense to say, for instance, that a person has a right to keep the money she has inherited but would be wrong not to give some of it to her poor relatives. This means that there is at least sometimes a right to do wrong (Waldron 1981, Edmundson 2004: 133–142).

It may be said that this is simply a matter of distinguishing between legal and moral rights and duties. In the above kind of case, it may be said that a person has a legal right to her inheritance but a moral duty to give some of it to her poor relatives (who have a moral right to receive part of the inheritance). However, the distinction holds in the moral realm as well, for we may agree that a person has a moral right, for instance, to retain the money she has worked hard to earn, but ought (in a moral sense) to give some of it to her poor relations, perhaps because, in moral terms, her merit is outweighed by their need.

Generalising we may say that because someone has a right to do something does not mean either that they are right to do it or that they are wrong not to do it. Sometimes the morally right thing is to waive your rights or not to demand them. This means that asking what it is right for me to do is not the same thing as asking what I have a right to do, whether or not the right is a moral or a legal one. Rights, if relevant, always have some normative force but they are not always morally or legally decisive. The small linguistic difference between 'right' and 'a right', or between 'right' and 'rights', marks a huge conceptual distinction of considerable practical significance.[2]

One possible analysis of the difference between rights and right is that statements of rights are moral generalisations about what it is *usually* right to do, whereas statements of right and wrong are related to the particular circumstances in question. This 'generalisation thesis' about the relationship between right and rights fits the fact that assertions of rights are characteristically general or universal in form, indicating, for instance, which categories of person have a right to do which sorts of things. This can be taken as a basis for giving guidance. An example would be that people have a right to be told the truth means that we ought usually to tell them the truth. Assertions of right, it may be argued, usually pertain to the issue of what we ought to do in a specific and particular circumstance, assertions of rights represent guidelines as to what is usually the right thing to do. So, we may agree that while it is generally the case that persons ought to be told the truth (this being what it means to say that they have a right to be told the truth), in a particular situation it may be right to tell them lies. This is because the general norm of truth telling is subject to and may be overridden by the complexities that arise in particular situations. This means that rights are always *prima facie*, that is they provide moral reasons for action, but these reasons may be overridden by other considerations in specific circumstances (Ross 1930). This generalisation thesis might explain how it can make sense to say that a person is right to deny someone their rights.

This is an interesting line of thought but it seems quite mistaken in terms of actual discourse. The idea that statements of rights are generalisations about what it is usually right to do seems very misleading as a representation of how the discourse of rights works. We do distinguish between general action-guiding maxims such as 'tell the truth' and 'be kind', and particular judgments which involve bringing all relevant moral maxims to bear on a particular situation. But the distinction between general maxims and particular judgments has little to do with the distinction between rights and right. In fact, it goes to the core of the discourse of rights that, although (almost always) general in form, rights apply with direct and sometimes overriding force to particular circumstances. Indeed, a central function of rights discourse is to generate clear cut decisions about how to act in particular circumstances. If people have the right to be told the truth then it is not for anyone else to make the decision whether or not they are to be told the truth on a particular occasion. The standard purpose of having and asserting a right is to take the issue out of an 'all things considered' approach whereby those involved weigh up all the morally relevant pros and cons before deciding what to do.

This response to the generalisation thesis is sound, but something of an overstatement. After all, have I not just pointed out that it is sometimes right to ignore or violate a person's rights? We cannot, therefore, say that rights are always the last word in particular situations, although that is a common mistake to make. Yet a failure to treat persons in accordance with their rights is not the same thing as simply deciding that a moral maxim ought not to be followed on a particular occasion. Rights have a stronger purchase on particular decisions than moral guidelines or generalisations. Rights feature as more or less powerful reasons why we ought to treat a person in a particular way rather than as mere guidelines to help us decide what to do. This needs explanation.

Another way of analysing the difference between right and rights is to say that right (and wrong) is the language of morality whereas rights are part of the language of law. The reason why it is sometimes right to violate rights is that it is sometimes morally right to ignore or break the law. The reason why rights are relevant but not decisive in moral deliberation is that it is normally but not always morally right to conform to the law. I shall call this 'the legalist thesis'.

The idea that right is a matter of morality and rights are a matter of law fits readily with the idea of law as a system of rules that establish decisively what people must and must not, or may or may not do. Our moral ideas about right and wrong conduct are, by political and legal processes, partially translated into official requirements and permissions that reflect morality but do not exhaust it. Moreover, law routinely operates in such a way as to override the individual's views as to what is morally right and wrong. These moral views may or may not have been taken into account in the process of establishing legal rules, but once established, law takes official and usually moral and legal precedence over the moral views of individuals. That is its function. Consequently, it is generally considered unacceptable for people to disobey a law simply because they believe it to be morally wrong. Talk of rights and duties fits easily into this legal mould, while the discourse of right and wrong operates in a different way to express our view as to what we ought to or may do, or to criticise what the law does or does not require, but not to override the rights of other people or excuse the individual from performing his or her legal duties.

There is no doubt that rights discourse in its current manifestations, has a distinct legal flavour. Thus the relationship between rights and rules is apparent and easily expressed by saying that rights are inseparable from rules that state the obligations that some people have to other people. Rules of this sort may be said to 'constitute' rights by creating general duties between persons. Thus, the correlative relationship between rights and duties, whereby one person's rights correlate with other people's duties, is created by rules that establish not only what people's duties are but to whom these duties are owed, namely the rights-holders. Moreover, rules, especially legal rules, have authoritative functions with respect to settling disputes and justifying coercive intervention in the lives of others (who have violated the rules). This explains the ways in which the language of rights and duties takes practical priority over the individual's moral beliefs about right and wrong.

The legalist thesis is closer to the mark than the generalisation thesis, for there does seem to be a close relationship between rights and rules. However, the legalist thesis goes wrong if it fails to take into account the fact that there are social rules that are not legal rules but serve a similar function in social discourse, and indeed are often made into legal rules. However important legal rights may be in explaining the nature of rights, not all rights are legal rights and, as we shall see, morality has at least as much a claim to the language of rights as does law.

Rights and rules

What moral rights and legal rights have in common is their relationship to rules. It is this relationship which explains why rights are often thought of as entitlements and therefore as matters that can be known and applied without having a full blown moral debate before deciding what it is right to do. On this view, rights are those things to which we are entitled in the light of the rules that authoritatively apply to the situation in question, something that applies both in a formal system of legal rules and in the informal rules embedded in the social practices, morality and customs of particular societies.

A rule, in this sense of a social norm, is a statement that, in a certain type of situation, a certain category of person (P) may, may not, or must, or must not, do a certain type of action (A) (Schauer 1991, Alexander and Sherwin 2001). Often such rules include reference to punishments or sanctions that will be inflicted on P if he violates the rule, but this is not always the case. Rules of this sort have a social existence when they are actually followed by most people in a society or group to which they apply and when those who do (or do not) perform A are routinely the object of hostile comments and attitudes. For a rule to have a social existence there must be criticism of those who do not conform to the rules and, to a lesser extent, approval of those that do (Hart 1961). A principal function of social rules is to provide the basis for making decisions in the case of disagreements between individuals and groups, thereby reducing conflict and fostering coordination between them. This is achieved through what is sometimes referred to as the 'exclusionary' force of social rules, by which is meant that they require us to apply the rule to the exclusion of other considerations that might otherwise have been relevant (Raz 1975: 35–48, 1986: 186–187).[3]

Thus the traffic rule that lays down a maximum speed of 30 miles per hour requires us to exclude factors such as our need to get to work on time when deciding how fast to drive. Or the moral rule to keep promises excludes us from taking into account the inconvenience and expense of keeping a promise. Social rules are not merely 'rules of thumb' to be used as general guides as to what is normally the correct thing to do but actually require us to exclude factors that it would otherwise be reasonable to take into account in an 'all things considered' decision (Schauer 1991: 74–82).

Such 'exclusionary' force is rarely total. The exclusion in question is 'presumptive' rather than absolute (Schauer 1991: 197) but is nevertheless an essential ingredient in the operation of social rules.[4] If rights are related to rules of this sort then this goes some way towards explaining the value of rights to the individual rights-bearer who is thereby protected from being dealt with according to someone else's calculations as to what would be, overall, the best thing to do. Rights, if seen as derived from social or legal rules, give us the assurance that we will be treated in a particular way to the exclusion of other considerations and enable us to place reliance on each other's conduct in that respect.

Assuming that it is plausible to argue that the distinctive language of rights is tied to the existence of social norms that form the basis for the rights claims in question, we can distinguish between legal rights that derive from legal rules and social rights that derive from the accepted customs and practices whose violation attracts general criticism. But what are moral rights?

One view of moral rights is that they are to be equated with social (or sometimes 'societal') rights. This gives a clear and useful distinction between legal and moral rights, and does capture what is often meant by 'moral rights'. We say that your mother has a moral right, in this societal sense, that you visit her in hospital because there is a general assumption backed by strong social opinion that this is what sons and daughters ought to do. There are other moral reasons supporting such acts, but to speak of it as a right adds this dimension of socially recognised rules as a reason for action. This is what makes it appropriate to speak of the mother's rights rather than simply saying that the children are wrong not to make such a visit. These sorts of moral rights can be termed 'social rights', although it is perhaps better to call them 'societal rights' to distinguish them from the common use of 'social rights' to refer to those rights that relate to welfare and family matters, as in the International Convention on Economic, Social and Cultural Rights (United Nations 1966b). Sometimes societal rights are called rights of 'positive morality', that is the morality that expresses public opinion as to what is acceptable or unacceptable conduct (Austin 1954: Lecture V).

This is not, however, the only common meaning of the term 'moral rights'. The discourse of rights also features in the evaluation and critique of existing societal and legal rights. This leads many philosophers to conclude that there are rights that exist independently of existing social and legal norms, rights which can be used to justify these norms. This is an attractive and very popular view. It makes a lot of sense if we have agreement that there is an authoritative set of rights that can be discovered through our, or some authority's, knowledge of 'natural law', or by the exercise of moral 'intuition', or our capacity for moral reasoning, but I shall argue that, in the absence of such agreement, it is more satisfactory to interpret this sort of moral rights talk as a matter of giving reasons for asserting what legal and societal rules there ought to be. To claim that something is a moral right (if it is not a statement about existing societal rights) can be understood as a claim that certain social or legal norms *ought* to exist. This use of rights discourse, which has been described as the expression of 'manifesto' rights (Feinberg 1973: 67), focuses on the moral justification of demands for the instantiation of social and political rights. It makes no assumption that there are pre-existing moral entities, called moral or natural rights, that exist independently of justified social and political rights but it does assume that morally persuasive reasons can be given for creating and sustaining social and legal rights. Unless 'moral rights' is just another term for social or societal rights, such rights can be seen as prescriptive affirmations about what rights there ought to be.

A completely different view, but one that is also in accordance with the logical relationship between rights are rules, is that moral rights derive from moral rules and that moral rules have a real existence that is independent of all empirically observable laws and social practices. This is a straightforward position to hold if it is associated with a theology in which God is the creator or legislator of those rules and the content of these rules is revealed to us by some religious authority or text. Such beliefs were standard in the time when natural rights were constructed. Subsequent philosophy has sought ways of replacing the role of God in this regard by providing other ways of establishing the existence of such moral rules, such as through an appeal to 'reason' or 'self-evidence'. If this form of moral 'objectivism' is successful, then moral rights can be defined in relation to such rules. I shall call this the ontological thesis because it asserts that moral rules have an objective reality that is independent of human beliefs and practices (Aquinas 1979, Finnis 1980, critiqued in Mackie 1977).

Generally, such ontological approaches have had considerable success when emphasising that certain rules are clearly more justified than others, but they have done so by an appeal to certain general values, such as autonomy or wellbeing, which can be readily understood and appreciated. This in itself does not establish that there are moral rules that already exist in such a way that they can be appealed to as a basis for claiming a moral right in anything like the way that we can appeal to the realities of existing laws or social practices. The shadowy and intangible idea of moral rules as things existing in detachment from such empirical realities tends to make this version of moral rights subject to much scepticism, particularly if it is claimed that we can have genuine knowledge of what these rules actually are. And if the ontological thesis is interpreted as a claim that rules are or are not justified by the extent to which they promote certain objective values, then this can be incorporated within the manifesto thesis, for no claim is being made that there are ontologically distinct moral rules, only that there is moral (disputable and controversial) justification for adopting certain rules.

We are left, therefore, with three radically different views of what moral rights are, the first identifying moral rights with non-legal social practices (societal rights), the second, with the rights that ought to be embodied in legal and social rules (manifesto rights), and the third (ontological rights) which assumes the societally independent existence of a set of moral rules about which we can acquire reliable information. In general I adopt the second interpretation, that the discourse of moral rights is best seen as a moral evaluation as to what social or legal rights people ought to have (Nagel 2002: 33). However, much of the analysis of rights which follows can be applied to the two other views as well for all incorporate some sort of a role for rules in the analysis of rights.

Accepting that rights derive from rules is a necessary but not a sufficient step to identify rights as distinct from the rest of normative discourse. Not all rules have to do with rights (Lyons 1969, Flathman 1976, Feinberg 1973, Campbell 2004: 153–70). Many codes of law and ethics in human history lay down duties without any mention of rights. Such duties are owed, if to anyone, to God or the State, not to rights-holders. Many rules simply lay down how we must behave without bringing in rights at all. Thus the duty to observe speed limits does not directly involve the rights of others, while promise keeping does. The difference between the two types of duty is that a promise is made *to* someone and that person has the right that the promise be kept. Only where rules prescribe duties that are in some way owed to another person do rules establish rights.

What 'owing to' actually means in practice is often unclear and controversial, but it is an important starting point when trying to distinguish those rules that establish rights that, in the case of rights-creating rules, some sort of duty or obligation is owed to another person. It is that person who has the right in question. With this in mind we can proceed to outline a typology of rights based on the different sorts of duty-imposing rules and the different sorts of duties that may be owed to other people. We return to the philosophical bases of these duties when we consider competing theories of rights.

A typology of rights

Analysing rights in terms of rules enables us to make some crucial distinctions between types of rights with respect to their form as distinct from their content. The classic statement of this typology was made by the legal theorist Wesley Hohfeld whose analysis has been enormously influential. The formal typology of rights set out below departs from his terminology where it may mislead and does not go into all the complexities of his scheme of 'jural relations' (Hohfeld 1919, see Kramer, Simmonds and Steiner 1998: 7–100) but it identifies the crucial and enduring parts of his analysis.[5]

First there are pure or formal 'liberty rights'. A person has a liberty right when there is no rule requiring her to do (or not do) or have (or not have) that to which she has a liberty right. Thus I have a legal right to feed the birds if there is no law prohibiting me from feeding the birds so that I am 'at liberty' to do so. In a liberal society in which there is an assumption that a person may rightly do whatever is not forbidden, liberty rights are taken for granted and not given much emphasis. Usually they have social significance when someone or some group is excepted from a general rule, as when the police but not members of the public are free to break the speed limit (in defined circumstances). Perhaps for this reason Hohfeld described this sort of relationship in law as a 'privilege'.

Formal or pure liberty rights (Hohfeldian 'privileges') relate to rules only in the negative sense that they assert the non-existence of relevant rules and for this reason they are sometimes not regarded as rights at all. This may be no more than a matter of semantics to be settled by arbitrary definition, unless what is being argued is that liberty (so-called) rights are never of any significance to actual people. In fact, formal liberty-rights can be of much wider import than in granting the privileges of being made an exception to general rules. In societies in which more and more rules are being enacted, it is important to defend the general assumption that a person is entitled to do whatever is not forbidden and entitled not to do whatever is not required by the relevant authoritative rules. This is a central ingredient of freedom, and one that gives rise to the thesis that liberty is increased simply by reducing the number and scope of laws.

Formal liberty rights do not in themselves generate any correlative obligations. They are nothing more than the absence of obligation on the part of the rights-holder (Hobbes 1996). What are more usually called liberty rights provide rather more protection for the actions of individuals by involving a correlative duty on the part of others at least not to interfere in the action or situation of the rights-holder. These substantive liberty rights are a species of what Hohfeld calls 'claim rights' because they make claims on the actions of others, thereby restricting the pure liberty rights of others. We must distinguish formal or pure liberty rights (Hohfeldian privileges) from substantive liberty-rights or other 'claim rights' that have some sort of correlative obligation. Following Dworkin (1977: 188–92), we may think of formal or pure liberties as 'weak rights' and claim rights, such as substantive liberty rights, as 'strong rights'.

Most rights discourse is about Hohfeld's claim rights and their correlative obligations (which fall either on some or all other persons). Indeed, rights are often stated in terms of what these other obligations are. The right to life is at least the right not to be killed by other people (or perhaps by oneself) and perhaps the right to be given the means of subsistence, if this is necessary for survival. This takes us to another crucial distinction, in this case between those claim rights where the correlative obligation is to refrain from intervention in the activities or situation of the rights-holder (often called 'negative rights') and those where the correlative obligation is to do something which is of assistance to the rights-holder (called 'positive rights').[6] In the case of the right to life, that positive obligation might be to render life-saving aid.

Here yet another distinction is crucial. This relates to what is involved in the correlative obligations of positive rights. Respecting the right to life may involve directly assisting the rights-holder (as when rescuing a drowning person), but it may also involve protecting the rights-holder against the harmful actions of others (perhaps by restraining others from drowning the rights-holder, or perhaps by erecting a fence to prevent access to the water).

Such duties to protect rights-bearers from the rights violations of others are often spoken of as 'the protection of rights', a duty that is usually given to states (Galligan and Sampford 1997: 53). Much controversy about rights relates to the extent to which the state should intervene to protect rights. Even more controversial is the extent to which states also have duties to directly further the interests of rights-holders by providing direct assistance: a duty of promotion or furtherance rather than simply the protection of rights.

All these distinctions are of major significance when dealing with questions about rights. Significant ambiguities occur when we speak of rights without specifying which form of right we have in mind: formal liberty rights or substantive claim rights (negative or positive). For instance, the issue of whether or not rights encourage egoism may depend ultimately on whether we think of rights as typically formal rather than substantive and, in the case of claim rights, negative rather than positive, and in the case of positive rights, protective or promoting. Where the stress is on positive claim rights and third party protection and promotion of rights, then the focus shifts to ways in which individuals and groups should and do act for the benefit of others.

There are further complexities. The formal liberty and substantive claim rights have in common that they apply directly to conduct and possessions: they are rights to do and to have things. However, there is a distinct form of rights that apply to acts and possessions only indirectly, by giving people the capacity to change other rights and duties. These rights Hohfeld and others have referred to as 'powers'. We might also call them 'facilitative rights' (Hart 1961). They include the right to enter into a contract, or make a gift, both of which may alter the property rights of those involved. Power rights include the right to make and unmake the very rules on which first order rights depend, as when legislators make laws. The right to marry, the right to make a will, the right to vote, all these and many more are powers or facilitative rights, rights which, when exercised, alter the legal or moral standing of both the rights-holder and others.

Power rights do not correlate with the duties of other people, but they do impact on other people and for this reason Hohfeld said that they correlate with what he called the 'liabilities' of others. Having a power right means that others are liable to have their first order rights affected by the actions of the power-holders. 'Liable' is not an entirely satisfactory term here as it carries the connotation that these consequences are not generally welcome to the other person, whereas most contracts, for instance, are entered into for mutual benefit and most wills are advantageous to the inheritor.

One particular type of power or facilitative right introduces yet another important variable in the analysis of rights. We have noted that a rule generates a right when the duty involved is owed to someone, that person being the rights-holder. One possible interpretation of this relationship is that the person to whom the right is owed has some sort of control over the obligation in question. Thus the correlative obligation may come into effect only when the rights-holder invokes it, as when someone calls in a debt. Or the rights-holder may have the power to decide whether or not to take action against someone who does not fulfil the correlative obligation. We may call such rights 'option rights' to call attention to the fact that the rights in question give the rights-holder the option of whether to activate or pursue the obligation that is correlative to the right. As we shall see, some theorists claim that all genuine rights are option rights in this sense, although there would appear to be many exceptions to this. We do not, for instance, generally hold that people may waive their right to life by releasing others from the obligation not to kill them.

A fourth category of rights in Hohfeld's formal schemer is the 'immunity right'. Immunity rights exist when the rights-holder is not liable to have her legal or moral position changed by the action of another person utilising a power or facilitative right. This is the case with the formal or pure liberty right this is posited on the absence of a rule, in this case the absence of a rule conferring the power right on another person. Again like a formal liberty right, an immunity right may not be much use if such power rights can be readily created. Indeed its prime significance may be, as its name suggests, to exclude certain persons, the rights-holders, from the application of a general power-conferring rule, thereby creating an immunity from the exercise of that power. However, immunity rights may be given a more substantive form by ascribing a correlative duty not to create power-conferring rules that threaten the liberty of a person. In this stronger version, immunity rights can have great significance because they offer protection against being burdened with liabilities.

It can readily be seen that the formal distinctions between these various types of right are of immense importance in any debate about rights and we shall have frequent recourse to this typology of rights throughout the book. However, in reality any actual situation will be covered by a number of these rights-relationships at the same time, so that an actual normative relationship between two people is often a complex combination of these types of right. In any actual situation the right to freedom of movement, for instance, will be a formal liberty-right (asserting the absence of a rule forbidding me to travel), a substantive liberty or claim right (asserting the negative duty of all others not to interfere with my movement and maybe the positive duty to assist me in moving around). The right to freedom of movement may also be a power right (to alter my legal status as a resident), or an immunity right (against anyone introducing laws that prevent me travelling). In other words, travel is an institution that is defined by a complex set of rights, duties, powers and immunities, and like all institutions can be changed by making modifications under any of these headings. A similar analysis can be given to all social institutions. Thus the institutions of property is best seen as a complex and variable bundle of rights relating to people's obligations to each other that relate to material things.

It is also the case that the right to movement is generally accepted as a 'human right' (article 13, UDHR (United Nations 1948)). Hohfeld, writing in the early twentieth century, did not think it necessary to treat human rights as a distinct category of right, but no survey of the variety of rights would be complete without some attempt to identify the distinctiveness of human rights and their significance in generating the current salience of rights discourse.

Human rights

Human rights can be viewed as just another subdivision of rights, one type of rights amongst others, or they may be viewed as fundamental to the very idea of rights and in some sense infusing the contemporary idea of rights generally. The first approach is analytically sound in that human rights fit well into a Hohfeldian type scheme: they are universal claim rights. The second approach leads us to consider the moral justifications for human rights, justifications that help to highlight the significance of rights generally. Although many actual rights are too trivial or technical to warrant comparison to human rights, there is in reality no clear and sharp distinction between human rights and other rights, either analytically or morally.

Many rights belong to particular persons (such as a person's ownership of her house) or to a particular category of person (such as the legislators' right to make laws). There are, however, certain rights that people have as people rather than a type of person or an occupant of any particular situation or role. These universal rights are often referred to as 'human rights' (Cranston 1973, Gewirth 1982, Macfarlane 1985).

The idea that human rights are, or ought to be, the possession of everyone regardless of race, religion, nationality or any other of the distinctions that divide humanity into conflicting and hostile groups, is powerful and important, but it cannot by itself enable us to identify which rights are human rights. Some universal rights, like the right to collect stones, are not significant enough to count as human rights. It is standard, therefore to add a second formal criterion to distinguish human rights from other rights, namely that they are 'overriding' in that they take precedence over all other considerations, including other rights. This in turn may be explained by the fact that such rights are of supreme importance to human beings, perhaps because they are necessary for having a worthwhile or, perhaps, a fully human existence (Cranston 1973).

To universality, overridingness and importance, is often added a fourth formal criterion for the identification of human rights, and that is 'practicality', the reason being that universality and importance are in themselves too open-ended and could include all sorts of desirable goals that could not be realised in practice. This is best seen as requiring that to be a human right. A right must, like any other right, be institutionalisable. By this is meant that it is possible or practicable to embody the right in actual societal or legal rules that promote and protect the interests to which the right in question is directed.

This avoids the controversy as to whether or not human rights ought to be defined in terms of purely negative rights. Are human rights to be classified as formal liberty rights or as claim rights, and more particularly are their correlative obligations to include positive as well as negative ones. Certainly a positive right to adequate health care and education seems wildly impractical in many states, whereas the absence of laws restricting freedom of speech seems readily obtainable in any society (Cranston 1973, Griffin 2001). Moreover, it is hard to see how any positive rights can be regarded as overriding if their fulfilment is a costly matter.

However the idea that human rights are restricted to those rights that can be enforced without serious expenditure cannot be taken to be determinative of what counts as a human right. For a start, this would give unwarranted priority to negative rights, that is, those rights whose correlative duties involve no more than not interfering with another person with respect to those interests identified by the right. This conflicts with the criterion of moral importance. One of the reasons for having a human right is that this can be used to justify expenditure being directed towards its protection and implementation. Moreover the expenses involved in protecting negative rights can be considerable, in the form of police and court services, for instance. Indeed, in many societies providing citizens who are unable to provide for themselves with a minimal level of nutrition, shelter and clothing is much less costly than protecting property rights (Holmes and Sunstein 2000).[7]

This takes us back to the idea that some universal rights are simply much more important than others. 'Importance' is a vague term that gives little practical guidance, but it serves well enough in the analysis of the concept of a human right if 'importance' is equated with those things which are generally believed to be of overriding importance for all human beings. Whether or not such rights actually exist is, according to my analysis, a question of finding out whether there are operative social or legal rules which ascribe such overriding rights to all human beings.

It is a different matter, however, if we are seeking to answer the question: what human rights ought we to have? This requires us to discuss which features of human existence have such overriding significance that the universal implementation of rules to protect and further these interests is morally justified. One approach to this moral question seeks to identify 'fundamental rights', in the sense of those rights that are more basic than others. 'Basic' may refer here to those things that everybody requires in order to survive. Such things are basic because they have a causal priority over all other considerations, since, if someone is not alive, then no other interests or rights have any importance to them. This makes the right to life an evidently basic right, but it also makes the right to sustenance a basic right, while not including, at least immediately, other rights that have been considered fundamental in other ways (perhaps because they are believed to be very important), such as freedom of speech (Shue 1980, Golding 1984).

However, 'basic rights' have a way of expanding to cover those things that are required for any human being to live a 'decent' life, a life that meets the essential requirements for living 'as a human being', with some dignity and happiness. This moves from a notion of what is basic for survival to a notion of what is fundamentally important for the wellbeing of human beings. Identifying the ingredients of a minimally satisfactory existence immediately expands the range of human rights from the preconditions of survival to that which is thought essential for a tolerable life for a human being, that is, a being with certain aspirations and qualities. It expands the scope of human rights to the right to participate in a society that gives dignity and fulfilment to its members. This takes us far beyond that which is 'basic' in the sense of what is causally required for human survival, to some picture of what constitutes a 'truly' human life, a more nebulous, relative and controversial concept.

The search for the normative criteria for adopting specific rights as human right leads us in this way to the core philosophical debate about human life and human values. Historically this debate has been conducted in terms of ideas about wellbeing (the sort of happiness that humans are capable of and the standing threats to such happiness as we can aspire to), on the one hand, and the expression of human autonomy (choice, independence, creativity, freedom), on the other hand. Those who emphasise wellbeing or happiness tend to think of human rights as protecting us against the principal causes of pain and suffering. Those who emphasise autonomy or fulfilling human activities identify the principal modes of human striving, such as creativity, reproduction, love, curiosity and morality, and see human rights as supportive of these functions.

Sometimes, as in the case of medieval natural law, essentially human activities have been defined in terms of human beings as creatures of God, so that human rights are derived from our knowledge of God's purpose in creating human beings, making the right to worship, for instance, a core human right (Finnis 1980). Other visions of what is important for human beings have focused on the human capacity to act morally, that is, in accordance with their beliefs about how they ought to behave. Sometimes this is a socially oriented view of human life, as in the Greek idea of the virtuous person, who fulfils their role in a harmonious and just society (Nussbaum 2000). Sometimes it is more individualistic, as in Immanuel Kant's ideal of the individual human beings as morally autonomous, that is, capable of choosing for themselves by the exercise of their power of reason the rules that they ought to follow (Kant 1948).

It is clear that determining what is important enough about human life to feature in a morally justifiable catalogue of human rights is a complex and difficult business that is liable to generate considerable disagreement. It is certainly an enterprise that goes beyond determining which rights are 'basic' in the causal sense in that they are empirical preconditions of survival. Indeed many human rights theorists see such basic rights as important only because they serve to promote the preconditions of the worthwhile human activities that are the real justification for human rights.

We return to these issues in the next chapter where we consider various theories of rights. Here we must note another conceptual problem about the conflict between universality and importance. Even if we can agree about what is intrinsically important for human life, this may not be something that fits the criterion of universality with which we started our analysis. Universality and importance may point in different directions. Not all important moral considerations are universal in that they apply equally to all human beings. Indeed it is sometimes argued that human rights should focus on those who are different and need special protection, such as homosexuals or people who are highly dependent on others. It is even argued that gender discrimination reveals the importance of stressing the differences rather than the similarities between human beings. This means that, if we wish to get at what is of overriding moral import, we must go about identifying the rights of women, or the rights of the mentally challenged, or the specially gifted, rather than the rights of everyone (Young 1990, Kingdom 1991).

It is possible to make such special rights formally universal by stating them in the form 'All human beings who are women or mentally challenged, or especially gifted, have the rights in question', but this undermines the distinction between universal and particular human rights, for any right, however particular, can be formulated in this way. We might fall back on saying that universality is a necessary condition for being a human right so that things which are of great importance to only some human beings are excluded from human rights on the basis that such rights require both importance and universality. But in this case would human rights always trump less universal rights? This is a difficult analytical problem to which we return when considering group rights.

A rather different approach to determining the distinctive characteristics of human rights is to include consideration of the function of human rights discourse. For instance, we might identify human rights with certain constitutional rights that protect the individual against governments, even democratically elected ones. Human rights may be considered such in virtue of their role in constraining what governments may legitimately do. As we will see, this approach is in line with the natural rights tradition from which the idea of human rights has developed. Traditionally such rights have been identified as universal immunity rights which prevent governments enacting laws that infringe on certain basic human interests, such as the right to life, and certain civil powers, such as the right to vote. This is to see human rights as rights that are to be institutionalised in a particular way. Human rights, in this view, ought to be constitutionally protected rights.

Yet there are other ways of protecting human rights and other functions performed by human rights discourse in contemporary politics and, in any case, not everyone who believes in human rights approves of constitutional methods of enforcement, and such political issues should not be settled by analytical dogma. Human rights are drawn upon to determine the purely moral duties of corporations and associations. They are also used to justify intervention in the affairs of sovereign states that fail to respect the human rights of their citizens and those of other nations. They are also used to campaign for legislation to promote such human rights goals as non-discrimination, equality of opportunity and adequate universal health care. It would appear, therefore, that our idea of what constitutes a human right will vary with the purpose to which such rights are to be put and the mechanisms for so doing, for there is no one function that can be used in establishing the existence criteria for human rights.

Across all these different areas of human rights discourser, it is necessary to take into account correlative duties in figuring out what ought to be adopted as human rights. The idea of human rights makes little practical sense if such rights do not correlate with the duties of other human beings to act or refrain from acting in certain ways. This means that we have to take account of the capacities and opportunities of potential human rights duty-bearers. Which raises the interesting question of whether such correlative duties fall on all human beings, or only on all those who are able to act in appropriate ways or, perhaps, particularly on governments or other powerful institutions. This may be regarded as an analytical point arising from the idea of correlativity and the criterion of practicality, but it is perhaps the more substantive political point that human rights can only be effective if correlative duty-holders who are able to fulfil such obligations.

Faced with the difficulty of saying in formal of functional terms what should count as a human right, it is tempting to define human rights in terms of their source in recent history, namely the United Nations, and in particular its Universal Declaration of Human Rights (UDHR) (United Nations 1948) and the two treaties developed from this declaration, the International Covenant on Civil and Political Rights (ICCPR) (United Nations 1966a) and the International Covenant on Social, Economic and Cultural Rights (ICSECR) (United Nations 1966b) which together are called the 'International Bill of Rights'.

This is commonly done and many legally oriented people do in practice identify human rights with international human rights law. This is unsatisfactory, because the United Nations cannot and does not claim to have invented human rights. Rather the UN and other organisations have sought to codify and implement human rights. Moreover, the International Bill of Rights is, for all its achievement, a flawed and developing expression of human rights. Further, human rights are moral rights in the sense of manifesto rights and so cannot be identified with any set of positive laws, either in international law or the constitutions of particular countries, such as the Bill of Rights in the amendments to the constitution of the USA. Both domestic and international laws may contingently succeed in stating what ought to be adopted as human rights but it is neither necessary nor sufficient to make them human rights.

We may, therefore, want to abandon a purely formal approach to the definition of human rights and to consider whether the distinctive characteristic of human rights include their underlying rationale or justification. Thus, human rights may be said to be the rights that embody the insight that human beings are fundamentally equal, in that, for all their differences, their lives are of equal worth, hence, it may be argued, the formal universality of human rights and the close relationship between human rights and non-discrimination.

This does not take us far enough since equality as non-discrimination is compatible with treating everyone equally unfairly. We must add an affirmation of the high as well as the equal importance of the human lives that are equally valued (Vlastos 1962). This then takes us back to debate about whether this high worth relates to the human capacity for wellbeing or the distinctiveness of human autonomy.

If we do take the equality of worth approach to the identification of human rights it is hard to keep such a rationale confined to human rights, at least as we think of them in contemporary global society. Equality of high human worth seems to fit in with the second approach to human rights identified at the beginning of this section, namely that human rights are not just a type of rights but are at the heart of the very idea of rights. Human rights may be a manifestation of what is referred to 'rights-based' approaches to politics in which the vital interests of the individuals are taken to be the fundamental basis for all political decisions. Human rights are simply a universal expression of this type of moral approach to politics that happens to be contingently associated with certain mechanisms for putting this approach into practice, such as international treaties and bills of right.

The rights approach

Rights-based theories of morality are defined in contrasted with duty-based and with goal-based or consequentialist approaches (Dworkin 1977: 169–173, Mackie 1977, Waldron 1984). Consequentialism is the theory that right and wrong are a matter of calculating the consequences of certain types of conduct and evaluating those consequences in an aggregative way, determining what is right by the criterion of the act that produces the maximum net benefit, all the consequences of the act having been taken into the account (Mill 1910). Utilitarianism is a type of consequentialism that measures the values of the consequences of an act in terms of its causal relationship to the production of pleasures and pains. The maxim that the right act is the act that produces the greatest happiness for the greatest number summarises the classic utilitarian moral theory. Other consequentialist theories do their calculations in terms of maximising preferences, that is, giving people what they want (Singer 1993) or a plurality of other desired ends (Moore 1903).

In contrast a right-based approach holds that an act is judged in terms of its effect on the interests identified by individual rights. This means giving these interests of the individual priority over the aggregate wellbeing of everyone. All duties, goals and social arrangements are ultimately valued according to their contribution to the value of the individual. This is said to embody an attitude of respect that acknowledges the intrinsic moral worth of the individuals concerned, which means that it is never right, for instance, to sacrifice the happiness of one person to promote the wellbeing of another. All human beings must be treated as ends in themselves. This is why they must have rights that prevent them being used as mere instruments of others.

Appealing as the distinction between rights-based and consequentialist approaches may be, it does not enable us to identify what is distinctive about either human rights or rights in general. Lots of rights, including many human rights, are what may be called instrumental rights, that is, they are rights that are ascribed to persons because this is of benefit that derive either to themselves or to others. Even the right to freedom of speech is generally justified in consequentialst terms as something that will produce more truth and so more benefits for society generally. Voting rights also may be seen as instrumental rights designed to protect the individual rights-holder and promote the general happiness (Nagel 2002).[8]

This takes us on to another important distinction between types of rights. The distinction is between intrinsic and instrumental rights. Intrinsic rights are rights that are designed to protect or express the interests of the rights-holders as defined by the right for their own sake. Thus an intrinsic right to freedom of speech is the right to express yourself in speech. Other rights, perhaps the majority, or rights including many human rights, are instrumental in that they are part of a system designed for further benefit to the rights-holder or others. The right to speech may enable rights-holders to protect their consumer interests, for instance, or may be to the collective advantage of those involved through the dissemination of information. Most particular rights have intrinsic and instrumental aspects. A particular right can have a number of different rationales or justifications.

Rights-based political theories do not deny the existence of instrumental rights. They simply argue that these are justified eventually by reference to the interests of rights-bearers. However, if they mean by this rights-bearers as a whole, then this is much the same as is argued by consequentialist theorists who hold that all rights are justified ultimately by the benefits they give to the sum of individuals, each of whom is equally important. In order to distinguish themselves from consequentialist, rights-based theorists must argue that the rights of one individual are ultimately justified in terms of the interests of that particular individual. But this is very hard to do, even in the case of human rights.

While the idea of intrinsic rights does not provide a basis for distinguishing human rights from other rights, it may be argued that it does pinpoint the distinctiveness of rights as an enterprise that emphasises the interests of the individual in a way that may not make them sacrosanct but certainly stands against the unimpeded implementation of a goal-based or consequentialist approach that unacceptably endangers the interests of vulnerable minorities.[9] This does not require a moral realism that envisages the existence of moral rights in the ontological sense, but it does mean holding that there are moral reasons (perhaps grounded in the idea of equal worth) that justify the creation of rights-creating rules.

Conclusion

There are many other ways in which we could describe the variety of rights, not least in terms of their content as economic, political or religious rights. However, the formal typology of rights outlined in this chapter opens up further moral and empirical questions that apply to all the spheres in which rights operate. Should we prefer a society that is marked by formal liberty-rights, that is, a largely unregulated or 'libertarian' state, or one that is characterised typically by substantive claim rights with positive correlative duties, such as a developed welfare state? Do some states and societies conform to one of these alternatives more than another?

The analysis undertaken in this chapter enables us to express these questions more clearly but not to answer them. In themselves typologies are no more than conceptual tools, to be adopted or discarded in the interests of clarity or their capacity to make distinctions that are useful in drawing up a picture of an ideal society or make helpful and explanatory empirical comparisons between societies. Hohfeld's own purpose was to suggest a scheme that would tidy up legal concepts and make for more transparent legal reasoning. Our objective is to refine and begin to address the other core questions to which this book is addressed. At this stage, all we can say in relation to our first question (what are rights?) is that it is clarificatory to say that rights, in their distinctive meaning, are constituted by societal and legal rules, actual or recommended, which specify in a variety of ways what duties (if any) are owed to other persons (the rights-holders).

This is not a philosophically neutral analysis. It effectively excludes the belief that there are ontologically 'real' or epistemologically 'true' rights to be found out there in some transcendent moral sphere. Nor is it morally neutral, because it assumes that rights should not be dogmatically identified with one form or variety of rights rather than another. Rights as such have no moral essence. They do not exist in a Platonic heaven, nor can they be defined into existence by selective appropriation from everyday moral and political discourse. Rights are social constructs as diverse and complex as the societies of which they are a part.

However, it is open to us to adopt our preferred conceptual configurations to express our own fears, aspirations and practical intentions. While it is necessary to start from the traditions of which we are a part, and wise to give these traditions critical attention, rights can become what we individually and collectively choose to make of them. The prime intellectual virtues here are to make clear how we are using this opaque and complex terminology in the context of the particular questions we are addressing and to take care when communicating our thoughts to others whose conceptual assumptions may be quite different. At the same time we can seek to re-imagine rights in ways that articulate, first, the sort of society in which we wish to live, and second, in the more specific case of human rights, those features that any society must possess for all its members to live a worthwhile human life. There is no definitive answer to our first core question as to the nature and meaning of rights, but, as we have seen there are lots of important distinctions to bear in mind as we seek to articulate the form and content of the various types of rights that we consider it important for us to have.

Chapter 3

Theories of rights

Theories of rights seek to provide comprehensive answers to the sort of questions that are addressed in this book: what are rights, who has rights, what rights have they got, what rights ought they to have, and how should we go about securing and protecting these rights? Notwithstanding the extensive variety of rights explored in Chapter 2, philosophers do attempt to construct general theories of rights. Some of these theories concentrate on establishing substantive empirical questions about who has rights and what these rights are, and normative questions about who ought to have rights and what these rights ought to be. Other theories focus on more formal questions of meaning, analysis and definition, although there are usually underlying evaluative agenda that relate to the justifying reasons why we would want to have a system of rights at all. This chapter starts with an examination of the two principal theories of rights that present themselves mainly as formal theories about meaning but in fact open the way to providing answers to all our questions about rights. One such theory is the 'will' (or 'choice' or 'power') theory. The other is the 'interest' (or 'benefit' or 'wellbeing') theory. Both theories provides a bridge between the conceptual and the normative issues about rights.

Will or interests?

According to the will theory of rights, rights are explained in terms of our capacity for choice and agency through the action of the will. Rights on this account enable the rights-holder to control through correlative obligations on others how such others may act towards the rights-holder. According to the interest theory of rights, rights are explained in terms of the fact that human (and perhaps other) beings are capable of having interests. On this account rights secure through correlative obligations the protection and advancement of the interests of the rights-holder.

Both the will and the interest theories may be seen as providing competing answers to the question: what is meant by saying that a person owes something, or has a duty or obligation, *to* someone else. Both theories also accept something like the Hohfeldian scheme of rights outlined in Chapter 2 which makes the idea of rule-governed rights and correlative obligations central to our understanding of rights. However, while it can be at least argued that all rights (with the exception of pure liberty rights) correlate with someone else's obligations, the relationship does not work the other way round (Lyons 1970). Whether or not all rights correlate with someone else's duties (Sumner 1987), not all obligations correlate with someone else's right. Thus a person's obligation to help the poor may not mean that any poor person has a right to be helped by anyone in particular. Many duties relate to the promotion of 'public goods', such as fresh air, that cannot be enjoyed by one individual without being enjoyed by others similarly situated. Some duties are owed to other people, and it is these obligations that most clearly correlate with rights. Hence the need for a theory of rights to say what it means to owe an obligation *to* someone else.

If we can answer this question then we may have discovered the key 'existence conditions' for a right (that is the characteristics that something must have in order to be a right). According to the will theory, a right exists when a person (the right-bearer) can choose that another person fulfil an obligation or release her from that obligation. On this view, rights talk is a language of claims that generates the capacity to control the actions of others by requiring that these others act towards them in a certain way, usually by not interfering with what they want to do but also sometimes by empowering them to achieve their objectives. Rights are thus things to be possessed, demanded, waived, or used as the owner thinks fit. The choices here are readily seen as exercises of will and power. Having or using a right may or may not be for the benefit of the rights-holder. All that matters is that the rights-holder has the power of choice or control over the fulfilment of obligations that correlate with the duty by the exercise of his or her will (Hart 1982, Kramer, Simmonds and Steiner 1998).

For the will theory, the obligations correlative to claim rights are owed *to* the rights-holder in the sense that the rights-holder has the normative power to require that their obligation be fulfilled or some recompense made for non-fulfilment. Rights are thus discretionary powers that holders may deploy as they see fit. This is most obvious in the case of claim rights. In the case of formal liberty-rights, choice is involved only in that the rights-holders may, but need not, do that which they have a right to do. Indeed it is a general characteristic of the will theory to hold that a person who has a right to do something also has a right not to do that thing. If we focus on power rights then it is evident that the element of choice is to the fore because it is up to the holder of the power right whether or not and how to use her power right. And, in the case of immunities, the rights-holder may always waive her immunity from the impact of the power rights of others.

According to the interest theory, on the other hand, the existence condition for a right is that there is an obligation that is directed toward the protection or furtherance of the interests, particularly of the person whose right it is (Bentham 1970, MacCormick 1977, Kramer, Simmonds and Steiner 1998). The interest theory accommodates formal liberty rights by saying that these exist when a person's interests are served by the absence of a rule. Claim rights are rights where there is a correlative obligation that protects or furthers the interest or specified interests of the rights-holder. Power conferring rules involve rights where these powers are designed to serve the interests of the rights-holder, and a similar analysis of immunities requires that an immunity right is a device to benefit the rights-holder. A person has a right when there is an obligation that is directed at protecting or furthering their interests. This may, but need not be, an option right along the lines that is central to the will theory where the rights-holder has the power to enforce and waive the right.

It is important to note that the interest theory does not say that all interests correlate with someone else's obligation, thereby becoming rights. Rather, only those interests that do correlate with such obligations constitute rights. But this does give us a basis for understanding the idea of an obligation being owed *to* someone, namely that the obligation is for the benefit of that person. Thus Raz requires that the interest in question is 'a sufficient reason' to ground or justify the imposition of the duty (Raz 1986). This may not be how it always works out in practice, but the rationale, reason or accepted justification for that obligation is that it serves the interests of identifiable persons, who are in general designated the rights-holders.

Viewing these theories as competing to provide answers to our first question (what are rights?), we might commend the will theory for its precision and clarity but prefer the interest theory because it is more comprehensive. Considered simply as an attempt to define the meaning of rights, the will theory seems to be dogmatic in its selection of what, in the previous chapter, I have called option rights or discretionary rights as the basic or sole type of right. The concentration is on those rights that give the individuals powers, particularly powers to demand or waive their rights of the sort that feature in option rights. It seems cavalier to exclude, as not really rights, formal liberties, or claim rights that cannot be waived (such as the right to life) and in general the rights of small children and those without the capacity to make choices or exercise a rational will.

Yet, if we reflect on how we talk about rights, there does appear to be a conceptual assumption that, other things being equal, if a person has a right then that person and only that person may enforce or waive that right. This explains why it seems to make perfect sense for a person to exercise her rights in order to benefit persons other than herself, something that should seem odd if the interest theory is correct that rights are always directed towards protecting an interest of the rights-holder.

Moreover, the interest (or benefit) theory does appear to have the serious disadvantage that it renders the boundaries of rights exceedingly vague and open-ended. This is not because all interests generate rights, for no one holds that position. The theory is that rights are designed to protect specifically preferred interests. The trouble is, however, that all obligations may benefit all sorts of other people in some ways some of the time. Perhaps we have to fall back on saying that what matters is whom the fulfilment of the obligation normally benefits. Or, perhaps, who it is intended to benefit (Lyons 1969: 23–46, Hart 1982: 180f.). In the case of legal obligations we may say that it is the intention of the legislature that counts, if that can be ascertained. But this does not apply so easily to societal rights, although an appeal might be made to public opinion as to what is the point of the obligation in question.

The interest theory also has difficulty with option rights where the right is obviously designed, or is actually used, as a means of helping people other than the option rights-holder, as when parents are given rights to enable them to protect their children, or as with economic rights that are in place because we consider that they are generally beneficial. Further, the interest theory has difficulty in coping with instrumental rights where the ultimate benefit of the right is for persons other than the rights-holders. Indeed, we seem to have to presuppose the truth of the choice theory in order to say that some rights are designed to protect and further the interests of persons other than the rights-holder.

This issue is often discussed in terms of 'third party beneficiaries', that is, persons who benefit as a result of a relationship of obligation between two other persons (Hart 1982, White 1984, Steiner 1994). Thus, if a person promises another person to make a gift to a third person, then it would appear that, on the interest theory, it is that third person who has the right rather than the promisee. However, an interest theorist may be prepared to accept the implication that the third party beneficiary does have a right (to receive the gift), while insisting that the promisee also has a right (that the gift be received). However, the interest theory has to hold that the promisees do generally receive benefit here, which is not implausible given that promisees must have some reason to extract the promises in the first place.

The interest theory also has the advantage that it can provide good reason why some rights are best taken to be option rights, for this enhances the individual's capacity to protect her interest by 'exercising' that right, without having to rule out of the discourse of rights the idea that small children and animals can have rights.

On purely semantic grounds it would appear that the advantage lies with the interest theory in holding that not all rights are option rights and with the will theory in so far as some rights consist in powers to benefit others. We have to conclude that neither approach can explain the full panoply and variety of rights that feature in standard right discourse. Underneath these conceptual skirmishes, however, there lie deeper disagreements as to the values that are served by rights. The will theory is, perhaps, not so much concerned with insisting on the role of choice in the form or structure of all rights as it is with recommending that, where possible, rights should have the form of option rights, thus preparing the way for insisting on the central role of autonomy in all our thinking about rights. Similarly the interest theory is concerned, perhaps, to ensure that rights are created and designed to serve a broader range of interests than autonomy. This emerging evaluative disagreement may be illustrated by reference to our second core question, concerning the subject of rights.

Who can have rights?

The largely conceptual disagreements between the will and interest theories of rights presented above as a contribution to our first core question (what are rights?) leads directly into the second core issue (who has rights?). The central question here is whether or not to confine rights to human beings (or perhaps 'persons') thus excluding the possibility or desirability of ascribing rights to other types of entity, such as animals, forests or angels. Within human beings (or persons), we still have to decide if rights can be ascribed to groups (such as societies, genders or nations) or only to individual human beings, and also which rights are to apply to all human beings and which to only some categories of person, such as adults.

On the will theory, rights involve the exercise of the choice of the rights-holder. It follows that those who can possess, or be the bearers or subjects of, rights must be rational beings who are capable of freedom of action, that is, able to exercise the sort of reasoned choices that having rights requires them to make. Except in the case of formal liberties, it makes no sense to give rights to those who cannot exercise them, and to exercise rights a person must be able to understand not only the normal choices available in everyday life but also have sufficient understanding of the idea of rights to exercise the discretion available through rights, otherwise they would be unable to make appropriate claims and waivers and to enter into the agreements and practices involved in making use of the opportunities provided by power rights.

This means that small children can have no, or very limited, rights (MacCormick 1982, Kramer, Simmonds and Steiner 1998). Animals are excluded as being unable to grasp the idea of rights, even although some may be able to make what are recognisably simple types of choice (Frey 1980, but see Singer 1975). However any other possible beings that can exercise choice, such as angels or other extra terrestrial beings must be included under the general category of 'persons'. And the theory can accommodate group rights as long as they can be said to make collective decisions, as we will see when we come to discuss the matter of collective rights in Chapter 10.

On the interest theory, rights exist when there is a rule that protects the interests of a being or entity, the rights-holder. It follows that the subjects of rights are confined to those who have interests. Some theorists are prepared to ascribe rights to any entity that may be said to have interests or well-being, while others restrict the subjects of rights to human beings on the grounds that their interests have a different nature, or a greater importance and priority. Precisely what counts as having an interest is left open so that the theory can accommodate a variety of substantive values under the guise of interests. Since merely having an interest is not sufficient to create a right, it may be that not all types of interest qualify as criteria for being a rights-subject. This means that the question of who has rights under the interest theory cannot be fully explored until we have come to a view about what sort of interests feature, or ought to feature, in the rules that protect and further rights.

It must be accepted that in the case of power rights it makes no sense to ascribe these to beings that cannot exercise such powers. Very young children and animals cannot, for instance, make laws. But, in the case of claim rights where there is a correlative obligation, it would appear that it is not the rights-bearers but the duty-bearers that must have this capacity, thus opening the way for the possibility (but not necessarily the desirability) of ascribing rights to forests and stones as well as rule-following adult human beings.

Focusing on claim rights, it may be argued that rights make no sense outside a context in which people make claims and counter-claims, and doing so on the basis of the legitimacy of certain rules and practices, thus again restricting the subjects of rights to those who are capable of entering into such complex social relationships. No one can claim or waive a right who does not have such skills, and maybe this means confining right to those who can understand the complex rule-based institution of rights and duties. This analysis may be applied to formal liberty rights as well as power-conferring rights.

This thesis makes much sociological sense, but we need not be led by the terminology of 'claim' rights to think that the value of rights is confined to those who can use them to make claims. In the case of animals, forests and children, claims may be made on their behalf. What matters, it may be argued, is the fulfilment of duties and the availability of remedies, however they are activated. Further, while claiming and waiving are part of some rights, they do not apply in every case. There are alternative mechanisms for seeing to it that the interests that are protected or furthered by the obligations correlative to a right are in fact protected or furthered. Thus a well-ordered bureaucracy is in principle capable to seeing to the protection of rights in the absence of any actual claimings.

It would seem then that any conceptual limitations on the subjects of rights are a matter of the obligations that it is intelligible to place on persons rather than on the capacities of rights-holders. This then leaves the question of why we would wish to ascribe rights to different classes of subjects, which takes us to the possible evaluative disagreements between the will and interest theories. Will theories see rights as a device to protect and express autonomy, thus confining right-subjects to those capable of autonomy. Interest theories take a wider perspective, but one that would still limit the ascription of rights to those capable of having interests. Generally this is taken to mean any being that can be valued for its own sake and not for the benefits it gives to others. This is usually held to restrict rights-bearers to those who have consciousness, for they alone are capable of feeling the pleasures and pains that are the minimum requirements for having independent moral status, that is, for being individuals that are valuable in themselves. For many this appears too broad: it certainly includes higher animals, even though it would appear to exclude inanimate beings.

If we wish to narrow the subjects of rights further we cannot rely on the concept of rights to do this for us, as I have demonstrated above. Even if we do not value autonomy above all else, claim rights are a useful device for enhancing this goal. However, independent grounds have to be given for making this the sole basis for ascribing rights, especially when to do so would appear to exclude from the categories of rights-bearers, children, mentally handicapped and otherwise incapacitated persons who cannot exercise the capacities of an autonomous being, the very groups that some rights theorists are concerned to protect against the selfishness of the more able sections of the population. The burden of proof here seems to be very much on the will theory to establish that only autonomy counts. Will theorists may protest that their argument is that the exclusive position of autonomy applies only in relation to rights. Other values have high priority in other moral spheres. This is a lame reply in so far as rights are taken to be the priority moral discourse, for it downgrades other values that may come into conflict with the pursuit of autonomy.

The term 'interests', as we have noted, is a slippery one of considerable scope and in itself provides no clear boundaries for establishing what sort of being may be rights-bearers. At its broadest 'interest' may be used to label anything that is good for the being in question. It is perfectly meaningful to say that it is in the interest of plants to have good soil and plenty of water and in the interests of sharks to have plentiful supplies of small fish to eat. Indeed this is commonplace in environmentalist literature (Singer 1993). These things are clearly benefits that permit the recipients to flourish. There is no difficulty in identifying possible obligations the fulfilment of which would be in the interests of such beings, therefore they may be the subjects of rights, the beings to whom these obligations are owed.

However, as we have seen, the interest theory holds that interests are a necessary but not a sufficient condition of being a rights-holder. It may be that plants and sharks have interests but that these interests simply don't count, or don't count enough. Here what matters is not the importance of these beings for other beings, such as humans, but rather the intrinsic value of their interests. Does it make sense to think of plants as having intrinsic value? It can certainly be argued that they have beauty, and that as complex living organisms they are important for their own sake, but would this have meaning in a world without sentient, or conscious, beings, even, perhaps, a world without beings who can appreciate the beauty and wonder of a complex living organism? These questions are profound and probably insoluble as they take us into metaphysical issues that go beyond the proof and disproof of empirical evidence. Nor do they involve simple moral disagreements about whether or not we ought to treat plants as having intrinsic value, for they raise the question of whether it makes sense to do so.

In the tradition from which the discourse of interests stems, the idea of interests is tied to sentience, not only on the part of the being who ascribes intrinsic value, but on the part of what can be considered to have such value. That is, 'interests' are confined to beings capable, at least, of feeling pleasure and pain. In this tradition sharks and sheep are thought to have interests but not plants and stones. On this view the sort of bearer of intrinsic value that has moral significance is confined to sentient beings. Only they can claim the right to exist.

However, even if interests are connected with consciousness or sentience, then not all interests are of equal intrinsic value. On this basis it is often argued that those beings that are capable of language, or complex thought, or self-awareness, or the awareness of being alive and or facing death, or valuing their own quality of life, have 'interests' in the fuller sense required. Sometimes these prerequisites are viewed as capacities that make for heightened pleasure and pain, making a difference of hedonic quality between the lives of humans and sheep. Arguments for maintaining the differences between humans and animals (with possible exclusion of some higher mammals) are also based on the greater intrinsic value of a life that is capable of reason and choice, something that is dealt with in greater detail later in this chapter.

When it comes to the content of rights there is great scope for disagreement as to what constitutes a person's interests or benefit. All these positions would seem to be perfectly intelligible and the choice between which versions of interest theory to adopt must be largely one for individual moral judgment. Some would identify interests largely with material well-being, others with success in personal relationships, and still others in the capacity to exercise admirable skills and characteristics. Some interests are clearly relative to personal ideals. This means that what is a right from one person's values or point of view is not necessarily a right on the basis of someone else's values. These content-related issues, which are taken up in the next chapter, are relevant to the question of what beings can be the subject of rights because the sort of interests we think valuable enough to be protected by rights will not be characteristic of all sorts of being. To enlarge our understanding of who or what may be the bearer of rights it may be necessary to imagine how rather different interests could be held to have moral significance as great as that which typically characterise human life.

What rights do they have?

Our third question is radically ambiguous in a way that should be, by now, familiar to the reader. It may be a question about the normative or institutional facts that pertain in a particular society: the rights that Americans, Britons or Indians actually have in their own communities or society. Or, it may be a question about what 'moral rights' they have in the sense of the rights that ought to exist in such societies. In this section I am concerned only with the first sort of question, an inquiry into the sociological facts relating to the normative systems that do or do not exist in a particular society.

We now have the apparatus at hand to give a fairly straightforward answer to this question about the social existence of rights. If we adopt the will theory then the existence of a right depends on the existence of a social rule laying down that some or all persons have the normative power to control the actions of other people, thus placing them under an obligation to behave in a certain way. If we adopt the interest theory then persons have rights when there are social rules in a society that require others to behave towards them in a way that does or is intended to benefit them. Once we have adopted one or other theory we have a ready answer to the factual understanding or interpretation of the question: what rights do they have? According to the theory of rights adopted, the discovery of what rights peopled have is an empirical investigation into certain categories of social rules and how they operate in practice. This is not an investigation that is attempted in this book but is the subject matter of legal and sociological research. It is appropriate however, in this critical introduction to rights, to mention some of the difficulties that face such empirical research into such institutional facts and social practices and behaviour.

We have already noted that there will be difficulty in determining when obligation creating rules do or do not benefit any particular persons, but at least part of the difficulty is solved by making a decision as to what is to count as an 'interest'. We may decide this by finding out what is regarded as an interest, or what they care about, in the society in question. In which case, people have rights when there are rules laying down obligations that serve objectives that are generally regarded as being in the interests of other persons (the rights-holders). Or the social observer may make an independent judgment as to what is to count as an interest for the purpose of determining what rights people have. This is likely to be done on the basis of the observer's own values as to what it is that has moral significance in human life although often a more objective and allegedly scientific basis is claimed.

In this case, deciding what rights people have could not be a conceptually or morally neutral matter. This is hardly surprising as rights are part of a normative structure present in a society and not 'brute facts' of the sort that we can directly observe with our senses, such as physical size, weight and shape. Nevertheless, once we have made these conceptual or moral choices, then we can make a factual determination as to what rights people have by seeing whether there are rules in existence that protect these favoured interests. Alternatively, we can base our judgments as to what counts as interests that justify rights by examining the beliefs on this matter held by those about whose rights we are inquiring. The latter would make for a better, because less subjective, judgment if our inquiry is a factual one.

But how do we establish whether or not there is a social rule or law in existence? For we have yet to determine how we go about finding out if there is an obligation-creating rule that might correlate with a right. Our analysis has taken us as far as saying that rights and obligations exist where certain social rules exist, rules that say what certain types of person may or must do or not do to each other. So, having defined rights in relation to correlative obligations or duties, we define both in relation to the concept of a rule. But where do we find these rules? How do we know they exist?

This is not only an intriguing question, in that it is difficult to answer, it is also a crucial question with respect to the claims that are made about both the advantages and the disadvantages of rights. We have seen that one of the benefits of rights is that they provide a clear and settled basis for social interaction. And that one of the alleged disadvantage of rules is that they are inflexible and restrictive of creative problem solving. But rights can be neither decisive nor restrictive unless we are able to readily identify the rules that lay down both the rights and their correlative obligations.

At this point it may seem advisable to turn to legal rights: the rights that are determined by officials to be the authoritative rules in a society. These can be discovered by reading statutes, law reports and legal textbooks. At least that way we can know what legal rights people have. But what if the rules in the books are not observed? And what about the non-legal rights and duties that we have categorised as related to social (or societal) rules, like the right to be told the truth and the duty to visit the sick?

The fact that rules are not always observed and obligations not always adhered to does not, of course, mean that these rules and obligations do not exist. People break rules and neglect their obligations. But this makes it all the more difficult to know what rights people have in a society since we cannot simply observe how they are treated by other people. We need to know whether or not they are being treated in accordance with their rights.

Sociologists and legal theorists have long grappled with these problems. Some have held that such questions are ultimately moral ones that cannot be answered without saying what rights people ought to have. Moral realists solve the problem by saying that the question about what rights people do have ultimately comes down to the question of what rights they have in a justified moral order. Empiricists take a different line. For them, the investigation of what rights people have starts with observing how certain categories or types of people treat other categories or types of people in certain categories or types of situation, so that they can generalise and say that persons A treat persons B in manner C in situation D. On the basis of ordinary empirical observation they make testable generalisations about conduct.

But not all regularities are examples of rule following behaviour. People routinely go to sleep at night without there being a rule that says they should do so. Moreover, the mere existence of a rule on paper does not change such routine behaviour into rule-governed conduct. For there to be a social rule, what has to be the case is that people act in a regular or routine manner because of the rule. But how can we know whether or not this is the case? Here the crucial factor is said to be what happens if they do not conform to the general pattern in question. A social rule is said to exist when failure to follow the rule leads to criticism and perhaps punishment by other people, and perhaps also by that individual's critical reaction to her own conduct. In the case of legal rules the hostile reaction is institutionalised through the activities of police, courts and prisons. In the case on non-legal social rules, the equivalent sanctions are imposed by the informal processes of praise and blame (Hart 1961).

This excursion into the ontology of social norms, that is the reality (or otherwise) of normative forces in a society that lead people to behave regularly in ways they might not otherwise do, is not undertaken for mere intellectual curiosity. It is a necessary part of the explanations both as to why rights are valuable things and why they may be criticised as morally unhealthy phenomena. Rights are valuable or harmful because they produce results, for better or worse. And these results are mediated through the mechanisms of social control and facilitation that operate in social settings. It is important to know what rights we have in order that we may know what to expect from other people and what remedies we might have if these expectations are not met. No equivalent benefits are to be had from discovering what rights we ought to have unless that leads to a change in the rights that we actually do have.

Conversely, the legalistic objection to rights, to the effect that they divert us from negotiating sensible solutions to particular situations in a flexible manner, make no sense if, after reaching agreement by negotiation we remain free to go ahead and do that without regard to the rules that will be forced upon us by the structure embedded in legal and social practices. The sociological points made here about the rights we do have are therefore an important background to understanding why rights are valued and how their value should be assessed. So much is not at issue between the will and the interest theorists.

Finally, we must remind ourselves that when people ask questions in the form of 'what rights do we have?' they often slip unwittingly into debating 'what rights ought we to have?', thus muddling these distinct questions and committing what is technically known as the 'naturalistic fallacy' by using reasons relating to what ought to exist as reasons for concluding that it does actually exist. This has the potential to undermine the benefits of having an actual system of rights in place by turning decisions into how these rules apply to particular cases into debates about what rights those involved ought to have.

What rights ought they to have?

The normative aspects of the will and interest theories come into play when we move on to the fourth core question about rights: what rights ought people to have? (Kramer, Simmonds and Steiner 1998, MacCormick 1977). This question can be applied both to the form and content of rights. Should we have liberty rights, claim rights, power rights, or immunities? Should they be intrinsic or instrumental? Should they be option or non-option rights? Should they be absolute or relative? Should they be legal or societal? And, whatever form they take, what should their content be: what categories of person should have a right to what sort of thing?

Autonomy

We have seen that the will theory regards rights as conferring power on rights-holders to control the conduct of others, thus enabling them, by the exercise of their will or choice, to protect themselves from the interference by others and enable them to pursue their own objectives. In its broader and more evaluative mode, the will theory suggests that the point of rights is to further the self-development and autonomy of individual persons over their own body, mind and circumstances. This fits with that stream of human rights and thus the rights-based approach to politics as a whole, which focuses on the idea and the ideal of the individual as agent, which is taken to be the very core of the personhood from which rights derive. By unpacking this ideal we gain insight into what will theorists hope and expect from a system of rights (Gewirth 1982, Griffin 2001).

The idea of autonomy is closely tied to the concept of agency. Agency is the capacity to act, that is, to make choices as to alternative courses of conduct and carry through 'actions', that is physical movements governed by the agent's conscious intentions. Indeed the very idea of an act involves the concepts of intention and purpose. Clearly action in this intentional sense can be a very valuable asset to a being, but it is also seen as something that is highly worthwhile in itself.

Agency is of particular significance when morality is involved. To make moral choices, to decide what is right and wrong for yourself and to do what you believe to be right even when this is adverse to your interests, all these morally related decisions have great significance in much of the thinking that lies behind a rights-based approach to politics. Moral autonomy is thought to be of value, even when the individual makes wrong or mistaken choices and holds inadequate or misguided moral views, just as the exercise of practical reasonableness generally is applauded even when the agent does not perform well.

This approach is closely associated with Immanuel Kant (1724–1804), the philosopher whose work is most commonly drawn upon in connection with rights-based approach to morality and politics. It is Kant's concepts of respecting people as ends in themselves and the dignity of autonomous beings that feature most prominently in justificatory rights discourse. The high, sometimes paramount, value many people place on autonomy is largely due to the powerful influence Kant's conception of autonomy continues to exercise over moral and political thought, and so it is important to briefly consider that conception.

According to Kant (1948), when humans act on the impulses of emotion without critical refection their behaviour is controlled by causal forces and is therefore 'heteronomous'. However, it is a distinctive feature of human beings that they can follow their 'rational will' and act autonomously as moral agents. The important thing about this autonomy is that it enables people to act contrary to and independently of the causal factors that shape all other movements. Mankind's unique 'freedom of the will' arises from their capacity not simply to choose their own goals but to do so in a rational way. Rationality here is manifest in Kant's 'categorical imperative' according to which it is rational for a person to act on a maxim that he is able to 'will as a universal law', or, in more modern parlance, 'universalise'; that is, be prepared both to see everyone act upon and commit yourself to follow in similar circumstances.

Much depends on precisely what Kant means by willing as a universal law. He argues that we cannot rationally make a promise without intending to keep it, for that would be to act on a maxim ('promising while intending to break the promise') that is inconsistent with the institution of promising. It is simply illogical to will that everyone follow such a maxim. Kant says that making a 'lying promise' is to contradict yourself. This demonstrates that it is 'reason' (rather than some moral idea, such as fairness) that makes it wrong. If this mode of argument works generally, then we have an important method for establishing right and wrong that is independent of the agent's own inclinations and desires and is therefore capable of being a standard for all (rational) agents.

Moreover, by speaking of this process of moral decision-making as a matter of moral legislation (albeit only for the decision-maker), a matter of laying down a maxim that is right for everyone to follow, this provides a basis for common standards applicable in principle to all, whatever their individual impulses and emotions might be. Thus every rational person has a duty to keep their promises and a right to have promises kept that are made to them. Promise keeping is thus part of a system in which all rational beings can join.

This helps us to make sense of Kant's other formulation of the categorical imperative, that we must treat 'humanity in your own person or in the person of another never simply as a means but always at the same time as an end' (Kant 1948: 96). It is because human beings are capable of acting out of a sense of duty in accordance with their rational will that their existence has dignity and great value so that they ought to be respected as 'ends in themselves' (Kant 1948: 97). While this maxim is a very incomplete guide as to how a rational person will behave it does rule out behaving as if other people are just like any other part of nature: there for our own convenience and benefit. Thus reason puts limits on our conduct in ways that may be effectively indicated by a system of rights that states the things that we cannot do to others and perhaps the duties we have to sustain and promote in relation to all human beings, including ourselves, as ends in themselves.

However, there are comparatively few moral maxims that look as if they might be justified by rational consistency alone. In most cases applying Kant's principle of moral legislation or universalisability is really a matter of asking 'could I approve if everyone did that?' and adopting a maxim only if you are prepared to live with the results. This makes universalisability a form of rule-consequentialism. If this is the case then Kant's attempt to ground morality in reason can have only very limited success and we can have no confidence that reason can provide us with a comprehensive system of rights that is independent from the natural wishes and desires of ordinary human beings.

However, if we adopt a wider conception of autonomy as the exercise of agency generally and not simply moral agency, then this can still give us a basis for the idea that persons are to be respected as ends in themselves, a view that can be filled out by showing the importance that we attach to using our capacities as an agent to have lives that are autonomous in the sense that they are relatively independent of other people. Thus freedom is, for Joseph Raz, 'the vision of people controlling, to some degree, their own destiny, fashioning it through successive decisions in their own lives' (Raz 1986: 369). While Raz rejects the notion that we have a right to autonomy, this less problematic model of agency is nevertheless sufficient to provide a basis for an attitude of respect for persons that is favourable to rights as the will theorists conceive of them.[1]

Rational agency may not, perhaps, have the all-consuming importance that will theorists tend to give to it, particularly if they adopt a narrow Kantian line as to what is involved in rational choice. There are other things about human beings, such as their capacities for complex forms of happiness, for creative activity and for forming loving relationships that are also deserving of respect, all for reasons that go beyond the degree of autonomy involved in these activities. And there are reasons other than respect for autonomy on which it is appropriate to ground obligations, such as the relief of pain and misery. This becomes apparent even in the case of human rights, the sphere in which appeal is made most often to Kantian values, when we consider rights to health or a decent standard of living.

Autonomy theorists argue that these rights are merely instrumental in that they identify prerequisites for living an autonomous life. I cannot live independently if I am in constant pain or am weakened by disease. Such 'basic rights' are important because they are the basis of the intrinsic value of autonomy that gives a distinct status to human beings (Kamm 2002). However, this counter-argument is scarcely adequate to explain the main reasons why we value such social and economic rights. While it is true that torturing usually (but not always) undermines their capacity for rational decision-making, this is hardly the core reason why we disapprove of it and make protection from torture an absolute right.

Nor is it convincing to say that all the rights of children relate to protecting and furthering their future autonomy, an argument that is not even available in the case of incurably mentally handicapped persons who afford a prime example of the fact that our priority commitments are to the relief of suffering as well as to respect for autonomy.

None of this negates the significance of autonomy as one value amongst others or the idea that human beings have a distinctive status that is closely related to the intrinsic rights that we consider to be fundamental. Moreover, autonomy also gains moral significance by giving us the basis for justifying obedience to the rights-conferring rules of our society if it can be shown that these obligations are freely chosen by those to whom they apply. Further, Kant's model of moral legislation, as that which can be endorsed by the rational will which is common to all human beings, offers a plausible theory of political obligation as well as a way of justifying having certain rights and a way of determining what rights we should have. In summary, it is possible that we can take autonomy to be an ingredient of human wellbeing that promotes human happiness as well as enhancing human independence for its own sake.

Interests

Turning to the evaluative mode of interest theories of rights, we can say that the issue of what rights people ought to have is determined by (a) which interests are to be given high moral importance, (b) which of these interests are under threat from the conduct of other people and (c) what in practice can be done through rule creation and enforcement to protect and further the interests so identified. Broadly conceived, interest theories contend that the point of rights is to promote and enhance interests. This means that both the form and the content of rights are determined by the ingredients of a satisfactory or fulfilling (usually human) existence.

We have already explored the concept of 'interest' in connection with a consideration of the subjects of rights as beings capable of having 'interests'. We noted there that interests could be interpreted as widely as to incorporate anything that is for the good of something and as narrowly as what complex sentient beings are 'interested in' having or doing (Campbell 2004: 164). When it comes to asking whether or not rights are a good thing, and if so what rights we ought to have, it is equally important to have some basis for deciding which interests count, both in morality generally and in particular in the determination of the value and content of rights.

Here I follow up a few leads that point us in the direction of larger issues in moral and political philosophy. The first lead comes from Jeremy Bentham, for whom interests, interpreted as pleasure and the absence of pain, are the ultimate goal against which we measure the moral outcome of actions (Bentham 1982: 11–50). Anything that is causally effective in increasing pleasure and minimising the pain of a sentient being is in that being's interests because it is instrumental in maximising their overall long-term hedonic wellbeing. Over the years this utilitarian theory has come to be identified with an approach in which material wellbeing is the measure of happiness and 'utility' is a matter of increasing the individual's and the communities' wealth.

This approach is clearly too crude if only because it excludes health and many other contributors to human happiness. Moreover, even in utilitarianism there is a strong ingredient of respect for 'higher' pleasures, or qualities of life, that are not readily measurable in terms of degrees of pleasure, such as creativity, loving relationships and moral achievement (Mill 1910: 7–11). It is necessary, therefore, to look for some further basis for choosing between interests and giving them priority. Two paths have repeatedly suggested themselves. One is to have recourse to individual choice or preference, the other is to resort to 'nature'.

Preference utilitarianism is the theory that what we ought to maximise is not pleasure but giving people what they want (Griffin 1986, Singer 1993). The idea is to maximise preference satisfaction. The phrase is misleading in that it suggests that getting our way is always satisfying, indeed this may be part of its attraction since it seems to suggest that the way to maximise happiness is to enable people to have and do what they want. Maximising preferences can be viewed as just a device for getting pleasure and avoiding pain, or it can be seen as a way of allowing the individual to decide what they value, which may not be pleasure but, for instance, creativity or power. These are all ways of giving content to the idea of people's interests. An alternative way of seeing preference utilitarianism is as an identification of ultimate value with making successful choices, but in this case it seems to revert to a form of will theory. Indeed preference utilitarianism is likely to give rise to a demand for liberty and claim rights in option form. In that people who put weight on making their own choices are likely to favour option rights. In its instrumental forms preference utilitarianism is open to the objection that people will often choose to have and to do things that are not in their own interests, if only because they miscalculate the consequences of their choices. Autonomy theorists may support their right to do so and to make their own mistakes, but this is not a move that can easily be taken within interest theory.

Another lead as to what should count as utility comes from philosophical naturalism. The thesis that there is a necessary connection between what is 'natural' and what is right has a long history going back to the ancient Greeks, who believed in a natural order of things that incorporated human beings in an overall organic whole in which everything has its proper place. Aristotle held that each type of being had its own nature but he did not identify the natural with everything that occurs but rather with the proper or correct functioning of a being leading to the realisation of its full potential as the kind of being it is. The most evident examples of this are things like plants which often wither and die before they flourish, but which nonetheless have a natural potential that can be realised in the right conditions. Thus human beings, for Aristotle, are rational animals, whose nature is fulfilled when reason governs the animal appetites of humans. This leads to an ethics that concentrates of cultivation of the virtues that enable a person to live a controlled and balanced life.

The Aristotelian approach was tied to an outmoded idea of science according to which each type of thing has its own essence, but was embraced in medieval theology in which natural essences were interpreted in terms of divine purpose. For instance, Aquinas (1979) held that through the study of instinctive or 'natural' conduct we could discern (with the aid of divinely bestowed reason) God's intention that we live in a certain way, a way that would lead to the fulfilment of our human nature. Thus, behind the instincts and appetites of sexual relations can be discerned God's plan for human procreation and the upbringing of children, hence the study of nature shows us that God requires us to marry and have sexual intercourse for the purpose of creating and rearing children.

The Aristotelian approach has been developed in a theological context into the medieval theory of natural law that we have already discussed. This tradition is carried on by contemporary followers of Thomas Aquinas, such as John Finnis,[2] and has echoes in the more secular theories of Amartya Sen (Sen 1999) and Martha Nussbaum (Nussbaum 2000), according to whom human beings have certain capabilities on the basis of which we can ascribe to them rights. This is a theory of human rights that identifies the basic ingredients of a human way of life as involving not money, or pleasure, or preference, but the capabilities that all humans have for health, action, creativity and enjoyment. On this basis they argue for protections to be provided and redistribution of goods carried out to ensure that all human beings can fulfil their capabilities. This is an elegantly expressed but inevitably controversial way of filling out the idea that rights follow from valued interests.

At this point it is possible to fall back on an empirical conception of what we identified in the last chapter as basic rights, rights that are instrumentally necessary to survival. Or, once again, we can bring in 'reason' to determine which interests should form the basis of the rules that create rights. Here the familiar ambiguities enter between reason as an empirical method to establish generalisations about the world, such as how best to achieve happiness, and reason as a form of moral intuition. But the former does not identify intrinsic interests, and the latter takes us into an entirely different world of moral epistemology, which we explore in the next chapter.

Nevertheless we should note that some theorists do seek to base rights on the idea of long term self-interest, rights deriving from those rules which enable us to protect not our immediate but our overall interests in the longer term. Assuming that individual human beings care only for their own interests, say their own pleasure and pain, and assuming that they have considerable instrumental rationality, theorists such as Thomas Hobbes (1996), and more recently David Gauthier (1986), have argued, that morality, and especially rights, are a matter of long-term self-interest, for only by respecting the interests of others can I contribute to a system that means they will respect my interests. In this calculus of mutual reciprocal benefit, rights feature as a device for ensuring that everyone benefits. This is especially true of legal rights that are backed by effective sanctions that deter people from dishonouring their obligations under these rights, thereby ensuring that no one can get the benefit of a system of rights that reduces suffering without themselves contributing by carrying out their obligations under this system.

The central difficulty with the rational self-interest model is that it is almost certainly empirically false. Actual individuals do have some altruistic concerns. Further, in so far as they do not, it is in the interest of individuals to depart from the system of agreed rights provided they can avoid sanctions that wipe out the advantages so gained. Moreover, instrumental reason alone cannot condemn this as being unfair or dishonourable or provide grounds for why an individual should sacrifice her own interests if this is not in her long-term interest. This is a weakness not only as to the practice of the theory but also to its very basis, for it seems unable to account for what is in many ways the essence of morality, that is the virtue of subordinating our own interests to those of others, and doing so for the sake of those others, the very thrust of the rights-based idea that every individual is entitled to respect as ends in themselves.

Conclusion

We started this chapter with the will and interest theories of rights as offering answers to our first question, about the meaning of rights, and developed it to take into consideration our second question, about who can have such rights. We then thought about how the two theories might contribute to finding out what actual rights people have in the societies in which they live. In relation to the will theory this seemed relatively easy, as we can look and see what rules are in force and which empower individuals to control the conduct of others in accordance with the content of those rules, although we noted the difficulty on determining if and when a social rule exists. In the case of the interest theory it seems more difficult to identify the interest or benefit that is associated with social rules that have complex consequences, and in any case there are problems in an empirical study of interests due to the vagueness and value-laden nature of the idea of 'interests'. In part this is solved by making it a matter of empirical investigation to find out what those concerned consider to be in their interests.

On passing to the moral question, we began to see the attractions of the will theory as a way of promoting the exercise of autonomy by giving people power over the conduct of others, a value that seems central to the idea of respect for persons which is so closely associated with rights. However it seems unduly restrictive to take autonomy to be the sole grounding of rights justification. Yet when we examine the prescriptive element of the interest theory and ask what interests ought to be protected and furthered through rules, we find ourselves in a jungle of competing theories. One of them, the idea that rights are instruments for the protection of long-term interests, seems promising but bears out the critique that rights are to be seen as the valued possessions of selfish individuals. In the next chapter we explore this terrain further through an examination of the competing ideologies that seek to bolster, reject or reform the idea of rights.

One final point must be made about how the will and interest theories relate to the critiques of rights, in particular the critique that rights are essentially egotistical or self-centred phenomena. Both will and interest theories can be viewed as oriented towards selfish individualism since the emphasis appears to be on giving priority to the individual's choices or individual's interests. Will theorists may seem to have the edge here as they can argue that a person's choice may be to further the wellbeing of others and that their theory does not assume that exercising rights is for the benefit of the rights-holder. However, despite the normal association of 'interest' with 'self-interest', a similar move can be made by interest theorists who can draw on the fact that people often taken an interest in the wellbeing of others, so that it is not the case that interest means self-interest if by that we mean seeking to pursue the advantage of the person whose interests are in question. Both theories are therefore able to open the way for viewing rights as capable of encompassing unselfishness or sociability.

Chapter 4

Political ideologies and their rights

The determination of whether someone has a right to something can be a matter of drawing fine distinctions and examining small print. Thus, in a court of law, before a decision can be made as to whether, for instance, one person has a right of way across someone else's land, detailed investigation must be made as to the principles and rules governing this area of land law and the particular history of the legally relevant relationships between the parties. However, such determinations take place against a panoramic backdrop of general moral and political philosophies that express differing positions about such matters as ownership, government and the economics of land use. These philosophies suggest general answers to our fourth question: what rights ought people to have? Moreover, the principles these political philosophies express and the assumptions they contain, when they are broadly accepted in a society, often find their way into answers to the apparently more factual question: what rights do people have? Already, in examining the wider ramifications of the will and interests theories, we have entered this open terrain of competing political outlooks. Now it is necessary to emerge from the conceptual jungle and embark on this next phase of our journey more directly.

Political philosophies are a bundle of factual beliefs about human nature, society and history, together with moral beliefs about what is good and bad, or right and wrong, and often religious or metaphysical assumptions about the meaning and purpose of life. These complex collections of inter-related ideas, which orient our thinking with respect to social and political matters, are sometimes called 'ideologies'. Examples include, 'liberalism', 'democracy', 'socialism', 'communitarianism', 'republicanism', 'environmentalism' and 'feminism'.

Such grand political theories can be referred to as 'ideologies' simply because of their comprehensiveness and their general role in organising our thinking about politics. But they may be regarded as ideologies in a more pejorative sense popularised by Karl Marx. Marx believes that world views are a reflection of the class or group interests of those who hold them, rather than genuinely universal moral outlooks that can rightfully claim to be in

the interests of all. As we look at some of these political philosophies, and their impact on our thinking about rights, a critical approach to rights will put us on the lookout for examples of this often hidden partiality that is insinuated by the term 'ideology'. While rights-talk nearly always purports to be morally universal, it may often be viewed critically as part of an ideology that creates and sustains an unequal and unjust set of social and political relationships. Even those who believe, unlike Marx, that rights-talk can rise above ideology (in its pejorative sense) accept that this is a common feature of rights discourse.

Taking a look at competing ideas about rights directs us back to the critiques outlined in Chapter 1 concerning the importance of rights, for good or ill, and challenges us to situate the discussion of the previous chapters in the general context of political philosophy. Space does not admit a comprehensive review of contemporary political philosophy from the point of view of rights. However, drawing on the discussions of autonomy, interests and consequentialism initiated in earlier chapters, I consider the significance for rights of the agenda-setting liberal theory of John Rawls in his monumental *A Theory of Justice* (1972), and responses from the point of view of libertarians, (Nozick 1974 and Posner 1977), communitarianism (Sandel 1982, McIntyre 1981), republicanism (Pettit 1997) and feminism (Young 1990 and Glendon 1991). I suggest some ways in which each ideology expresses or responds to our four critiques: egoism, legalism, dogmatism and elitism.

Rawls and the social contract

The central role of Rawls's work and its treatment of rights in contemporary political philosophy justifies explaining his theory in some detail. Ideologically, Rawls's theory of justice may be seen an expression of progressive liberal thought in the 1960s and 1970s, particularly in the USA, with its roots firmly in the origins of liberalism as a political and economic theory in the seventeenth century. At the time of its publication *A Theory of Justice* (1972) was taken to be a universally applicable theory of justice, although Rawls, realising its close connection with a particular vision of a just human society, later restricted its relevance to states within the liberal democratic tradition (Rawls 1993).

Rawls's theory is about justice, a concept to which he attributes a moral priority that overrides all other considerations. However, rights feature centrally within his conception of justice. His theory of justice calls for a set of basic non-overridable rights, and establishes principles for determining the rights and obligations of members of a just society. It also suggests a way of determining what these rights should be, thus suggesting how we might decide what rights we ought to have.

Rawls calls his theory 'Kantian constructivism', partly because he is indebted to Kant's analysis of autonomy, and partly because he 'constructs' his principles of justice through consideration of the hypothetical choices of ideally rational agents, thus underlining the importance of autonomy as a value. The rational choices in which Rawls is interested are those that are made in the process of reaching a binding agreement about the purpose and limitations of government. Rawls revives the tradition of social contract theory in a hypothetical form that sets out a normative method for arriving at an acceptable agreement about the rights and duties which apply in a just society.

The social contract theory that was in vogue in the seventeenth and eighteenth centuries at the time the enlightenment theories of natural rights were developed. These theories involve the idea of an actual historical agreement postulated to have occurred when individuals in the 'state of nature' (that is, prior to the emergence of society or government) agreed, either between themselves or collectively with a single individual (the future ruler), to accept government authority. Citizens' obligations to the state thus originate in an historical agreement to which they are now bound through the contract then made. This not only explains their obligation to obey the state, but provides a way of determining the rights and duties of sovereigns and subjects by looking into the terms of the contract into which they entered (Lessnoff 1986).

While retaining an interest in political obligation, Rawls avoids these historical speculations by offering us a decision-making procedure in a purely hypothetical, indeed fanciful, situation (called 'the original position') in which free and equal rational individuals are asked to discuss and agree on the ground rules for social cooperation. Those involved are purely self-interested in their motivation, but Rawls brings the moral ideals of impartiality and fairness into the design of the original position in which the social contract is debated and decided. His aim is to define a situation in which the decisions taken may be considered fair. Fairness requires, first that the participants be free and equal. By 'free' is meant uncoerced and without prior obligations (that is having formal liberty, in our typology of rights). By 'equal' is meant that they are all equally sources of claims on the benefits of social cooperation as well as having equal procedural right to participate in the decision making. Further, we are asked to imagine that in this original position the participants are behind a 'veil of ignorance' in that they do not know the key distinguishing characteristics that mark them off from other participants, such as their talents, personal tastes, ethnicity, gender, life-expectancy or position in society.

The contracting parties are unusual in other ways. They have complete and accurate information about society in general, including that, in the real world they will be moral creatures, with a conception of the good and the capacity to understand and obey rules. They know the 'primary goods', such as wealth, that everyone wants (this is a 'thin' theory of the good), but they do not know their own particular tastes or conception of the good (which would be a 'full' theory of the good). This is all set up so that they do not choose outcomes that will benefit people of their own type and situation. It is designed to 'nullify the effects of specific contingencies which put men at odds and tempt them to exploit social and natural circumstances to their own advantage' (Rawls 1972).

Rawls then puts 'rationality autonomy' into the situation by requiring the participants in the original position to debate and decide what they want on the basis of rational self-interest, that is their calculations of what would make them, as individuals best off, leaving out of consideration such 'irrational' motives as envy or the desire to harm others. The participants are in other ways entirely amoral, having no moral values, such as a commitment to justice, beyond the objects of their own natural preferences, although they do know that they will have a sense of justice and that they will have 'full autonomy', which is 'that of citizens in everyday life who think of themselves in a certain way and affirm and act from the first principles of justice that would be agreed to' (Rawls 1980: 521).

The participants in the original position are asked to adopt the principles that will be used to construct the basic institutions of their society, and which will then be used to decide on the distribution of benefits and burdens in that society. They are told that they can have in mind a 'well-ordered' society in which there is a 'public' (generally accepted) conception of justice which requires that there will be rules that are general, universal, public and capable of ordering social claims with finality and comprehensiveness. This ensures that they do not choose 'first-person dictatorship' in which the will of one person is supreme, and it prevents 'free riders' (people who take advantage of a public good without paying for it) who escape the obligations of justice. The participants in the original position are to choose 'a public system of rules which defines offices and positions with their rights, duties and immunities' (Rawls 1972).

From this dramatised concoction of impartiality and selectively informed rationality Rawls believes that we can derive some quite substantial conclusions. With the knowledge that there are certain 'primary goods', that is things, like health and resources, which all people want and need whatever their different conceptions of the good in other respects, Rawls suggests that two principles would be agreed in the original position. The first, which is directly concerned with rights, is that 'each person is to have an equal right to the extensive total system of equal basic liberties compatible with a similar system of liberty for all' (Rawls 1972). The sort of rights he has in mind are freedom of expression, liberty of the person, freedom of conscience, democratic participation, ownership and rights associated with the rule of law, such as freedom from arbitrary arrest and the right to a fair trial.

These basic liberties have what he calls 'lexical' priority over the second principle. This means that the first principle must be met before the second can be applied. They represent those things that people in the original position would insist on being guaranteed to them whatever they turn out to be like and whatever circumstances they might find themselves in. Rawls believes that we would all choose such things because we would be anxious about what might happen to us if they were not secured absolutely.

The second principle of justice agreed in the original position is that 'social and economic equalities are to be arranged so that they are both (a) to the greatest benefit of the least advantaged and (b) attaches to offices and positions open to all under conditions of fair equality of opportunity' (Rawls 1972) with the proviso that equality of opportunity is lexically prior to achieving the greatest benefit for the least advantaged (which Rawls calls the 'difference principle'). And so, once basic liberties have been secured for all in accordance with the first principle of justice, unequal distributions of goods may be introduced if they maximise the benefits for the worst off group (the 'maximin' criterion), always provided that there is realistic equality of opportunity with respect to the attainment of the better-off positions. This achieves Rawls's object of establishing that the 'right' is prior to the 'good', for the right puts limits on how the good may be pursued. This enables him to restrict the impact of consequentialism while endorsing a generally utilitarian approach to the benefits or social cooperation.

The second principle is not directed to establishing 'basic liberties' but is directly concerned with the rights to equality of opportunity, and it sets up a basis for the welfare rights of the least well-off group in society. In so doing, it takes account of consequential considerations, while subordinating them to the sort of limits that rights-based theories have sought to establish. Moreover, it sets up a general method for reasoning objectively about what rights persons ought to have.

In fact, Rawls's method is more complex than has been outlined so far. The outcome of the original position has moral standing because the conditions under which it is agreed are considered fair as they do not privilege anyone. This part of the theory Rawls's refers to as 'pure procedural justice' because the correctness of the outcome is judged by the fairness of the procedures and not by any independent knowledge of what is substantively just. However, the suggested outcomes of the original position may clash with what Rawls calls our moral 'intuitions', that is, our ordinary moral beliefs after we have reflected on these. When this happens, Rawls suggests that we go back to the original position to see if, by making it fairer we can come out with principles that are more acceptable to our considered moral intuitions. Similarly, we might question our intuitions and modify them in the light of our awareness of what a fair decision-procedure is likely to produce. Eventually such a process of reflection may lead to what Rawls calls 'reflective equilibrium', the point at which the principles from our modified original position coincide with our examined and reformed moral intuitions. This gives our reflective equilibrium the underpinning of two sources of moral insight: impartiality and intuitive conviction.

If successful, Rawls's approach, might overcome some of the major objections to rights. It provides a response to the critique that rights are dogmatic in that it identifies the sources of rights and gives us a method whereby their content may be articulated and refined. The basic rights are still drawn in very broad terms, but we have a method for making them more precise as we take into account more and more of the actual situations to which they are to be applied. Similarly the egoism critique of rights can be met by arguing that rights can and ought to be based on strict impartiality, with any resulting inequalities being to the benefit of the worst off. Further Rawls's approach, while concentrating on rules, clearly transcends narrow legalism by focusing on a deliberative process whereby those rules are developed in a consensual manner. Finally the elitist critique may be met by a confident affirmation that in the original position, people choose to live in a democratic society and insist on fair equality of opportunity.

However, Rawls's approach is not entirely successful. There is considerable dogmatism in his description of the initial position. For a start, we can query the basis and meaning of the assumption of basic human equality, the need for a 'well-ordered society' and the conception of society as an association of individuals rather than groups. Also, despite the fact that Rawls rules out any appeal to particular attitudes to risk of the participants in the original position, we might argue that Rawls's claim that the participants would choose his two principles of justice really depends on an illicit appeal to such attitudes. For instance, it only seems to be rational for participants to choose to maximise their minimum expectations (choose the maximin criterion) rather than, say, choosing to maximise their average expectations (the utilitarian criterion) if we assume they have a conservative attitude to risk, but this is an assumption that Rawls explicitly rejects (Barry 1973).

Moreover, if ultimately the dominant input into the outcome of 'reflective equilibrium' is our moral intuitions then we have not made as much progress as we need to have confidence that we can reach agreement even on broadly stated basic rights. It may be, for instance, that most people in the world would gladly forego certain of the basic liberties for a more prosperous and secure material environment. Others will find that looking to the wellbeing only of the worst off group, and then to a very limited extent, remains far too elitist in that it permits such other inequalities as increase economic output (Pogge 1989).

Indeed, it can be argued that the indeterminacy of the method is acute, for how can we know what such unusual people as those in the original position would choose? In real life our preferences are affected by a range of factors that derive from things that are particular to us: the communities in which we live, our gender and ethnic identities, our social and economic circumstances. To make an impartial choice we would not only have not to know about these things but we would have to be not influenced by them. But this seems impossible. In fact, it might well be that, if we removed these formative factors from our make-up then we would not be in a position to make any decisions at all on such matters.

These criticisms of Rawls are examined further when we look at other political ideologies. In fact, many of these points have been conceded by Rawls, but it is important to note that Rawls came to view his theory of justice in a rather limited way 'as working out a liberal political conception of justice for a democratic régime, and one that might be endorsed . . . by all reasonable comprehensive doctrines that exist in a democracy regulated by it' (Rawls 1995). This means that it can be regarded as an ideology in the morally neutral sense that it contains the presuppositions rather than the justifications of a particular political outlook, namely political liberalism. We can see this in the stress on the separateness of persons, the role of contract in setting up social institutions, the place of reason in human affairs, the attachment to certain sacrosanct liberties and, as the work unfolds, the effectiveness of competitive market economies.

Nevertheless, we can regard aspects of Rawls's work as ideological in the pejorative sense, because of its emphasis on only certain liberal values, an emphasis that is arguably built into the unquestioned assumptions of the theory. It can be argued, indeed, that it is a theory that glorifies models of individual competitiveness that are inevitably beneficial to the minority of able and energetic people from privileged backgrounds, with little more than a nod in the direction of the 'worst off' whom, it is assumed, would be even worse off without the system of competitive individualism.

Later Rawls deploys his general approach to consider what he calls 'human rights' as distinct from the rights of citizens that emerge from *A Theory of Justice* (1972). By 'human rights' Rawls (somewhat arbitrarily) means those rights whose observance protects a state from intervention on the part of other states (Rawls, 1993). Interestingly he does not include democratic electoral rights or representative government as human rights, but requires only that there be a public conception of the good that is sincerely sought by those in power. Without going into any detail about an interesting example of an attempt to justify armed interventions in the affairs of sovereign states, we can see this as an example of how a theory of rights can undergird the selective use of human rights in international relations to legitimate interstate interventions. It is as well to remember that theories of rights have such political uses, whether or not we approve of them.

Libertarianism

The ideologically controversial nature of Rawls's theory of justice amply illustrates the nature of the terrain we enter when it comes down to the roles and contents we attribute to rights in our preferred society. Some critics regard his conclusions, particularly concerning redistributive justice, as verging on socialism and giving insufficient weight to the fundamental rights of individual liberty (Nozick 1974). Others see his commitment to the welfare of the worst-off as superficial, ignoring larger questions of inequality in society generally and leaving too little scope for the values of community and caring (Campbell 2001: 68).

Libertarians, for instance, who regard the state as a largely unnecessary evil, react in at least two ways. Those libertarians who hold to the natural rights tradition of Hobbes and Locke insist that people are born with certain inalienable rights and that nothing may be done that runs counter to these rights. Libertarians in the utilitarian tradition of Bentham and J. S. Mill come to basically the same political conclusion, but on the basis that all rights are derived from utilitarian calculations and that the extensive substantive liberties against others in which libertarians believed are simply the most effective means of promoting the general happiness.

The inalienable rights approach is exemplified by Robert Nozick for whom rights are properties that individuals bring into the world with them. Using the example of our horror at the idea that we could be subjected to compulsory transplants of our vital organs (as some people argue utilitarianism requires), Nozick contends that 'individuals have rights and there are things no person or group may do to them (without violating their rights)' (Nozick 1974). The force of these rights is so great that it is never justified to infringe them even if that would reduce the violation of that right in society generally. Starting from the idea that we have an inviolable and inalienable property right in our own bodies, Nozick extend this to a total liberty (or 'negative claim right' in our terminology) to do what we like with our bodies unless we infringe the same right of others. Extrapolating further, he holds that we have a right to what we produce with our bodies and that no one may take this away from us without our consent. No amount of social good for others can justify the violation of such rights.

Further, anything we do for the welfare of other people must be with our consent, as a matter of benevolence or self-interest, not as a duty. It follows that whatever the outcome of our actions, as long as we do not violate the rights of others in the process, it is just. Indeed, it is a violation of our rights if what we earn by our own labours or with the consent of others (whom, for instance, might foolishly be prepared to buy a ticket to see me play golf, thus making me very rich) is taken away from us in the form of taxes to support the wellbeing of others. Such taxation is theft and the work we undertake to pay that tax is forced labour.

Whatever we think of the very restricted basis of this political philosophy, Nozick provides a vivid example of a rights-based theory. Moreover, he brings out how determining our rights in particular circumstances involves reference to how we got where we are. In order to determine whether a person has a right to something, on Nozick's theory, it is necessary to trace the history of that thing. If it was created by someone then it belongs to that person unless he has given it away or sold it. If it was taken from the person who had made it without his consent, then the possessor has an obligation to give it back, for it is not his. Nozick follows this through for all rights so that it is wrong to look, for instance, at the pattern of distribution of benefits and burdens and conclude that this pattern is right or wrong as it is, rather than because of how it came to be. He is thus totally opposed to redistribution unless this is to rectify past infringements of rights to person and property. Rights do often have this historical dimension, although he is dogmatic in his assertion that they do not also have a forward looking dimension as well.

Nozick presents a 'conjectural history' of how libertarian governments could have evolved by agreement without any violation of natural rights, thus justifying the existence of a minimalist state. This part of the theory is convoluted and not particularly convincing and one wonders whether he would have stuck with his analysis of rights if it turned out that only anarchy can be justified within the theory. Further, Nozick's theory is vulnerable to all four of our critiques of rights: egoism, dogmatism, elitism and legalism. But it is particularly vulnerable to the legalistic critique because it turns every dispute about rights into a forensic inquiry as to how we have come by our holdings. While we might seek to rescue the reputation of rights from Nozickean libertarians because of the highly selective moral basis of his theory and the potential of rights to serve other goals than protecting natural property rights, there must be some doubt whether this could be sufficient to counter his analysis of the way in which certain familiar negative rights seem to confirm some of the critics worse fears about rights.

Roughly the same libertarian conclusions can follow from the very different premises of utilitarianism. Thus, the work of Richard Posner (1977) and other law and economics specialists, draws on classical theories of the market to justify a very similar set of rights to those advocated by Nozick, at least in the economic sphere. Posner's analysis starts and finishes with the market theories derived from Adam Smith, whereby the assumptions of rational self-interest, plus open competition in the production and distribution of goods, leads, through the mechanisms of supply and demand, to the maximisation of wealth, that is, the greatest sum of material satisfaction (Smith 1976).

Again, the model is quite a simple one. Based on a theory of human nature according to which humans are not inclined to work unless they benefit as a result, but have the capacity to calculate their long-term interests and to channel their actions accordingly, people will trade what they have until they possess what they value most. Further, given the same assumptions about human self-interest, people will buy what they want at the lowest available price. Since wealth (as the sum of useful commodities) is increased by intelligently directed labour, people work to produce as much of what others are able and willing to buy to sell at a price that is lower than other producers, while still making a profit (that is taking in more than the cost of what they put into the production through labour, wages, buildings, machinery and so forth). Given an adequate supply of raw materials and a large enough market, this results in a plentiful supply of what people (consumers) want at the lowest feasible price. And so, as if by an 'invisible hand', the mechanism of the market turns the self-interested conduct of individual (and corporate) economic agents into an outcome that serves the greatest happiness of the greatest number.

In this free market economic system rights feature as prerequisites for an effectively functioning market. For the market to operate efficiently, people cannot take things without either paying for them or working for them. In other words, there must be property rights (as negative claim rights) and theft must be a crime. Similar protection must be given to the person of those who cannot otherwise engage in economic competition. Moreover there must be an absence of laws that prevent people entering into and engaging in the market place (a set of formal economic and personal liberty rights). There must also be a law of contract (a set of power or facilitative rights) that empower people to make binding agreements, and ancillary rights to have these agreements enforced.

In economics, this is a very powerful approach, although it has to be supplemented by endless modifications to take into account the fact that markets are not always open, competition is usually imperfect, and actual markets are always in danger of degenerating into monopolistic systems. One aspect of the economic analysis of law is that the law may be required to intervene in imperfect market relationships in order to counter its imperfections. It does so my 'mimicking' the market and enforcing rules (as in the law of negligence) that produce the same results as would have eventuated from a perfect market. Thus problems such as transaction costs (the time and effort required to gain the information to make the most rational economic deals) are dealt with by regulations requiring disclosure of relevant information, and externalities (the costs of production, such as pollution, that the producers who are causing the pollution do not pay for) are dealt with by regulations placing limits on or licenses for polluters.

To be a comprehensive theory of rights the same approach has to be taken to all spheres of human life. There have to be markets in personal relationships (including marriage, adoption and friendship), in health care (including transplants and euthanasia), in knowledge (intellectual property), in law enforcement (through deterrence and incapacitation) and so on.

The utilitarian (or 'economic rationalist') approach would appear to be more flexible and therefore less dogmatic than Nozickean libertarianism, for it is always possible that any interest-protecting rule, or right, may turn out to be less than fully efficient and therefore require modification. However, once the utility of having fixed rules is apparent and the dangers of self-interest distorting any system of making exceptions to those rules is clear, and once we take long-term consequences into account, the unchangeable facts of human self-interest and calculating intelligence mean that the same basic rights-creating rules are routinely justified on consequentialist grounds.

It is not difficult to see that libertarian theories of rights are easy game for the critiques of the egoism of rights and (particularly in the Nozickian version) of their dogmatism as well. However, libertarian theories of rights, whatever their philosophical underpinnings, may be most vulnerable to the charge of elitism for, while they accept the need for formal equality rights (the absence of rules excluding anyone from participating in the market), the operations of competitive markets, while they may be maximally efficient in the quantum of wealth produced, are highly inegalitarian in the distribution of that wealth. This is partly because of the different talents and efforts made by those involved, some of which may lead to merited inequality but most of which is a matter of luck, but also due to the cumulative effects of profit making which enable those who survive in the competition to amass vast fortunes. Unless the negative claim rights against the taking of wealth by means of taxation are overridden either by other rights (such as the right to health care) or by humanitarian considerations that are better expressed in the language of general utility, then a libertarian rights system is inherently elitist, not only in economic spheres but in all those areas of life that are dealt with according to the market model.

Communitarianism

The communitarian response to Rawlsian liberalism does not have the clear cut ideological agenda apparent in the case of libertarianism. What communitarians object to is the artificial individualism of both the liberal rights model and its more libertarian variations. In particular communitarians cast doubt on the very idea of societies as associations of individuals who bring to their societies all the capacities of reason, language, values and the whole complex of inter-personal emotions that are in fact the result of living in a particular society at a particular time. This associates communitarians with the egoism critique, but the community-based alternatives may have either a left-wing or a right-wing slant.

To communitarians, the social contract seems a total nonsense. In its historical form, the idea that individuals could enter into contracts before they had lived in a rule-governed social situation, and could have a conception of the obligation to keep the promises they made in this absurd historical fiction, is simply incoherent. In its hypothetical form, the social contract is also unconvincing, since the individuals as described, for instance by Rawls, are so denuded of their human characteristics that it is impossible to know what they would decide. In the language of one communitarian critic, an 'unencumbered' self (Sandel 1982) without location in a particular culture and context is not really a self at all, for such a person can have no sense of being a person with values and rationality of the sort that would be required to enter into a hypothetical social contract.

This is not necessarily a criticism of the egoism of the social contractor, for it is possible to imagine a non-egoistical inhabitant of an original position. Rather it is an objection to the abstract individualism of the model. It is equally applicable to the individualistic utilitarian who assumes that all individuals have basically the same core desires, or gives priority in the scheme of rational calculation to the 'preferences' of individuals, as if individuals have settled preferences outside the social context in which they were brought up and in which they live. The critique here is not so much moral as psychological and sociological. It is about the origin and cultural embeddedness of the characteristics that typify actual human individuals.

As noted in Chapter 1, the term 'communitarian' is of recent origin and refers to the work of certain post-Rawlsian theorists, such as Michael Sandel (1982) and Alistair MacIntyre (1981). The ideological drift of their work has overtones of Burkean conservatism in that they tend to emphasise that rights, so far as they exist, have to be seen as part of a social order rooted in existing practices (Burke 1969). These practices may change but they change slowly. Value assumptions come in when this fact is lauded for the stability and meaningfulness it gives to human life, even although the societies in question are conservative and inherently unequal. Thus appeals to natural or abstract moral rights possessed by individuals may be condemned because they undermine established social orders thus endangering the very values, such as human happiness and guarantees against oppressive power, that they are intended to promote.

This does not mean that conservative communitarians are hostile to rights as such. Indeed, the objection to abstract rights is often that they undermine the settled system of rights and obligations that have evolved to suit and indeed constitute the life of a particular culture and society.

However it is true that cultures vary in the emphasis that they give to rights and so this communitarian position does appear to make the significance of rights dependent on whether or not a culture emphasises, for instance, negative or positive claim rights, or whether it gives higher priority to such ideas as the common good when it comes to deciding the weight that is to be attached to individual rights. And there are communitarians that endorse the critiques of rights as such and express a preference for societies that give relatively little significance to rights, to the point where some rights theorists would say that they are not rights at all because they do not protect members of minority groups and particular individuals being subordinated to considerations of the larger group welfare, particularly with respect to family and cultural life.

The same basic sociological critiques of individualism can be made from a radically left wing point of view. Thus many critiques by contemporary communitarians echo Karl Marx's scathing analysis of the individualism of

Jeremy Bentham (Marx 1977). Marx was equally critical about 'natural rights' which, despite their apparent universalism, actually in practice serve to defend a particular system of bourgeois property rights whereby the owners of the means of production are entitled to treat their factories and their employees as if they were their private property to dispose of as they think fit. Under the not always hypocritical belief that the 'rights of man' are an affirmation of human equality (and Marx accepted they were to an extent in their rejection of feudalism) the universal rights of the individual are a way of supporting a 'false consciousness' amongst the proletariat (the class of those that sell their labour to the owners of production) that legitimates and sustains a particular form of unequal economic system, namely capitalism.

Along with this sociological critique goes Marx's questionable belief that economic and political systems based on liberal capitalist values were bound to collapse through their own self-contradictions and that a collectivised form of community would evolve in which people could, as members, participate equally in the shaping of their own lives as social beings, that is, beings who could flourish only when involved in non-coercive mutually supporting relationships. For Marx, rights would pass away with the laws that are a feature of societies, particularly capitalist societies, prior to the emergence of communism. Communism would be characterised by cooperative and conflict-free social relationships in which everyone contributed what they could and received in accordance with their needs as social beings. In the absence of private ownership of the means of production there would not be the conflicts that generate the need for rights, and there would be no place for the sort of coercive laws required to enforce bourgeois rights. Marxism is particularly associated with the legalism critique of rights whereby rights are seen as a way of treating people not as human beings but as abstract legal entities whose relationships can be captured in assertions and counter assertions of rules imposed by the state.

Another recurring theme of communitarians is that there is good reason to ascribe rights to groups and not just to individuals. Indeed, many argue that group rights trump individual rights (thus seeming to undermine the idea that rights protect the individual against the group). If individuals are largely constituted by their social relationships, and their values and ways of life have been absorbed as members of a particular group and culture, it makes sense to defend the interest of these social beings by making sure that their group is protected, and that means securing its continuation as a group and the inviolability of the cultural practices that make them a group, even if this means curtailing the freedoms of its individual members.

The adoption of group rights has attractions for critics of individual rights. Group rights certainly avoid the critique of egoism, and communitarianism generally focuses away from legalism towards less formal expressions of rights in established custom and shared values. Nor is dogmatism so closely associated with group rights as with individual rights. What group rights actually might be is, however, a difficult and complex problem, as the further analysis undertaken in Chapter 10 makes clear.

While the communitarian critique of overly individualised analyses of social and political life remain intellectually and morally powerful, communitarianism as an ideology has the disadvantage that the implications of this critique split into widely divergent programmes for reform, sometimes reactionally conservative and sometimes radically socialist. Moreover the philosophical basis for its prescriptions seems equally divergent, sometimes pointing to traditional, almost pre-scientific conceptions of nature and natural law, and sometimes embracing radically relativist post-modern epistemologies that derogate from the Enlightment project of seeking rational justifications. It is therefore necessary to identify what sort of communitarianism we are talking about before we can have any clear idea of its implications for the selection of the rights that people ought to have.

Republicanism

A recent revival of what has been identified as a 'republican' political philosophy presents as providing some sort of compromise between liberalism and communitarianism (Pettit 1997). Pettit's thesis is that liberalism stresses individual freedom as a negative matter of 'non-interference', and communitarianism stresses the importance of communal belonging, while republicanism brings the two together by accepting the liberal tenet that the state should not endorse any particular conception of the good, but conjoining it with the distinctively republican idea that individuals liberty must be securely protected so that they enjoy 'non-domination'.

Non-domination requires that citizens be secure in their liberties in that they are not liable to losing these liberties through the arbitrary action of the state. Non-arbitrariness requires that 'The acts of interference perpetrated by the state must be triggered by the shared interests of those affected under an interpretation of what those interests require that is shared, at least at the procedural level, by those affected' (Pettit 1997). Interference on the basis of the interests of those in power and without democratic debate and decision-making is 'arbitrary' and therefore illegitimate. Since non-domination is a communal good that can be enjoyed by one individual only if it is enjoyed generally in that society, we have here an element of communitarianism that is central to the republican development of liberalism.

It may be doubted both whether the liberal tradition has been concerned only with negative freedoms, as Pettit claims, and whether communitarians will be convinced that we can have secure ways of protecting the interests of all social groups in a society without supporting some shared conception of what amounts to a good or acceptable way of life for all. But the republican ideology is an attractive compromise that has breathed new life into the debate about the conflict between the individual and the community.

Its implications for our question 'what rights ought people to have?' point in two important directions. The first is the significance of rights in providing security against illicit interference, not only by the state but by other forces at work to undermine individual freedom. This previews our subsequent question 'how are rights best protected?'. It also highlights security as a fundamental human interest that generates a need for particular security rights as well as a system of rights in general. The second implication for substantive rights is to suggest that, having become aware of the various normative theories about the proper content of rights and the fact that there is no agreement as to which theory to adopt, we may have to turn, as I do in the final chapter, to some conception of democracy as the proper method to go about making the (collective) decision as to what rights we ought to have. Non-arbitrariness, it would appear, can only be achieved by genuine democratic debate and decision-making.

Feminism

The history of feminism may be divided into liberal and radical stages. In the liberal phase, from the nineteenth century until comparatively recently, those who saw women to be oppressed and belittled argued for equal rights, especially equal legal rights (Wollstonecraft 1975). Women should have the same rights as men to vote, to work, to own property, to education and so on. In this stage feminists saw rights as a neutral form that could take into account their interests, which had hitherto been neglected. Gender is, in this view, an irrelevant characteristic when it comes to the allocation of rights, and to take gender into account in this context is discrimination, along the same lines as racial and religious discrimination.

Along with the demand for equal rights, goes an attack on the distinction between the public spheres, such as politics which is governed by rights, and the private sphere, such as the family which is not. This dichotomy is seen as providing a provenance for gender oppression in the home and, for liberal feminists, should be abolished. In the public world of civic life, politics and work there are rules and rights. This is the man's world. In the private sphere of friendship and family, there are emotions and responsiveness. This is the woman's world. What is required is an end to this public/private distinction (Pateman 1988).

More recently, however, confronted with the fact that formal equality of rights has not brought about the equal participation of women in economic and political life, a more sceptical feminist attitude towards rights has arisen that sees rights as part of a male dominated culture that is overly dependent on rules, conflict, egoism and substantive inequality. Abolishing the distinction between public and private does not help if it is the public world of rules and rights that comes to dominate everything.

Part of this more radical feminist critique of rights derives from the work of Carol Gilligan (1982) who famously published her findings as a social psychologist that girls and boys had different attitudes to games, with boys insisting on and arguing about the rules of the game, and girls more focused on keeping the game going in a cooperative manner. This was developed into a more normative idea that women have an alternative, and perhaps a better, way of approaching life, with more emphasis on caring, nurturing and problem solving than on regulation and rights. Gilligan points to the difference between the 'justice perspective', often equated with 'male reasoning' that looks to rules and rights, and the feminist viewpoint in which 'relationships become the figure, defining self and others' and the focus is on establishing and fostering harmonious interactions, not arguing about the violation of rights and how this is to be rectified (Gilligan 1982). These ideas have been developed into a stark contrast between 'an ethic of rights' on the one hand and an 'ethic of caring' or 'an ethic of responsibility' on the other (Noddings 1984).

Other radical feminists became sceptical about the universalism of rights, for it appeared that the rights that women were offered are men's rights, that is, rights designed to further the interests of those with male characteristics, such as aggression and competitiveness. One solution is to walk away from the discourse of rights altogether. Another approach is to craft a different set of rights appropriate to women, such as special rights for carers. For many this seems to go back to an era of paternalism when women's particular or special rights were seen as protecting them against the rigours of the male world; not allowing them to work when pregnant, to take jobs that put a strain on their weaker bodies, and so on. Others, however, stress the need to recognise difference, partly for its own sake, and partly to protect the particular qualities of less powerful groups, such as women. A parallel debate occurs in the area of race, ethnicity and sexual orientation.

Without necessarily abandoning the view that all human beings are of equal value, radical feminists argue that what is important about people is often what is different or distinctive about them. For this reason some of the most fundamental rights might not be universal after all. Indeed, the danger is that if they are taken to be universal, then what happens in practice is that the alleged 'universality' is interpreted in a way that favours the dominant class or gender group, a typical example of an ideology in the pejorative sense.

Similar criticisms are made of the concept of 'impartiality' as it is used in the discourse of rights to indicate that all have equal rights and that these must be applied without bias and with complete consistency. This approach does not, for many feminists who seek to retain a commitment to justice and rights, deal with the underlying causes of oppression in society. Thus Iris Marion Young notes:

> A growing body of feminist-inspired theory has challenged the paradigm of moral reasoning defined in the discourse of justice and rights. In this paradigm moral reasoning consists in adopting an impartial and

> impersonal point of view on a situation, detached from any particular interests at stake, weighing all interests equally, and arriving at a conclusion which conforms to general principles of justice and rights impartially applied to the case in hand.
>
> Young (1990: 96)

Young sees this phoney idea of impartiality as recommending an unhelpful and destructive detachment that detracts from the importance of the differences between people and situations, and hence to a neglect of oppressed groups and the different causes of oppression.

The feminist critique has much in common with communitarian criticism of the individualism of the rights tradition, for women have a special interest in the formation and sustenance of the sort of solidarity and community that can only be obtained in groups. In this respect women's movements are becoming increasingly sensitive to the fact that women belong to many different groups and cannot themselves be seen as a unified category. It is also critical of rights on the grounds of (male) egoism, particularly with respect to the will theories of rights and their emphasis on individual claims. It is also very much associated with the idea that rights involve an overemphasis on rules. There is, however, considerable ambivalence in feminist writing about rights in that many feminists, particularly those involved with human rights, see the idea and institutions of rights as potentially protective of vulnerable minorities, including, but by no means confined to, women.

Conclusion

This chapter is a very incomplete survey of some of the ideologies that compete over the discourse of rights and react to it in ways that vary from enthusiastic affirmation to outright rejection. It is designed to illustrate that theories of rights are but part of wider political philosophies and that these wider political philosophies have a direct bearing on the sort of rights we ought to have. It also demonstrates why it is important to be suspicious about grandiose appeals to rights, particularly when expressed in abstract terms, because of the background ideologies that come into play when we seek to give them more concrete expression.

If we take our critiques of rights seriously we will have to consider further whether we can retain something of the advantages of a straight-forward no-nonsense approach characterised by the work of Nozick, in which rights are clear and clearly decisive, while meeting the objection that such approaches are simplistic and biased. It seems also that, if we are to retain the legitimacy of rights discourse, we will have to find some place for the group and difference-oriented rights that meet the sort of difficulties raised by communitarians and feminists.

The way forward here may be greater emphasis on the idea of democracy, both as itself the supreme expression of autonomy, in this case a sort of group autonomy that is compatible with the nurturing of public goods and as a reaffirmation of the significance of the rule of law, with a greater emphasis on legislation than on courts as the authoritative source of rights. This provides both a recognition of the communitarian focus on the social nature of individual wellbeing, and an opportunity for the emergence of rights that are in form, force and content appropriate and acceptable to that type of society. This is the model of 'democratic positivism' that is presented and discussed in the final chapter.

PART II

THE INSTITUTIONS OF RIGHTS

Part I explored both the moral and the legal modes of rights discourse, observing that the association of rights with rules means that legal analysis makes an important contribution to the understanding of rights. In particular, legal rights help us see the connection between rights and effective entitlements, drawing attention to the assumption that rights offer some sort of guaranteed expectations and operative normative capacities to their holders (hence their attraction to republicans). On the other hand, the idea of rights clearly transcends legal discourse and applies also in the social sphere where there is a less formalised system of expectations concerning how we ought to behave towards each other, expectations on which we can base the notion of customary or societal rights and sometimes the political demands for establishing legal rights and affecting government policy with respect to our social and economic relationships.

The contribution that rights, and social and legal rules generally, make to human wellbeing in terms of security, fairness and cooperation, provides the basis for moral reasons why it is important to have rights, and to have them to some extent irrespective of what the content of those rights may be. These moral reasons for having a system of rights flow through to the justification for establishing specific rights, both in law and in social opinion. The reasons why having rights is important and the evaluation of the rights that we do or ought to have are based on core moral values, such as autonomy and wellbeing.

The undeniably moral bases of rights do not do away with the need to institutionalise the protection of interests in response to the claims of moral rights. In fact, to do their job, rights must form an operative part of normative frameworks that can guide, govern and facilitate social interaction. It is of the essence of rights discourse that it calls for institutional embodiment in order to achieve its objectives. The main justification for having rights lies in the benefits that accrue to human beings from living under a system of rules that embody rights and duties as defined in positivist terms. The point of arguing for the adoption of rights with a specific content is to create a system that reliably protects the interests and empowers the choices that the rights serve. Part II explores the variety of ways in which this institutionalisation or social actualisation of what would otherwise be mere manifesto rights takes place.

Many, but not all, of the institutional embodiments of rights are legal and some are constitutional. The institutional requirements of an effective rights framework include legislatures, government bureaucracies, courts, police forces and prisons. While these institutions have evident physical manifestations in the buildings in and from which they operate, they are essentially an interconnected set of organisations that serve distinctive functions in a complex interactive system of social norms and practices. It is noteworthy that the various roles which make up these institutions are themselves defined in terms of the rights and duties that characterise these roles.

In order to describe the functions and operation of these institutions we can draw on the basic concepts of law, including the idea of law itself (Atiyah 1983, Waldron 1990). A legislature's function is to make laws, a government has the task of administering laws, police are there to enforce laws, and the courts to apply them to particular cases. But what is 'law' and why is it important?

Law is a body of rules that are mandatory (non-optional) in the territory or sphere in which they apply and which are created and administered by the interlocking institutions listed above. The best working analysis of a developed legal system is that put forward by H. L. A. Hart (1961) (see Sumner 1987). According to Hart, a legal system is a combination of primary and secondary rules. The primary rules apply directly to ordinary conduct, laying down what must or may be done or not done. The secondary rules are rules about rules. These secondary rules determine who, for instance, may make, enforce and change the authoritative first order rules in a society. Secondary rules are administered by officials whose interlocking roles constitute the principal operatives of a legal system (Hart 1961).

Rights come into this picture in several ways. First, in order to carry out these functions, the institutions themselves involve the exercise of certain power rights: rights to legislate, to administer, to enforce and to apply laws. Most of these rights are 'power conferring' in that they derive from rules that entitle officials of the institution in question to change the legal position of other people by creating obligations, issuing authorised directives, and determining particular normative issues such as who owns what and what people may or may not do to each other (Hohfeld 1919).

Second, rights come into the picture as ways of justifying legal systems. Power rights require justification. Why should there be officials who are able to bind other people and alter their entitlements? Why should there be such public power-conferring rights? One (but not the only) answer is that such second order rights serve to protect and promote other rights, principally the first order rights of those who are affected by the exercise of the power rights for which justification is being sought (Dworkin 1986). Public power rights are also justified in consequentialist terms because of the contribution they make to such public goods as order, dispute resolution, economic efficiency and defence.

Private power rights also require moral justification. It will be recalled that private power rights are the normative powers of individuals to affect the legal position of other individuals. Such rights include the right to buy and sell property, to get married or to make a will, all of which affect the entitlements of other people. These rights require justification because they can adversely affect the interests and choices available to other people. This justification may sometimes also be given in terms of other rights, such as liberty rights, but it may also be provided through consequentialist arguments about the social benefits of, for instance, enforcing contracts and facilitating family relationships for economic and reproductive ends.

These first order, justifying, rights are mainly substantive claim rights, such as the right to life, to physical protection, to welfare benefits, and so on – the sorts of reasons why, on the social contract model, people in the state of nature agree to enter into political and legal relationships. The rights used to justify the existence of public power rights of officials also include private power rights of citizens, such as the right to enter into contractual relationships. Such rights have no value if, when they are not respected, they cannot be enforced. The role of law here is to provide clear and authoritative rules for regulating such private powers and settling disputes about such matters.

The justification required for the right to make law is particularly stringent because first order legal rules are binding on all members of a society and cannot operate effectively unless they are generally obeyed. It is a fact of human societies that general conformity with mandatory rules does not happen within a large scale group unless there is an element of actual coercion that ultimately involves the use of force against recalcitrant individuals. While such sanctions need not be viewed as a logically necessary or a factually dominant part of any system of social norms, a coercive element is a standard part of the institutionalisation of those norms that are regarded as legal norms within a society. Legal rights, therefore, with their correlative duties, always require a rationale that is sufficiently powerful to justify the element of coercion that is present to some degree within all legal systems. Ultimately, it may be argued that such justifications cannot be given unless it can be shown that the legal system actually serves important fundamental rights particularly human rights.

A third way in which rights have bearing on the institutional arrangements within a legal system is in relation to how the public power rights involved are put into practice. Thus, in the making of laws, legislatures may be required to submit their legislative proposals in a certain form and have them approved after debate and voting in a prescribed manner. The rights correlative to such duties are called procedural rights since they affect the way in which binding decisions must be made and applied if they are to be a legitimate exercise of the powers in question. Similarly, in the application of laws to particular situations, those involved may have a right to be heard, or to be represented by a lawyer, or to cross-question witnesses. Procedural rights of this sort have great importance in law and some of them, such as the right to a fair trial, are included in the standard list of human rights (International Covenant on Civil and Political Rights, 1966: articles 9, 14, 15 (United Nations 1996a)).

There is a fourth way in which rights feature in the legal institutions that form the context of much rights discourse. We have seen that the justification of law brings in rights to exercise public power. In order to ensure that public power is not used to cause harm it may be necessary to institutionalise certain rights by making them constitutional rights, so that courts have the power to nullify laws that conflict with these rights. The constitutional power of courts to override legislation on the basis of its violation of constitutional rights is not a universal feature of legal systems, but it is one, where it exists, in which rights play a central role.

In all these and some other ways, the institutions of law take us into a maze of associated power rights, claim rights, procedural rights and constitutional rights. The discourse of rights generates institutional arrangements of this sort. However, the institutions of rights are not confined to legal institutions, which are, in fact, often no more than formalisations of social arrangements that continue to apply in the ordinary interactions of any social system. Other systems of rights and duties are developed and applied in non-legal spheres, such as business and education, that go beyond everyday societal rights but are not extensively embodied in legal systems.

These non-legal or societal rights and duties include the professional and business norms that govern both the customs and the internal disciplines of the occupational communities in question. Such rights, which belong to what is sometimes referred to as civil society, are typically manifest in occupational codes of conduct, the teachings of religious communities and the articles of voluntary associations. They also feature in a broader political landscape as the basis for democratic rights.

Thus, the moral right to democracy is a justified claim to equal political power. It is institutionalised through the familiar procedural and power rights involved in elections and the associated rights of freedom of association and freedom of speech. Many of the justifications for such democratic rights are consequentialist, expressing, for instance, the view that democratic processes are the best method available for seeing that government is carried out in a way that maximises citizen wellbeing. However, other justifications of democracy take the line that equality in political power is an intrinsic right based on the inherent value of self-determination, however well or badly it is carried out, which is commonly accepted as a human right.

In this part of the book we consider the institutions of rights in three chapters. Chapter 5 (Legal rights) starts with a focus on domestic law in the light of ideas that are embodied in the notion of the 'rule of law' and looks at the arguments for and against constitutional bills of rights in the light of other means of implementing human rights. Chapter 6 (International human rights) expands this perspective to include international law, particularly the developing system of international human rights law. Chapter 7 (Rights and civil society) takes in both domestic and international concerns in considering the implications of rights for the more informal and private aspects of social life, particularly in the sphere of non-governmental organisations and business enterprises but also with respect to those human rights that establish the criteria for acceptable governance generally.

In summary, the moral imperative behind a rights approach to morality and politics is to secure and protect in a concrete way the treasured freedoms, interests and capacities from which rights derive their justifications. Such institutionalisation need not always be formal, legalistic and coercive, but it does have to be effective, at least to the point where it makes sense for us to say that when an individual or group claims that their rights have been violated or that they have a right to do or have this or that, they are doing much more than simply making a morally justified demand. A degree of institutionalisation is required if rights are to fulfil in practice their functions as claims which we, as rights bearers, are entitled to make and on which we are able to rely, thereby providing the basis for an authoritative settlement of social and political disputes and the effective protection of specified interests. This is the subject matter of Part II.

Chapter 5

Legal rights

Rights talk is a moral discourse which claims that there are moral grounds for setting up entitlements that can be relied upon for the protection and furtherance of specified interests. In complex societies, setting up entitlements often crucially involves establishing legal rules, and hence legal rights. Emphasising the significance of legal rights for the analysis of rights in general does not imply that non-legal or societal rights are less important. However, societal rights are in many ways similar to legal rights, the crucial difference being that legal rights have the backing of distinctively legal institutions, such as legislatures, courts, government administrators and police, whereas societal rights are part of the less tangible but more stable practices and attitudes current in a cultural tradition.

Legal rights do not necessarily offer better protection than societal rights. Public opinion, peer pressure and individual conscience may be more effective in seeing that rules are obeyed than expensive and elaborate bureaucratic and court procedures which may have very low compliance rates. Nevertheless, given the damage to individuals and social structures that can be done by the unconstrained wrecking behaviour of small minorities, it is hard to imagine that societal rights would work effectively in large scale developed societies without the backing of legal rights, if only to deal with the harmful effects that a small number of people can cause by ignoring their duties that correlate with societal rights. Legal rights are the rights on which we can fall back when societal rights fail, because legal rights can be enforced by the coercive power of the state, albeit often not without considerable expense, and frequent failure, on the part of the rights-holders.

Moreover, legal rights have an important informal role in social life by providing a reference point for justifying our conduct to each other. They provide a framework for everyday social interactions that operates largely without the processes of legal adjudication, litigation and enforcement. If we act within our legal rights, this is a step on the way to social acceptance in most societies, most of the time. Legal institutions are consequently fundamental to our understanding of rights in general. And, because legal rights are one of the ways in which the discourse of rights impacts on palpable reality, the legal articulation of rights has a reciprocal, deep and pervasive influence on the overall discourse of rights (Flathman 1976, Wellman 1995, but see Raz 1984 and Thomson 1990).

Of course, legal rights themselves are unlikely to be effective unless the rights in question have the support of officials and of public opinion. Indeed it is part of the concept of a legal right that it has the effective support of legal officials. Moreover, the political support of officials and citizens for legal rights must itself be made effective in the provision of sufficient resources to enable the legal system to operate, and to make available the material and organisational infrastructure required to implement specific rights. Legal rights that actually provide what people are entitled to are not a matter of paper rules but implemented rules and that implementation takes us far beyond police and courts to the administrative and economic organisation of a society. This is well summarised by Carl Wellman:

> Typically a legal right is a complex cluster of legal liberties, claims, powers, and immunities involving the first party who possesses the right, second parties against whom the right holds, third parties who might intervene to aid the possessor of the right or the violator, and various officials whose diverse activities make up the legal system under which the first, second and third parties have their respective legal liberties, claims, powers and immunities and whose official activities are in turn regulated by the legal system itself . . . Any adequate analysis of a legal right must distinguish the several roles of the individual citizens living under the law (the roles of the first, second and third parties) and of the officials (policemen, prosecutors, judges, jurymen, legislators and administrators) whose activities transform what Llewelleyn called a 'paper right' into a real and functioning legal right.
>
> Wellman (1975: 52)

In this chapter we follow this line of thought by looking at the association of rights and remedies, the concept of the rule of law and the distinctively rights-based mechanism of the judicial review of legislation.

Rights and remedies

Rights are, at least potentially, precious possessions. They can give us power, confidence and self-respect; but not if they are violated or ignored. Moral rights, rhetorical rights, even manifesto rights, while they can play a part in bringing about social change, are in themselves a mockery if the interests that they are intended to protect are harmed with impunity. Rights that matter are rights which are protected and for which, if violated, there is some remedy which brings compensation or restoration to the rights-holder and censure, liability or punishment to the right-breaker. The remedy not only compensates for the violation but plays a part in preventing it by both affirming the significance of the protected interest and providing incentives to people not to violate the right in question.

Given that the principal function of rights is to provide protection and security for interests it is sometimes argued that rights without remedies are not rights at all. This is a strong version of the thesis that rights exist only when there is a social rule that successfully protects an important individual interest.

This line of thought utilises a rather narrow conception of a social rule which does not allow for the common situation where a rule has broad social support, but is frequently violated with little effective response. Of such a situation we might say that there is a right but that it is poorly protected. However, the fact that there is a right implies that something is amiss when there is ineffective protection, lack of critical response to violations and poor remedial action. Indeed if no criticism is made, no remedial action is attempted and the violations are widespread, it makes sense to say that there is no right, although, we might add, there ought to be. Further, a crucial distinction between legal rights and other rights is that in the case of legal rights there is an authoritative remedial mechanism that is called into action to deal with alleged rights violations, so that rights may be said to exist even if they are frequently violated, just so long as there is an appropriate and available legal response to such violations (Hart 1961).

The close, almost logical, connection between rights and remedies does something to explain the significance of identifying the duties that are correlative to right, for that is to identify the persons who can be held liable to pay compensation or receive punishment if they do not fulfil the specified duties. However, as we will see, these remedial duties may also fall on those who have a duty to protect rights-holders against the violations of others and take action to ensure that compensation or punishment is enforced where violations occur.

Typically, legal remedies are divided into civil and criminal, although the term 'remedies' is used primarily for civil remedies, in contrast to the penalties, sanctions or punishments that are the outcome of criminal convictions. In civil law, which concerns such matters as breach of contract and tort (that is negligently causing harm to another person), remedies are looked to as a matter of compensating the victim for the harm done by the wrongful conduct of another. The aim of such remedies is to prove compensation of an amount that will put the injured person back in the same or equivalent position as they were before the injury was incurred (Weinrib 1989).

Such remedies seem highly appropriate as responses to violations of rights. If rights are for the protection of interests then they should provide for a restoration of the loss or injury involved in the violation of a right. Remedial justice lies at the core of the logic of rights. Compensation by the rights-violator, where possible, is always in order when the duties correlative to violated rights have not been fulfilled and harm has resulted.

However, literal compensation by violators is not always possible. Murdered persons cannot be brought back to life. Poor people are often unable to compensate for the harms they have negligently caused. This is where criminal sanctions come in: fines, forced labour, deprivations of liberty, even death itself. Such penalties are not compensation for victims but punishment for offenders. They may sometimes be construed as a form of compensation since they make the offenders 'pay' for their crimes and this may give some satisfaction to victims. Certainly, we often do think of the victims of crimes as having their rights violated, or of them having a right (against the state) that those whose criminal conduct harmed them be punished.

Exactly what is going on here depends on the theory of punishment involved, but there would appear to be elements of retribution as well as deterrence. The retribution can be viewed as a type of compensation (Sadurski 1985). The deterrence, both of the individual offenders to encourage them not to re-offend ('specific deterrence') and of other potential offenders ('general deterrence') can be viewed as a means of protecting the rights-protected interests of potential victims. We consider that because a crime harms the community generally, all citizens have a right that offenders be punished. Nevertheless, it is clear that criminal sanctions are crucial ways of protecting rights to life, bodily integrity, property, of particular victims. With respect to rights, therefore, punishment is not merely a form of second best compensation (Davis 1986). It also has an important role in deterrence and prevention of crimes that violate rights. Criminal law is thus an important means for reducing the incidence of rights violations. It may be seen as proactive protection of rights rather than a second-best remedy for rights violations. It relates particularly to the protective duty of government to safeguard and nourish the interests that are identified in the assertion of a right.

To emphasise remedies as central to the nature and operation of legal rights may seem odd to those who have been led to believe that focusing on remedies is an alternative to focusing on rights. This is because the long tradition of the common law used the language of remedies rather than rights. What mattered in common law jurisprudence was to have a 'cause' of action, not to establish a rights violation. A cause of action requires demonstration that a defendant's conduct was of a specific type that gives rise to liability.

On the analysis of claim rights as correlates of obligations owed to a rights-holder, this debate seems largely vacuous (Kramer, Simmonds and Steiner 1998). Building on the correlativity of rights and duties, in which rights and duties are equal constituent part of the normative relationship involved, rights and remedies for the neglect of specified duties, are a practical extension of this correlativity which centres on responses to failures of duty. It is mistaken to argue that there is a significant difference between a system of law that emphasises remedies and one that emphasises rights. The mistake is to accept that there is an operative legal right without a remedy.

Explicating legal rights takes us deep into the principles of civil and criminal liability in law. This is so whether the rights in question are human rights or ordinary rights. The human right to life, for instance, is a combination of a general prohibition on killing, a duty on officials of the state, and to a lesser extent other people, to prevent killing, and a duty on the state and perhaps others to compensate victims (or their families) and punish those who have killed, partly to protect the rights of persons other than the victims. There are in fact many more remedies for rights-violations than the two mentioned so far. For instance, of great significance for rights are administrative law remedies that protect citizens from maladministration and unlawful conduct on the part of officials, by limiting the powers of officials and overturning their decisions that are not in accordance with the law.

It should be noted that most of the remedies that are characteristically associated with legal rights are not exclusively attached to legal as opposed to societal rights. Compensation and punishment, for instance, are features of many non-legal social relationships in families, social groups and workplaces. What is distinctive about law, and hence legal rights, is not so much the remedies as the way in which these remedies are set up and applied through an authoritative system of general rules administered by independent courts. This takes us to the idea of the rule of law, a concept of great importance in the discourse of rights and one that brings out even more clearly the impact of legal institutions on our understanding of rights.

Formal rule of law

Sometimes law appears to be more as a source of obligations than of rights. The rule of law, particularly as it is appealed to by politicians, is often invoked to emphasise the citizens' obligation to obey the law and respect the decisions of legislatures and courts. This is an obligation that has no correlative right since law-abidingness is in general productive of a public good enjoyed by all citizens indiscriminately. But particular legal obligations usually do have correlative rights, so that conformity to law is in general a matter of respecting rights.

In fact, there is much more to the rule of law than law-abidingness. The 'rule of law' is routinely opposed to the 'rule of men', a rather obscure way of putting the point that governments are entitled to govern only by making general rules that are applied by executive officials and subject to the control of independent authorities, particularly courts (Aristotle 1948: 1287a, Dicey 1964). The rule of law rejects governance by way of issuing particular commands and permissions about what specified individuals must or must not do. Or, more weakly, if certain officials do have the some power to issue particular orders this is only because of a general law that gives them that authority as officials. Moreover, according to the rule of law, any citizen who is required to do something by an official has recourse to a tribunal or court to determine if the requirement is lawful in terms of existing power-conferring legal rules.

This fuller idea of the rule of law is that, to be legitimate, government must be both through law and subject to law. Government through law is government by means of law, that is, through the enactment and enforcement of general rules rather than by particular commands of particular persons. Government subject to law is where those who govern are themselves subject to law, not only as individual persons, but also in their role as governors. Thus governments must govern by means of law and in accordance with law. Further, governments are not the final arbiters of whether their actions are lawful. It is essential to the rule of law that legality is a matter for courts to decide.

A variety of moral reasons can be given in favour of governance through and under the rule of law. Many of these reasons relate directly to the idea of rights. Thus, the rule of law is at the core of some of the most fundamental civil rights. These include important procedural and formal rights, such as the right to 'due process' or 'natural justice', the right to equal protection of the law, the right not to be treated 'arbitrarily' and so on.

In fact, the moral and practical significance of the rule of law goes far beyond the fact that it incorporates certain civil rights. For instance, the limitation of government to governance through laws is what gives significance to formal liberty rights, that is, rights to do things not forbidden, or not do things that are not required by law. This is an important part of what it means to live in a 'free' society.

The rule of law is also central to one aspect of justice, often referred to as formal justice, namely the idea that like cases be treated alike, that is treated in accordance with recognised criteria for determining what is and what is not 'alike' (Perelman 1963). Formal justice cannot be systematically achieved unless there is an effective system of rules in place laying down the criteria for treating categories of people similarly or differently. Whatever we think of the content of a particular law, there is moral significance in the fact that our interests are impacted by government (and other powerful organisations) only by rules that say what categories of persons and actions are to be treated the same or differently. This is a more limited notion on 'arbitrary' than that put forward by republicans (see p. 75) but it is fundamental to the rule of law.

Formal justice is one expression of the idea that all are, or ought to be, equal before the law, a civil and political right that features in all statements of human rights. This is not a very radical conception of equality as the rules in question may permit and enforce gross inequalities, but it may be seen as a minimal embodiment of the idea of the equal worth of persons, and this is so even if there is doubt about the moral content or moral justification of the particular laws that apply; hence, our *prima facie* obligation to obey laws, even if we disagree with their content.

Further, much of the significance of the rule of law derives from the circumstances of politics in which people living together in a society need a central authority and yet have reason to fear the power that such a central authority must have if it is to fulfil its functions (Hobbes 1996). The protection that brings security from personal injury, the order required for the acquisition and use of personal property, the force necessary to maintain those voluntary agreements that are crucial to the prosperity of the society, the organisation that goes into the provision of adequate defences against external attack – all these things require submission to an authority with sufficient power to coerce the recalcitrant and manage the patterns of sustainable cooperative existence.

For these very different reasons there is moral value in the rule of law quite apart from the sheer efficiency of controlling and coordinating the conduct of large collectivities of persons in this way. These reasons can readily be articulated in terms of rights. And so, while, of course, governments can use rules for purposes other than the promotion of rights, the rule of law is a necessary precondition of many of the benefits whose furtherance and protection is standardly elucidated in terms of rights. Health, safety, welfare, as much as formal justice and civil and political rights, depend on an operative system of law. Sometimes this involves establishing individual rights that may be enforced by those individuals through courts, the core example of 'option rights' (see p. 45). But it can also involve setting up rights for all those whose interests are at risk by putting systematic arrangements in place to ensure that society has the capacity to protect these interests. This is particularly the case with respect to positive welfare rights, where the state has the duty to provide adequate services to meet the health and welfare needs of its citizens (Hunt 1996).

Such rights, as we will see, often remain, for good or bad reasons, political (or societal) rights rather than legal rights as they do not correlate with legally enforceable duties backed by legal remedies. But fulfilling the duties correlative to these rights does involve establishing rules in order to facilitate the creation of the resources and their effective deployment to meet the needs on which the rights in question are based. This is an issue which we shall return to in Chapter 7.

Substantive rule of law

There is reason to fear that actual governments will not always govern through rules, for it will often be in their interests to depart from the rules in particular cases, even when they stick within the legitimating goals of government. Worse still, there is reason to fear that governments will use the powers they are given for one set of purposes to promote quite different ends, such as their own private interests, and do so through the instrumentality of rules. Whiles states are legitimated by their function in establishing and protecting rights, they are also one of the main sources of violations of the interests that they ought to be protecting.

For these reasons some philosophers and jurists contend that the rule of law is a more substantive or 'thicker' concept that the formal one that I have outlined above (thus Fuller 1969, compare Raz 1979). They argue that the rule of law or 'legality' requires that the rules in question have a particular content, if only in the negative sense that they do not include rules which violate certain fundamental rights. Human rights are routinely brought in to give content to this more substantive idea of the rule of law.

This position is fleshed out by Lon Fuller, who spells out in some detail what he calls the 'principles of legality' whereby it is a requirement of law that rules be not only general and clear, but also publicised, prospective, stable and possible to obey (Fuller 1969: 46). Like Hart, Fuller points out the efficiency of these formal requirements. No authority, for instance, can get people to follow a certain code of conduct unless that code is made public and done so in advance. Similarly there is simply no point in requiring people to do that which they are not able to do. But he goes further than Hart in arguing that these principles of legality are also a way of treating citizens with respect. By promulgating authoritative rules in advance the ruler is treating citizens as responsible individuals who can choose for themselves what to do in the light of these commands. In general, flouting the principles of legality is not only inefficient it is unfair. Thus it is simply an outrageous insult to a responsible human being to punish them for doing something that they could not have avoided doing.

Hart agrees with most of this, but he disagrees with Fuller when he argues that the formal requirements of legality actually impact on the content of the primary rules of the system, so that some rules, such as racialist ones, simply cannot be part of a legal system. Hart disagrees here on the grounds that the formal criteria of laws do not relate to their content, and that it is wrong to think that a system cannot be a legal system because the content of the laws are iniquitous (Hart 1957–58).

Fuller himself is perhaps doing little more than expressing the view that if we support the moral advantages of the formal rules of law we are likely to support particular laws whose content enhances respect for these same moral values. But his account of the rule of law is clearly 'thicker' than Hart's and may be seen as embedding in the concept of law a value commitment to the moral worth of the individual as a responsible being. This fits well with the value assumptions that underlie support for having systems of rights, particularly if we adopt the will theory with its emphasis on the individual as a morally responsible agent.

It is then a relatively easy step to thicken the concept of law even further and broaden the principles of legality to include other requirements that manifest the same sort of value commitments. At this point the discourse of rights and the idea of legality come even closer, for we then find that these substantive requirements which limit what may be accepted as law, consist of the familiar list of fundamental human rights that are included in the International Covenant on Civil and Political Rights (United Nations 1966a).

To some commentators, the disagreement between Hart and Fuller is a trivial one, having to do with a matter of mere definition concerning whether or not we will call a rule accepted and applied by officials in courts 'law' if it violates certain values or rights. What difference does this semantic issue make in practice? For Hart, one difference is that the recognition that what we have here is an unjust law helps to make us morally more critical of the law, which is a desirable thing. We should not assume that something is morally right simply because it is legally acceptable.

However, the debate has more significant implications if what is at stake is the legal powers of judges to make and unmake law. Should judiciaries be given the power to determine that so-called laws made by legislature are not laws at all if they have a certain content, more specifically, if they are incompatible with certain rights? This takes us on to the main constitutional issue discussed in this chapter: does a commitment to rights, including human rights, suggest that we ought to support judicial review of legislative action? Should a democratic constitution include a court-enforced bill of rights?

Bills of rights

Human rights articulate some of the practical implications of the fundamental values and basic institutional requirements that both legitimate and limit the powers of governments, businesses and other social institutions. These values and institutions provide standards against which to measure our social, economic and political arrangements. They help us to identify and address individual and systemic injustice, oppression, inequality and suffering and establish priority goals that ought to be attained in any tolerable and humane society.

The exercise of social, economic and political power is necessary for the achievement and defence of human wellbeing but, due to the frailties of human nature and the limitations of our organisational capacity, power can be misused and has a tendency to be abused, usually by those minorities who by virtue of wealth, education or social prestige are able to impose their own values and promote their own interests against those of the majority of citizens. Such is 'the tragic paradox of politics' (Campbell 1996: 13).

Democratic systems of government are designed to counter such minority power and engender a system of decision-making and social control that serves the general interest. By the general interest is meant the legitimate interests of all members of society as identified by criteria such as wellbeing, autonomy, justice and equality. The mechanisms whereby this is achieved are a combination of open elections for government office, ongoing debate and free political association and the promotion of an educated and informed population (Harrison 1993, Held 1996, Dryzek 1996).

There are different views as to what constitutes the general interest (the basic values of wellbeing, autonomy, justice, equality, etc.), as to how such values as are agreed on are to be achieved, and as to who are best equipped to make decisions on behalf of the community as a whole. This is why the ongoing process of open discussion is punctuated by elections that seek to give equal weight to the opinions of all adult members of society through the principle of one person, one vote and the acceptance of decisions favoured by a majority of those voting. In giving preference to the values and opinions of majorities a democratic system also gives majorities the political capacity to protect their own interests and counter the tendency of those with political and economic power to use their position disproportionately for their own benefit.

Democratic government is justified because it (1) comes as near as is practically possible to recognising the autonomy or self-governance of every individual with respect to binding collective decisions, (2) provides an effective device (regular elections) whereby majorities can protect their interests against the abuses perpetrated by powerful minorities and (3) institutionalises equality of all citizens as persons with moral and political views deserving of respect. The values of autonomy, general wellbeing and equal moral dignity justify the acceptance of democratic rights as human rights, that is, as universal and overriding moral entitlements.

Actual democratic systems fall short of this ideal in many ways. Often democracies fail to constrain the power of wealthy and influential minorities because the elections are not open and fair (but manipulated and bought) or the decisions are not those of an informed and prudent electorate. Often the majority of decisions reached are not simply expressions of reasonable opinions as to what constitutes the general interest but are clearly unfair to minorities whose interests are unjustly sacrificed to those of the majority.

It is all too clear that, because actual democracies can be manipulated by powerful minorities or abused by self-interested majorities, the existence of democracy does not guarantee respect for such basic values as autonomy, justice and equality. Like all human institutions, democratic systems have a built-in bias towards the abuse of power. This means that there is a perpetual imperative to reassert these human rights values and to work out how they may be better protected. The articulation and promotion of human rights is an important part of the endeavour to make democracies more democratic and protect both majorities and minorities against every present threat to their wellbeing.

Bills of rights have an important role here in giving clear and forceful expression to those fundamental interests that are recognised as basic to a decent and truly human existence. They provide check lists against which we can measure the reality of our democracy, the justice of our laws, the fairness of our economic and social system and the appropriateness of our conduct towards other people. They have a particular role in helping us to identify old and new ways in which power is abused or simply not effectively used for the common good. Bills of Rights enable us to express dissent and withdraw consent both from a particular government and, in extreme cases, from the system of government itself. They can also serve to identify the priority goals of all morally legitimate government. In this capacity they have a moral standing above that of existing law and constitutions and serve as the ultimate basis of the citizen's moral obligation to obey the state.

Bills of rights are, at the very least, affirmations of universal manifesto rights: rights that everyone ought to have. But they are also associated with a particular method for institutionalising rights and turning manifesto rights into concrete rights. Most human rights enthusiasts favour an entrenched and judicially enforceable bill of rights. This is because, while they see the utility of using human rights conventions to combat non-democratic régimes, they identify threats to human rights within democracies themselves (Freeman 1990, Dworkin 1990).

Democracy is seen as a threat to human rights because of (a) the special interests of elected politicians who neglect human rights in order to retain or gain power (short-sightedness, pressure groups, public opinion polls etc.), (b) the unfettered power of majorities to impose their will on the rest of society and (c) the special vulnerability of disadvantaged groups under any political system. It is argued these dangers require a countervailing force that can curb self-seeking politicians and oppressive majorities and specifically promote the wellbeing of the underprivileged. By giving courts the power to render legislation invalid on the grounds that it violates provisions in a Bill of Rights, and disabling elected governments from overturning such decisions, human rights, including democratic rights are, it is argued, better secured.

These anxieties are well founded and the need for seeking to ensure better protection for human rights is well established. However, there are grave objections to the mechanism of relying on judicial power to counter these threats. Many of these objections derive from human rights considerations (Waldron 1999).

These drawbacks of bills of rights relate both to the effectiveness of their outcomes and to the process or methods used to entrench judicially enforced bills of rights. Most of these difficulties arise from emphasising one incredibly important feature of all bills of rights: they are very simple and general statements of rights, cast in abstract terms. Such statements can have great value in providing a sense of direction, but they engender enormous disagreement when it comes down to saying what they are to mean in practice, as applied to concrete decisions that actually affect social outcomes. The 'interpretation' of abstract rights is inevitably political and controversial. Bills of rights are in general so vague that they do not have meaning at the level of specificity required to determine whether any actual type of conduct or rule is or is not a violation of human rights. A court-administered bill of rights leaves it to judiciaries to translate such general principles as 'the right to life' into the sort of specific decisions that outlaw capital punishment, or restrict access to abortion services, that allow or permit voluntary euthanasia, or sanction or prohibit rationing of health care, or permit the production of human embryos for stem-cell research (Dworkin 1990).

The abstraction of general statements of human rights is such that in the application of a bill of rights to an actual case in a court of law it is necessary in effect to legislate what the rights in question are to be taken to mean in concrete terms, or to draw on the previous decisions of courts that have, individually or collectively, legislated in this way. This does not mean that bills of rights have no meaning. They identify in general terms fundamental values and legitimate interests and in so doing point us in certain directions and invite us to articulate further what these values are and what they mean in practice. But they are radically indeterminate.

It follows that having a judicially enforceable bill of rights may or may not produce the particular outcomes that citizens want, for the judges will have their own ideas about all these controversial matters. It is not the case that we all agree what our human rights are and are simply handing over their enforcement to courts. What we are handing over is the power to determine what our rights are. We may think that judges will do a good job in making such determinations, perhaps because we think we will agree with them more than we agree with our elected representatives, but we cannot know this to be the case, and we cannot do anything about it if the judicial idea of what a human rights involves differs from our own. The hope that what we regard as our human rights will be better protected by this mechanism may not be fulfilled.

The core point here is that, while we can agree on general human rights principles, such as the dignity of human existence, the basic equality of all human beings and the wickedness of inflicting unnecessary human suffering, we disagree what these fundamental principles require in practice. Even when we do agree on more specific points, such as the right to vote, the right to express our opinions and our right to equality of opportunity, there is enormous and reasonable disagreement about the content and limitations to be placed on such rights (Waldron 1999).

Moral disagreement arises and persists because our moral beliefs are irretrievably attached to our feelings as well as our knowledge, to our capacity to feel for others, our capacities to sense what is worthwhile and what is not. And much of our morality depends on our factual beliefs about what works and what does not work in human relationships: something that is affected by our experience of living in the world, an experience that is different for every individual. And so disagreement arises also because we see the world inevitably from our own (often but not necessarily self-centred) perspective or that of the group of groups to which we belong.

At the level of specificity and detail where rights and duties come into play in affecting the concrete reality of everyday life, there is reasonable diversity of view as to what these rights are, how much weight is to be given to each of them, and what to do when they clash with each other or with other moral considerations. We are often loathe to admit this diversity of views because it makes human rights seem too subjective, too much a matter of taste, too culture bound, when we want to see them as moral fixtures: objective, rational, universal.

However, it is perfectly possible to hold the objectivity of human rights (to deny that they are simply a matter of what we happen to like), while admitting that it is not easy to work out precisely what these rights are and how they are best implemented. There can be reasonable disagreement on human rights just as there can be reasonable disagreement about what is beautiful, or useful, or historical fact.

It is because we disagree on such matters and because it is in practice very difficult to distinguish the disagreement that is based on selfishness or error from that which is not that we may have differing views about what objectively our human rights are. Hence the existence of reasonable political disagreement, and one reason why we have recourse to democracy, a process of open debate and decision-making that seeks to embody respect for human equality, by making the people the source of the laws that bind them.

Of course, courts have a long history of changing and developing the law within the limits set by pre-existing legislation. There is frequently no harm and much good in courts developing and updating the law on the basis of the real life cases that come before them. But, in many jurisdictions, parliaments have always been able to assert their democratic authority by countermanding such judicial developments with new legislation. Under a court-centred Bill of Rights, court decisions are placed beyond democratic revision, except by way of constitutional amendment.

This US style of entrenched and court-enforced Bill of Rights is defended on the grounds that it is necessary to protect minorities against majorities. Certainly, no one can deny that individuals and groups are capable of acting with extreme selfishness. Indeed the main argument in favour of majority rule is that rich and powerful minorities will otherwise use the instruments of government to feather their own nests. But note how the cure – giving power to judges to override majorities – contradicts the justification for that cure – respecting the equality and dignity of the individual human being.

If we are not all equal when it comes to having an opinion on justice, rights and the common good, then what is left of the ideal of human equality on which human rights are founded? It removes such contentious matters of moral opinion from the democratic process, so that citizens are excluded from having any power to determine the specific rights that are to apply in their society. This is in clear contravention of the idea that the moral views of every human being are to be given equal respect. It is to this extent a violation of autonomy, dignity and self-respect. Majorities can get it wrong, as do judges and politicians and bureaucrats. But a democratic system, with its emphasis on representation, freedom of speech and assembly, transparency, accountability and the rule of law, is designed to minimise and correct the mistakes that we make in governing ourselves.

This anti-democratic or 'counter-majoritarian' objection (Bickel 1962) is often brushed aside by saying that experience shows that judges do not deviate significantly in their 'interpretation' of human rights from the views of the majority. This is true. Courts do indeed tend to lag behind public opinion and rarely provide moral leadership in part because they are well aware that this brings criticism of the legitimacy of their conduct. Further, if courts do seek to override legislation on a regular basis, new judges are eventually appointed who are more subservient to governments. But if this is the case then a bill of rights is likely to be of little help in countering the views of majorities who are neglectful of the wellbeing of vulnerable minorities. Further, courts are likely to block reforms as societies change and entrench conservative opinion in the face of perfectly legitimate developments in moral opinion.

Moreover, court-centred bills of rights can be used to undermine the capacity of majorities to defend their legitimate interests against powerful minorities. Bills of rights of a sort capable of being implemented by courts inevitably emphasise liberty over wellbeing, thus giving the opportunity for those with appropriate resources to counter reforms that promote the general wellbeing by reducing property rights, including the right to use money to manipulate political opinion and serve the interests of business over consumers. Court-centred bills of rights have frequently been used to stall progressive policies aimed at general wellbeing and have rarely been of much assistance with respect to wellbeing of the majority of citizens.

Such conclusions may seem depressing to advocates of human rights. It seems that no one can be trusted to do the right thing in politics. It would, however, he naïve to think otherwise. The eternal problem of political philosophy is how we can guard the guardians. To have a political system someone or somebody must have the final say. If we seek to supervise that body then the supervising institution has the final say. If we respond by dividing power between different centres, then this either amounts to a negation of power or an uncoordinated number of 'final' authorities between whom conflict is inevitable. To admit that democratic procedures do not always get it right does not mean that there must be a better way. In the case of democracy we can always know that something is right, namely the maximisation of individual autonomy with respect to collective decision-making and showing respect for the views of everyone equally, but we cannot ensure, or even know, whether the decisions taken are the outcome of honest moral opinions or foolishness or selfishness, or some mixture of these and more. In a democracy we can at least argue, persuade and hope to change the decisions with which we disagree.

This, it is argued, does not help if the rights under threat are in fact democratic rights (Ely 1980). If democratically elected politicians remove political rights, perhaps by extending their term of office indefinitely or removing freedom of speech, then we have no peaceful way of correcting the situation. However in such a scenario it is unlikely that courts would be able to do anything effective since governments that are capable of suspending elections are equally capable of dismissing judges or ignoring their decisions. In less extreme circumstances, however, such as making alterations in electoral law relating to campaign finance or constituency boundaries, it may be thought that politicians should be excluded from the decision-making process. This is certainly a difficult area in which the vested interests of elected politicians is evident, but there may be perfectly legitimate reasons for such changes and it is clear that there is reasonable disagreement about what is the most desirable form of representative democracy. It seems wrong in principle to exclude the electorate from an indirect say in such matters.

The problem of reconciling democratic rights with judicial review using bills of rights has led to many compromise solutions being suggested and tried, to which we cannot give adequate consideration here. Statutory bills of rights, subject to legislative amendment may be enacted to guide judicial interpretation of law or guide the administrative practices of government, as in New Zealand (Bill of Rights Act 1990) and the United Kingdom (Human Rights Act 1998). Entrenched bills of rights may include a 'notwithstanding' clause that enables legislature to override decisions of courts even when they are interpreting and applying the bill of rights, as in Canada (Russell 1991). Such compromises are clearly more acceptable democratically, although courts are sometimes inclined to transgress the limited powers given by such constitutional arrangements and, to the extent that courts do comply with the limitations contained in compromise bills, they are in a much weaker position for protecting their understanding of the rights expressed in the bills, thus diluting their claimed effectiveness as constraints on the human rights sins of governments.

In general all of these compromise devices come up against the capacity of courts to circumvent legislative provisions if they have recourse to a broadly worded bill of rights, and all suffer from the consequence that they are either ineffective or they take responsibility for the pursuit of rights away from the democratic process, something whose debilitating effects are the greater as we increase the range and scope of what counts as a human right (Campbell, Ewing and Tomkins 2000).

Conclusion

Given that the very meaning and existence of rights is, I have argued, tied into mechanisms for their implementation, and granting my thesis that the operation of legal rules is in many ways a paradigm for such institutionalisation, it is quite natural to think that human rights should be constitutionalised in a way that gives courts ultimate authority over their content and application. This may appear to give the sort of guarantees that republicans look for in 'non-denomination' (see p. 75). However, quite apart from differences of opinion as to how effective courts are in giving effect to human rights through bills of rights, there is a real clash of rights here between the right to be protected against abuses of human rights perpetrated by governments and the right of self-determination whereby citizens of all countries can draw on human rights to claim an equal share in the determination of precisely what human rights are to mean in practice.

There remains a strong case for saying that a significant bundle of human rights, perhaps all human rights, are dependent in large part on the enactment of specific rules laying down the duties of citizens and governments to respect such rights and of governments and other agencies to help protect them. Where such rules clearly identify who has the correlative duties, establish remedies for violations of these duties, and are backed up by the human and material resources to secure the objectives of those rules, and a general cultural commitment to a rights-based approach to politics, then we have the best institutional basis for the realisation of human rights that is available to us. 'Human rights legislation', such as equal opportunity and racial vilification legislation, can be given special constitutional status by adopting a slightly thickened version of the rule of positive law, the inclusion of a requirement that human rights legislation cannot be overridden except by subsequent clear and express legislative enactment. This would help to ensure that human rights are not subject to implied repeal and give way only to later changes in human rights legislation that are openly debated and democratically decided. All this may be summed up by saying that the rule of positive law is an essential part of any acceptable rights régime and is capable of giving a special place to those rights we choose to designate as human rights.

Chapter 6

International human rights

One aspect of the universality claimed for human rights is that they apply to everyone, whatever the existing societal and legal rights may be within particular states. This means that human rights hold for all states whatever their culture, history and current practices. And because human rights are those rights that ought to be respected globally, all human rights are in this sense international or, perhaps, transnational or cosmopolitan. Such is the moral force of human rights.

This part of the book concentrates on the institutions of rights, the social, political and legal arrangements whereby our ideas about rights are given effect in practice and through which practices our rights become a reality. From this perspective human rights are likely to be identified with the rights that all people have in international law, something that we can find out about by examining the sources of international law, emanating from the activities of the United Nations (UN), international treaties and customary international law (Simma and Alston 1992). From the institutional point of view, international human rights are part of international law. It is appropriate, therefore, for us to look at how human rights, morally conceived, are, and might be, institutionalised through the mechanisms available and capable of development under international law.

Given the individualistic associations of rights, including human rights, international law is not a natural breeding ground for human rights since international law has its origins and principal focus in the relations between states, not persons. In international law, states not individuals are the traditional players and rights-holders.

Yet something like individual international human rights emerged early on in the development of international law through a number of different channels. For a start, all governments take an interest in the interactions between their citizens and those of other states, especially with respect to trade. Then, in times of war, states have concerns with how their soldiers are treated when captured and by what methods wars are waged. Customary practices with respect to the treatment of prisoners have been supplemented by The Hague Conventions in the late nineteenth century and the Geneva

Conventions after World War II that concern the protection of wounded combatants, prisoners of war, civilian populations and the use of disproportional military force, all of which is known as the international humanitarian laws of war. Also the International Labour Organisation (ILO), established by the Treaty of Versailles in 1919, has espoused a variety of economic and social rights in its long history.

However, what is now generally known as international human rights law derives from the foundation Charter of the UN in 1947 and its Universal Declaration of Human Rights (1948) (Steiner and Alston 1996). That Declaration contains a wide ranging list of human rights in an aspirational framework that calls on states to secure such rights for their citizens. A prime motivation for this Declaration and indeed the UN as a whole was to secure lasting peace between nations and it was believed that the recently concluded world war had been caused at least in part by a failure of states to respect the human rights of their citizens.

So far this fits into a manifesto model of rights, since the Universal Declaration is non-binding and expresses political objectives to which the parties make a moral commitment. However, the Universal Declaration was followed up by two covenants that were intended to bind the states which ratify them. These two covenants render the Universal Declaration more specific and make it the basis for a binding agreement between states, giving human rights the form of law through international treaties.

In the event, only the first, the International Covenant on Civil and Political Rights (United Nations 1996a) requires states to take immediate action to implement these rights within their territories. The second, the International Covenant on Social, Economic and Cultural Rights (United Nations 1966b), simply sets out goals to which states are required to move as their means permit. Nevertheless, the UN has always been committed to the equal significance of both sets of rights. Since that time there have been a large number of conventions, treaties and agreements enunciating human rights standards with respect, for instance, to women's rights (United Nations 1979), children's rights (United Nations 1989), and discrimination (United Nations 1965).

The development of international human rights law has had considerable impact on the nature of international law. Instead of focusing almost entirely on states and their rights, international law now takes a direct interest in the rights of individuals within states. This has weakened the traditional doctrine of state sovereignty whereby it was agreed that one state should not interfere in the internal affairs of another state. States now have a basis for criticising and seeking to influence the internal policies of other states on the grounds that their governments are violating human rights, as in the case of economic sanctions against South Africa in the era of apartheid. Indeed, since the end of the Cold War, there have been several

UN endorsed armed interventions in the affairs of sovereign states, as in Kosovo and Rwanda, that have been justified on human rights grounds.

International human rights raise several interesting issues from the perspective of political philosophy. International human rights seems to offer the prospect of clear answers to at least some of our four core questions about rights at least as far as human rights are concerned. From reading what is sometimes called 'the international bill of rights' (The UN Declaration of Human Rights and the two Conventions, on Civil and Political Rights, and on Social, Economic and Cultural Rights) we can discover that human rights belong to all human beings irrespective of race, religion, gender, age or national origin and we can know the rights that all human beings possess by examining the content of the international bill of rights. With respect to content, it is interesting to note that the international bill or rights includes many more economic and social rights than are to be found in the constitutions of most countries.

And in the light of the history of steps taken to implement international human rights over the last few decades we can have some idea of what might be appropriate by way of methods of realising human rights. These include critiques of state practices on the basis of Resolutions of the Security Council of the UN (which has representatives from most of the major world powers), some of which make provision for the use of sanctions, and some of which require armed intervention, for instance to prevent genocide. Less forceful means of enforcement include criticism by the UN Commission on Human Rights, formed under the ICCPR, which consists of representatives of member nations and has the power to investigate complaints lodged by other states or citizens of the states in question and to issue critical opinions based on the scrutiny of reports that member nations are obliged to provide periodically. Further, the General Assembly, the Economic and Social Council and its Commission on Human Rights and its Committee on the Status of Women, as well as the High Commissioner for Human Rights who is responsible directly to the Secretary General, can all bring some influence to bear on member states through their condemnations of perceived human rights violations.

The development of these institutions and processes bear out the thesis that, although international human rights originate as manifesto rights that are used to justify claims to entitlements, it is part of the logic of such rights that they should be embedded in social and legal practices that provide means whereby individuals may secure and thus actually have rights. In this respect the United Nations through a variety of committees has taken significant steps towards both articulating these rights more specifically and at least going some way towards monitoring compliance with them by encouraging the development of appropriate institutions within states and commenting on reports received as to their implementation.

However, the phenomenon of international human rights, impressive as it is, in practice falls short with respect to providing theoretical and practical answers to our core questions about rights. With respect to the meaning of rights, it is not clear, for instance, if rights require the articulation of rules that specify the interests that are to be protected or promoted and the nature and location of the duties that arise under such rules, or whether they can simply be identified with the desirability of some vaguely defined social and political goals. With respect to the existence conditions of rights, international human rights seem to fall somewhere between the status of manifesto rights whose adoption by its member states is to be encouraged, and the status of positive rights to which enforcement procedures attach.

Also, very little is attempted in the way of providing justifications for the rights proclaimed in various conventions and treaties, although there is some reference in preambles to the inherent dignity of all members of the human family. No official attempt is made to articulate a theory, for instance, as to what counts as a dignified human life, a concept that is capable of radically different cultural interpretations. In fact it is clear that such issues were deliberately left vague so as to facilitate the adhesion of states with radically different religious and moral traditions. For political reasons, the international bill of rights is not forthcoming on the meaning, status and justification of human rights.

The exponential development of international human rights law has not been inhibited by this lack of theoretical underpinnings, but the international human rights system is highly vulnerable to critical comment. Thus the range and variety of 'rights' claimed, including the collective rights of 'peoples', raise some awkward questions as to their philosophical basis and theoretical legitimation. We may seek clarification as to the obligations that are assumed to be correlative to the various rights that are claimed. We may raise doubts about the rights that are actually proposed, on the grounds that they are not culturally neutral. We may question the speciesism[1] of purely human rights that excluded the higher animals. We may be worried by the contradictions that arise when so many of the listed rights clash with each other in practice. And we may criticise the selective use that is made of these rights in a context where it is self-interest and political independence that rule.

Finally, with respect to the best means of protecting rights, it must be questioned whether a system that depends largely on monitoring compliance and encouraging states to change their ways can be considered sufficiently effective. Indeed, it can be argued that such mechanisms, when selectively applied as a result of political pressures that are institutionalised in the implementation procedures, and widely ignored without penalty in practice, do not come sufficiently close to what is required by the moral demands of human rights to warrant being regarded as rights at all.

In what follows, I take up three themes from the wide variety of issues raised by international human rights law, concentrating on the sufficiency of their institutionalisation. The first relates to the relative absence of courts in the international human rights régime. The second concerns humanitarian intervention in the affairs of other states. The third takes up the underlying problem of cultural relativism.

International courts

One way in which to develop international law as an instrument of human rights protection is to make it more like national law. What matters here is not that it be precisely the same as national law but that it progressively embodies those aspects of the rule of law that are appropriate to a world of largely independent sovereign states. This means that states, as well as individuals, should be required to act or refrain from acting and held liable for failure to conform only where there is a system of rules which it is feasible for them to obey, with clearly identified and legitimated origins, which are applied by independent tribunals.

International law has long been subject to the criticism that it is not really law but simply a form of customary morality, largely based on the mutual self-interest of nations. It is said to have no legislature, no effective administration, no genuine courts and no effective implementation. Moreover, it is (or was) only binding on those nations that accept its authority. These critiques go along with the belief that international relations are, in 'realist' terms, a matter of the relative power and self-interest of states.

The development of international law is in part a process designed to meet these points and some of the critique is now out of date. Custom remains a source of international law (but this is true of national legal systems as well) and the United Nations has become equivalent to a legislature in that it is possible to identify those decisions that have the status of binding rules. The system of treaty making, particularly where the treaties are initiated and administered through the United Nations also meet the requirements of a clear social source of rules that are accepted as binding. International human rights is an area now replete with recognisably positive law in the shape of covenants adopted by the UN General Assembly and ratified by the vast majority of states. Moreover, when such treaties are ratified by a given number of states they become binding on all member states of the United Nations in terms of international law.

It is, therefore, increasingly possible to reach a reasonably objective decision about what is and what is not part of international human rights law. Moreover, there are now many international and regional courts which are in the business of actually making such determinations in relation to particular disputes. This has resulted in a body of case law that is sufficiently developed to begin to resemble the jurisprudence of national legal systems.

And so, while there are many problems relating to the implementation of such decisions, and only a patchy global coverage of regional international courts, there is something approaching a system of international law that approximates to a hard version of the rule of law. There remain serious shortcomings with respect to the democratic legitimacy of the system which is only very indirectly related to the electoral decision-making of individual persons, but this does not in itself undermine the rule of law advantages that are emerging.

One example of a recent advance towards the rule of law in the international sphere has been the creation of a permanent International Criminal Court (ICC) to deal with persons believed to be guilty of certain human rights violations. This was agreed through the adoption of the Rome Statute (United Nations 1992) in 1998 by a meeting of sovereign, independent, nation states, requiring the ratification of sixty states before coming into force. The ICC is not intended to take the place of domestic courts but can take action through a reference from the United Nations Security Council, a State Party to the Statute, or at the behest of its own independent investigative Prosecutor.

Because of international law's prime focus on relationships between states there has previously been no permanent court to which the conduct of individual persons could be referred.[2] The humanitarian law of war, as in the 1907 Hague Convention (IV): Respecting the Law and Customs of War on Land, the 1949 Geneva Conventions, the 'crimes against peace' and the 'crimes against humanity' in the London Charter of 1946, and the 1948 UN Convention on the Prevention and Punishment of the Crime of Genocide, which applies to acts that are intended to destroy a group of persons, do identify crimes for which the individuals shall be tried and punished, but implementing these laws has been an *ad hoc* process.

Such implementation as has occurred has been dubious with regard to the rule of law, since its selectivity makes it look very much like victors' revenge, as in the case of the Nuremberg trials of Nazi war criminals. However the *ad hoc* International Criminal Tribunal for the Former Yugoslavia in 1993 and the International Tribunal for Rwanda in 1995 established by the UN are regarded as models for setting up a permanent court to deal with such crimes as genocide. It is argued that the establishment of a permanent court with its own officials and budget is a necessary part of realising human rights objectives by ensuring that there is a politically impartial basis from which prosecutions can be brought, the occurrence of crimes can be established according to proper legal procedures and criminal sanctions applied in a consistent manner.

In making an assessment of this claim we must bear in mind two legalistic errors. The first is thinking that having laws on the books in itself promotes human rights. The second is thinking that legal remedies are the only important remedies. If the objective is to reduce the incidence of grave human rights violations, then it will be a long time before we can make any assessment as to whether or not the existence of a permanent court has reduced the perpetration of crimes against humanity. Arguably, the deterrent effect of such institutions is unlikely to have a significant impact on the behaviour of people caught up in armed conflicts, particularly civil wars, where the stakes are high and the chances of subsequent arrest and conviction slight.

However, it can be argued that the institutionalisation of human rights through an international court is a necessary part of giving reality to the moral claims expressed in the language of rights. On this view, to have a right it is necessary for there to be a remedial social response to violations of that right. Rights exist even when they are violated. But if, when violations occur, there is no effort to respond by assisting the victim and punishing the perpetrator, then arguably such a right does not exist at all. The logic of rights certainly includes taking all practicable measures to protect the interests identified in the right, but it also includes institutionalising the social recognition of such violations as occur, including through the punishment of those who violate human rights. It can be argued that every case in which an international criminal is convicted of some form of human rights abuse we have a recognition of the rights of the victims. 'Remedies' in the form of criminal convictions and punishment does nothing material for those who have been murdered and little for those who have been abused but it is a recognition that victims matter and to this extent is in itself a vindication of human rights.

The creation of a permanent international criminal court can be seen as part of the process of instantiating the objectives of some specific human rights, when these human rights are conceived as moral rights, that is when making the claim that there are justified moral demands for creating effective entitlements to protect certain interests of all human beings. This applies whether or not the existence of such courts has an impact on the incidence of human rights violations. Certainly, setting up such a court offers the prospect of the emergence of a body of international criminal law that will clarify the obligations and hence the rights of all human beings. This, in conjunction with the development of similar jurisprudence within individual nations and regional jurisdictions will take us some way towards the realisation of certain highly important human rights.

The principal human rights objection to the International Criminal Court relates to its shortcomings with respect to the rule of law. The absence of an effective international police force and prosecution service means that enforcement of international criminal law will be so spasmodic as to make it impossible to reconcile with the principle of equality before the law. It will be largely a matter of chance and the relative power of nations who is indicted for what. This is a violation of the rights of victims and accused alike.

It could also be said that the definition of what counts as a crime for the purposes of the Court is inadequate. The crimes included are limited to very serious breaches of a few core rights, oriented in particular towards those that are a risk to peace and that include an element of discrimination, as in the case of genocide. Should such a court not have a much wider brief that covers serious violations of all human rights?

This criticism assumes the indivisibility principle according to which human rights are a unified body of rights that must be taken as a whole and given identical content in different contexts. We have seen, in Chapter 2, that this is a mistake that fails to take into account the relationship of rights to obligations. The question that needs to be addressed with respect to international criminal law is: which human rights obligations it is intended to cover? The answer would seem to be: those that domestic courts cannot be expected to prosecute, or to prosecute fairly. The context here is to do with the crimes of military and political leaders in situations where normal peaceful conditions do not apply. It is in such circumstances that there is no way in which domestic courts are able to deal with the situation.

Another important feature of the context is that such crimes take place in situations of armed conflict to which it is more important to bring to an end with some sort of political solution than that they are followed through as an exercise in securing justice. Traditionally a concern for what we now regard as human rights violations was subordinate to securing victory and enduring peace. It is a mistake to think that securing justice for victims must always have priority over securing peace in human rights terms. Peace is a precondition of most human rights progress. Prolonging a war in order to punish crimes against humanity is not a net gain for human rights.

We may therefore accept that human rights approached from the point of view of international criminal law should have a different content, form and implementation than human rights in other contexts. This does not necessarily mean that such laws should focus on the most evil crimes. The practicalities of what international law can be expected to do in the absence of a world government can reasonably be taken into account. However, the rational for current efforts to define the nature of the crimes to be tried at the ICC appear questionable. Thus, it is argued that international criminal law should concern itself only with group crimes, such as genocide, where the criminal acts, such as murder and rape, are perpetrated against a group rather than against an individual. This does provide some basis for selectivity in international criminal law. And it does accord with the emphasis of human rights on discrimination as a standard mode of violating human rights which pertain irrespective of a person's race, gender, nationality or religion. Moreover it connects with the particular horror of mass murders and rapes that take place in genocidal situations. But it ignores the injuries done to the individual victim and appears morally suspect in taking the genocidal motives of offenders into account more than the harm done to individual victims.

What is needed here is an identification of the sort of evils that take place in modern conflicts, the particular responsibilities of those who occupy positions of leadership in such conflicts and the need to avoid prolonging conflicts because these leaders are threatened with personal sanctions. These are not matters that can or should be determined by courts themselves. They are issues that must be resolved in advance when establishing the brief for such courts. Here more than anywhere it is evident that there are no self-evident human rights rules simply waiting to be applied.

Human rights intervention

By this stage in our journey it is clear that we cannot hope to arrive at a list of human rights, together with their correlative duties, that applies in all contexts and can be used for all purposes and in conjunction with all remedies that human rights discourse does and could serve and utilise. Indeed, it is often destructive of these aims if we do not seek to specify in appropriate detail the rights that we seek to prioritise for particular purposes and mechanisms of application. Clear statements of rights, duties and remedies that are context specific are essential prerequisites for protecting and furthering the human interests involved.

The very same events that have prompted the founding of the International Criminal Court raise the issue of when the UN or individual states should take steps to protect people against their own governments or the results of domestic lawlessness. Telling examples of this arise from a number of recent interventions in the internal affairs of states on human rights grounds. The lamentably late UN intervention in Rwanda after genocidal massacres had taken place between Tutsi and Hutu tribes during 1994 and 1995, and the scarcely more timely response to the ethic cleansing in the former Yugoslavia between Moslem and Christian groups, were more or less legitimated through the UN on the grounds of human rights violations. Equally significant have been notorious failures to intervene to prevent the massacre of Kurds in Iraq, tribal groups in Uganda, the enemies of Pol Pot in Cambodia and non-Arabs in the Sudan.

These events have led people to ask whether there ought not to be more such actions to protect vulnerable people against their governments or those whom their government will not or cannot restrain. What of systematic starvation through maladministration and corruption? What of governments that use torture or permit multinational companies to destroy the traditional means of subsistence for large numbers of their poor citizens? (Moore 1997, Chatterjee and Scheid 2003).

Here what is at stake is not the rights but the duties of interventionist states, with or without the authorisation of the UN. Do the rights-protection duties of states extend beyond their own borders and to persons other than their own nationals? Clearly that is the case with respect to their negative duties, to refrain from violating the human rights of anyone, but does it extend to positive duties, including duties to prevent third parties injuring their own nationals? Given the fuzziness and frequent irrelevance of the distinction between negative and positive duties in national communities, it is difficult to accept that it marks a definitive bright line in international affairs. If we take seriously our humanitarian concerns for the wellbeing of all members of the human race, it does not make sense to limit our obligations to those with whom we happen to share common citizenship. To do so can be seen as an example of collective selfishness on the part of those able to intervene to protect those less fortunate than themselves.

There are pragmatic and principled counter arguments to this interventionist position. The pragmatic reasons relate to the immediate suffering and unpredictable long-term consequences of armed intervention, which can destabilise the global system of independent states on which so much of the political structure depends and without which the peace and orderliness required for the wellbeing of everyone is at risk. The principled reasons relate to the right of self-government that is possessed by all 'peoples', as affirmed in the ICCPR with respect to self-determination and through the customary internal principle of non-intervention in the internal affairs of other states.

The principles of non-intervention may be justified in terms of international stability, but it can also be seen as an intrinsic right similar in kind to the right of individual to their autonomy (see p. 54). Chapter 10 considers the right to self-determination in some detail as an example of a collective or group right. Here we may note that the right of self-determination may itself warrant intervention in the internal affairs of a state that is oppressing a minority people. Genocide may be, for instance, a way of denying a people their right of self-determination, along with much else. In this case we have a classic example of a clash of rights, neither of which can be fully respected without infringing the other.

There are a number of ways of approaching such moral dilemmas. One is to follow Burke (p. 12) and fall back on the traditional system of rights and duties that has worked through such conflicts over many years of progressive development. But this is unsatisfactory if the current system is manifestly unsatisfactory.

Another approach is to seek to compare the rights in terms of some common factor. Here it is most common to think in terms of consequences, perhaps in terms of the reduction of human misery, as utilitarians do (see p. 9). We consider whether overall, more pain and suffering would be avoided by the competing lines of action. It is hard to deny the moral relevance of such an approach, but it has to be remembered that a rights approach is founded on the view that the general happiness does not trump the rights of individuals, especially not on an *ad hoc* or arbitrary basis.

Further, as we will see, self-determination is not a right that is usually justified principally in terms of the happiness, even of the peoples claiming that right. Rather it is thought to be an intrinsic right (see p. 40) because it is a good thing that peoples govern themselves even if they do it badly from the point of view of their own welfare.

A third approach to the clash of rights is to prioritise rights by way of comparing the moral values at stake and making an intuitive judgment as to which is the more important. Philosophers often claim that this is an impossible thing to do objectively and rationally. They point to the 'incommensurability' of distinct values and the existence of equally reasonable choices in such matters. Nevertheless it is something that we do all the time with respect to our own value choices, and something that peoples as a whole do when they cast their votes in elections or make policy demands on their governments.

In our discussion of Rawls (see p. 63) it was noted that many liberal theorists attempt to minimise the problem of conflicting rights by drawing on the distinction between 'the right' and 'the good', holding that objective judgments that we can reasonably impose on other people concern 'the right' (essentially rights), whereas that which has to do with 'the good' is a matter of personal judgment. The image of a liberal society then becomes one in which there is an agreed framework concerning 'the right', leaving it to individuals and voluntary groups to decide what is 'good' for them. It is for this reason that Rawls insists that participants in the original position are unaware of their particular conception of the good, though they remain aware that they do have such a conception.

However, I have argued that, even if we can agree that questions of right can be settled objectively, this breaks down as soon as consequences are taken into account in deciding what is right in particular circumstances, and they nearly always are. And even if we can get over that difficulty, if we are dealing with a clash of rights, then we have a dispute within the sphere of 'the right'. If rights clash, and we are not going to resort to consequentialist arguments, then we must fall back on our moral intuitions, albeit intuitions we subject to reflection and reconsideration.

However defensible such an approach may be at the level of moral theory, it is seriously questionable when applied in practice to international relations, a sphere that has traditionally been regarded by dominant 'realist' theorists as one of self-interest and relative brute power. Given that there is no international government and no operational global court to which deference is given when states are in conflict, the issue of whether to intervene in the affairs of another state is ultimately a matter for the intervening power, and history is replete with examples of intervention occurring to protect the perceived interests of the intervenor but being justified by appeals to justice and rights. The lack of impartiality in such self-serving decisions renders the alleged moral judgments suspect. Hence the reluctance of states and informed observers to accept a principle of intervention that can be abused by powerful states and which certainly fails to live up to anything like the impartiality that might apply if the rule of law were in force at a global level.

In these circumstances it is common to adopt a fourth approach to the clash of rights, which is that of compromise. In this case the compromise is to refrain from armed intervention but to rely instead on a series of methods starting with rational argument and friendly diplomacy, including the offer of aid in exchange for changes in the offending conduct, and building up to more coercive measures through such instruments as trade sanctions and other attempts to isolate and bring effective pressure to bear on the recalcitrant régime.

Such measures are, of course, open to the same partiality objections. They are equally subject to the decisions of those who are initiating the intervention and therefore questionable as regarding bias and partiality. Also, economic measures often harm the very victims that intervenors are seeking to protect much more than the rulers who are perpetrating the alleged human rights violations. Yet, where armed intervention may itself bring extensive and often unforeseeable and incalculable damage, compromise may be deemed preferable. This may seem to run counter to the tenet that human rights are absolute and inviolable, but where human rights clash, this undermines any strong form of that tenet in any case. One way out of this impasse is to formulate criteria for making the difficult choices that have to be made in such circumstances. This includes identifying which violations of human rights may properly trigger the various types of external pressure and intervention.

This is a principal function of the UN which is carried out through the various conventions that have been adopted by its General Assembly over the years, and in relation to which they are a large number of largely uncoordinated monitoring régimes. However, while these may have some impact through the publicity generated by their reports, which are often largely dependent on submissions from non-government human rights organisations such as Amnesty International, states rarely utilise these mechanisms for fear that they will then be used against them (Risse, Ropp and Sikkink 1999).

It is the UN Security Council that has the duty under the UN Charter to intervene militarily, and although this has to be on the basis of securing and protecting peace, this is a power that can be used in relation to human right violations if these are seen as a threat to peace, which they often are. However, where the UN cannot act under its Charter, perhaps because the human rights violations are not a threat to peace and stability, or because of a lack of consensus amongst the Security Council members, there remains the possibility under international law of a state or group of states acting on their own, as was the case when the North Atlantic Treaty Organisation (NATO) sent troops into Kosovo in 1992 to prevent the massacre of Albanian Muslims, and the 2003 US led intervention in Iraq.

In either circumstance there is a need to determine when such military interventions are justified. Clearly not just any violation of human rights will suffice for this purpose. Is it a matter how serious the violations are? Does this relate to the type of violation (say torture), or its incidence (the number of people involved), or its motivation (say racial or religious hatred)? Does it matter whether the régime in question is a democratic one? And what counts as democracy in such circumstances? Is this a matter of respecting civil and political rights? Are such rights more important than the right of sustenance? Is it in fact only as a means to delivering humanitarian aid that intervention is justified?

John Rawls is one leading political theorist who has addressed this issue. In his Amnesty International lecture 'The Law of Peoples' he sets out a thesis on human rights that is directly related to the function of justifying intervention (Rawls 1993). His famous work, *A Theory of Justice* (1972), set out the basis for legitimate liberal democracy, including an idea of fundamental rights with constitutional protection. However he does not take these rights to be the same as human rights which he sees as a special class of rights of universal application. This special class of rights 'express a minimum standard of well-ordered political institutions for all people who belong, as members of good standing, to a just political society of people' and 'constitute a minimally decent régime'. These human rights are, in his view 'sufficient to exclude justified or forceful intervention by other peoples, say by economic sanctions, or, in grave cases, by military force' (1993: 68).

Interestingly, what Rawls counts as human rights for these purposes do not include democracy of the sort that he argued for as a basic right in a liberal society. 'Human rights' he argues 'are thus distinct from, say constitutional rights, or the rights of democratic citizenship, or from other rights that belong to a certain kind of political institution, both individualist and associationist'. Human rights include 'only such basic rights as the right to life and security, to personal property, and the element of the rule of law, as well as the right to a certain liberty of conscience and freedom of association, and the right of emigration' (1993: 70). However, although a liberal democratic system of representative government is not required, Rawls does insist that an acceptable hierarchical society must have a government that is guided by 'a common good conception of justice' that is 'a conception that take impartially into account what it sees not unreasonably as the fundamental interests of all members of society'.

We might disagree with this basis for the justification of removing the immunity from economic sanctions and armed intervention, and may think it arbitrary for him to define human rights in such restricted terms. However, the idea of seeking to establish standards that relate specifically to the issue of intervention is a step forward in clarifying an important aspect of human rights discourse. It underwrites the significance of accepting that what counts as human rights can vary in form and content in line with the purpose to which they are to be put.

The method Rawls actually uses to arrive at his conception of human rights is a version of his own methodology that he uses in *A Theory of Justice* (1972) to determine the normative structure of a liberal democracy (see p. 63). The version of the social contract model used here is one in which he imagines what states, behind a veil of ignorance that deprives them of knowledge of what sort of state they will be in reality (e.g. large, wealthy and liberal or small, poor and hierarchical), would agree on as justifying immunity from intervention. This model has the advantage of seeking to exclude the sort of partialities that bedevil human societies and their governance generally, and it does push the contracting parties to adopt an approach that is basically tolerant of diversity. It is doubtful, however, if it can deal with all significant grounds of moral disagreement. Moreover, it skirts rather than solves the issues of pluralism and diversity that render all efforts to reach international agreement on human rights problematic.

A solution to these problems that can be used to give an institutional framework to protect human rights through armed intervention is a necessary part of giving an acceptable reality to the notion of international human rights. This concerns both the effectiveness and the justifiability of such interventions. Absent such provisions positive human rights law falls short of instantiating the realisation of the moral norms expressed in the discourse of human rights.

Cultural diversity

Rawls revised his claims about the scope of *A Theory of Justice* (1972) in the light the criticism that the book seems to reflect the values of a liberal intellectual from within the culture prevalent on the eastern seaboard of the United States at the time of writing. He has no difficulty in claiming a broader base than this for a position that embodies ideas drawn from a long tradition of western philosophy, but did accept that he presupposed values that could not be seen as cultural universals. His 'law of peoples' is a further move towards a tolerance of diversity in values which seeks to embrace non-western traditions. Does he concede too much to save the universalism that is part of the logic of the discourse of human rights? Can human rights be relative to the culture to which they are applied, so that gender equality, for instance, need not be part of human rights in a hierarchical society? Or is this to abandon the role of human rights as a basis for the moral criticism of all existing social relationships? (Donnelly 1982, Teson 1985, Ghai 1994, Freeman 2000: 100–130).

The issue of cultural diversity is closely linked to philosophical debate about moral relativism (Levy 2002). Moral relativism takes a number of different forms. Sometimes it is an epistemological theory to the effect that there is no objective truth in moral assertions. Often this goes with the theory that moral judgments are expressions of emotion or attitude that have no truth value in themselves. They are no more than facts about the person expressing the moral view and are not ways of knowing what is the case about the world external to such human emotions. It is generally assumed by people who take this line that these morally expressive emotions are partly shaped by the culture in which people have been raised and to which they belong. This, it is argued, does much to explain why moral judgments and the sort of basic 'intuitions' on which most theories of rights are based reflect the general attitudes and moral values of the nation, religion or group to which those holding these values belong.

Scepticism about moral objectivity (or moral 'realism') has been continuous within the history of philosophy for more than two millennia. Against the evident fact that moral values vary with cultural differences is pitted the difficulty that people have in accepting that their most basic moral beliefs, such as that it is wrong to kill a baby for fun, are no more than expressions of their feelings, so that in the case of the above example if their or any one else's feelings were very different on this matter, it would not be wrong to kill babies. The philosophical problem is that it is very difficult to provide any intelligible basis for moral discourse other than the shared emotional responses of cultural groups. Of course, if globalisation eventually involves a cultural homogeneity amongst all peoples then more or less everyone might agree on their moral responses to different types of conduct, but this fact of universal agreement would not in itself prove that such attitudes are 'correct' or 'true'.

Human rights are a ready source of examples of the sort of moral judgments that do not appear to those who hold them to be simply matters of their feelings. In fact they would argue, very often, that their feelings are generated by a judgment that certain types of conduct are wrong. Whatever we think of this at the theoretical level it is an approach that breaks down when we find that there is significant moral disagreement about the content of human rights. This happens often over rather specific issues within particular cultures, like the morality of capital punishment and abortion, and whether the right to life is compatible with such practices in any circumstances. But disagreement about human rights can be more sweeping and abstract when we move outside the liberal western tradition from which current human rights discourse emerged.

Thus some non-western cultures take a view on the place of women in society that is radically at odds with that which has prevailed in theory at least in western societies, particularly over the last 30 years or so. The exclusion of women from most areas of public life, the punishment of women for sexual 'misconduct' and the practice of genital mutilation (or 'modification' according to your point of view) are examples of the sort of thing that in some parts of the world are accepted as right and in other countries are seen as self-evident violations of human rights (Nussbaum 2000).

On the other hand, there is a growing awareness in western societies that they have been guilty of cultural as well as economic and political imperialism and colonialism by assuming that their way of doing things is intrinsically better than that which prevails in other cultures (Taylor 1997). Further respecting the dignity of persons must surely involve respecting their distinctive culture. It seems wrong, on this view, to impose one's own moral beliefs and practices on other people. Hence the argument for toleration of cultural diversity. Indeed, there is an argument for encouraging cultural diversity as something that enriches the world in much the same way as bio-diversity.

Here we need to distinguish between different sorts of toleration and different types of moral relativism. There is toleration (let's call it 'strong toleration') that involves not interfering in the lives and beliefs of others simply because one disagrees with them. Toleration of this sort assumes that one's own beliefs are the correct ones, but 'tolerates' the views and practices of others by not criticising them, seeking to change them, or forcing them to abandon their mistaken ways. Strong toleration is compatible with moral realism and a literal belief in universal human rights in their moral mode.

'Weak' toleration, on the other hand, stems from moral agnosticism in the form of a lack of certainty as to what is right and wrong. It is based on the view that the beliefs and practices of others are or may be equally valid from a moral point of view. This toleration is weak in that it does not have to take the tough step of allowing error to flourish, but simply reflects a general agnostic approach to cultural differences. This seems a poor position to adopt from the human rights point of view since it must include agnosticism as to the moral justification of human rights themselves. We tolerate different views on human rights because all are, for all we know, equally right.

Moreover, strong toleration is compatible with a considerable measure of cultural diversity if we take into account some forms of moral relativism that are compatible with a realist moral philosophy. Thus, it may be claimed that objective truth in morality is obtainable but that this truth varies with the culture that is under consideration. Realist moral relativism of this sort argues that it is objectively right to do something in one culture that is objectively wrong to do in another culture. This is because the circumstances are different and these differences are morally relevant. Thus in a hunting-gatherer economy it is wrong to own land and acceptable to kill game wherever it is. In an agricultural society there is a right to own land and it is theft to kill game on another person's land. Right and wrong, in certain matters, depend on the economic system in place. Examples of realist moral relativism can easily be multiplied. In a society in which marriage is regarded as a sacred and lifelong commitment it may be morally wrong (not just legally difficult) to seek a divorce as this is a much more serious step for the other spouse than it is in a society where divorce is commonplace and unstigmatised. In India it is wrong to kill cows in a way that is routine in non-Hindu societies because this is offensive to others in that community.

It may be argued that realist moral relativism does not apply to fundamental moral values but relates simply to the specific content of what counts as 'theft' or what sort of conduct causes harm in different situations. This means that there can be rational agreement on basic moral values, and there can be agreement also that these values require different conduct in factually different situations. But this does not mean that the realist can tolerate certain sorts of cultural differences, such as the crucial examples we have noted as to the relative moral importance of men, women and children.

There is, however, another move that the moral realist can make. It can be argued that there are two levels of moral rules and principles. There are those (first order) rules that apply directly to the rightness and wrongness of conduct, such as the prohibition of homicide. Then there are (second order) rules and principles concerning how we respond to the first order moral or immoral beliefs and conduct of others. On this analysis we can hold that it is, at the second order level, right to tolerate the beliefs and conduct of others that are wrong at the first order level. This is, of course, what strong toleration amounts to.

Strong toleration can be justified at the second order level in a variety of ways. It may be pragmatically important for the avoidance of social conflict, to say nothing of religious wars. But it may also be justified on the grounds that it shows respect for the autonomy of other people, that is, their right to make up their own mind about right and wrong and to act accordingly.

Where would this leave human rights? On the one hand it seems to undermine the absoluteness of human rights and their role in justifying intervention in the lives of others, or even criticising the treatment of minorities in other cultures. We should not stand by as one group of people inflicts death and serious injuries on another group or systematically oppresses its members on the basis of gender, caste or ethnicity. On the other hand autonomy is one of the values that underlie many, some would say all, human rights, and to take autonomy seriously must mean maximising the scope of individual moral judgment, and that requires maximising non-interference in the collective life of others. Whatever principled approach is adopted must take into account the effectiveness of intervention in putting an end to the human rights violations, and the consequence of armed intervention on the lives and interests of those caught up in the ensuing violence which impacts on the human rights of these people. No dogmatic simplicities are possible here.

One practical solution to such problems which is not only pragmatic but takes into account these competing moral considerations, is to accept a dualism between international and domestic human rights standards. In the international sphere, at least for purpose of legitimating intervention in the domestic affairs of states, there would be a minimalist set of international standards taking significant account of cultural differences (Ignatieff 2001). The specific content of human rights in each state or region would be determined within states, preferably by democratic procedures that seek to give everyone an equal say in determining the rights and duties that bind. This might be considered satisfactory for the development of effective human rights legislation or for the enactment of statutory bills of rights.

Conclusion

International human rights law is often equated with human rights in general. This is a mistake which ignores the deeper moral grounding of human rights as well as their important and distinct deployment within the domestic jurisdictions of individual states and regional groupings of states. Nevertheless, the international dimension of human rights must be taken into account by any theory of rights.

On the face of it, international human rights do not appear to fit well with the model of rules that I have argued is basic to the understanding of rights as rule protected interests (in the case of human rights these interests being universal and of great significance to all persons). However, a great deal of international law generally and international human rights in particular seems to consist more of rhetorical and aspirational claims and demands that have neither the form of rules nor an effective system to back them up.

This is to some extent a misunderstanding of the model of rules. In the first place the model of rules is more a prescriptive than a descriptive theory of rights discourse. The thesis is that if rights are to play a distinctive and effective function in improving human existence then it must be through their articulation in rules that are specific enough to have real purchase on actual situations, and specifically rules that indicate where the correlative obligations lie and what these obligations are. It is the telos rather than the total actuality of rule-governance that is essential to rights.

Second, the rule model of rights does not claim that these rules must be legal rules or be associated with legal remedies. This is a desideratum in so far as we seek to achieve the important goals of formal justice and liberal freedoms, but there are many aspects of human wellbeing that human rights can protect and that are not centrally achieved through legal process. What matters is that those with the obligations correlative to rights actually see to it that the interests that the rights are designed to protect are actually protected, particularly when those obligations are positive obligations requiring organisation, effort and resources to fulfil. The idea that this can only be done by means of legal rules justiciable in courts is a legalist fallacy. The correlative of that fallacy is the idea that having human rights rules in the corpus of law is equivalent to protecting these interests. Regrettably that is often not the case.

These points having been made, it is also important to note that international human rights are in some respects moving in a law-like direction. From the UN and regional governance institutions, such as the European Community, there is a constant effort to render human rights in a legal form that is appropriate to be dealt with in courts. We have looked at the International Criminal Court as an example of this trend. Moreover, where this development has not taken place there are grounds for dissatisfaction with the state of international human rights.

Also, if we avoid the legalistic fallacy that all human rights methods must involve legal process, we may take a less sceptical view of the implementation processes adopted by the UN. Persuasion, adverse publicity, withdrawal of membership of trading groups and other soft sanctions may be criticised in so far as they are ineffective, but they are not inappropriate given that human rights is concerned to respect the autonomy and moral independence of all persons and, by extension, of their governments. Indeed, they may be important steps on the way from transforming international human rights 'law' from manifesto rights to operative rights.

Fully operative international human rights cannot be realised in the absence of a world government, a remote vision that, if realised, would turn international human rights into a form of world state law. But, given that the global reality is one of independent states and that this system is considered to be presently necessary for the realisation of human rights in the world as we can hope to know it, then it is to be expected that the realities of political power affect the means by which human rights are implemented at the international level. This acknowledges the propriety of compromising some human rights when they clash with other human rights, in particular when they clash with rights that are vital to the maintenance of the peace and stability on which so much human wellbeing depends.

In these circumstances it may be counterproductive from the human rights point of view to seek a rigorously enforced law of international human rights on the model of the rule of law as applied to domestic jurisdiction, for the necessary background political community required for a system of domestic law does not exist in the international sphere. The legal model is unlikely to meet with more than minor educational progress, with its effective use being spasmodic and inconsistent. Yet, in exploring the non-legal forms of human rights implementation domestically in the next chapter, we may conclude that the practical relevance of human rights is far from exhausted by their role in stimulating human rights legislation and seeking legal solutions to all social problems.

Chapter 7

Rights and civil society

The natural rights tradition and its successors, the Enlightenment 'rights of man', and the modern human rights movement, all focus primarily on the role of the state, with some ambivalence as to whether the state is the grand defender of or the great danger to human rights. Of course, in its protective role, one of the state's chief functions is to oversee the relationships between its citizens. Indeed, the corpus of civil law, including the law of contract and tort, deals with the inter-personal legal rights of citizens, many of which centre of fundamental freedoms and personal property rights. However, while citizens, indeed all human beings, have human rights against each other and human rights obligations to each other, it is still the state that has the duty to see that such obligations are fulfilled and such rights respected within its jurisdiction, thus ensuring the state a central role in human rights protection, in addition to its direct negative and affirmative human rights duties.

There are many social organisations that impact on the wellbeing of individuals apart from the state. Political parties, religious organisations, recreational clubs and associations, educational groups, professional organisations, corporations, trades unions, pressure groups and loosely organised social movements can not only interfere with individual rights but also act to promote and protect them. It is debateable, as we will see in Chapter 10, whether these, or any, groups have rights in all the ways that individual persons have rights. Groups can certainly have legal rights, even constitutional rights, but perhaps not intrinsic rights (that is, rights justified by the interests of the rights-holder), and presumably not human rights. Nonetheless, they can certainly have legal and moral obligations, some of which relate to safeguarding and promoting the societal, legal and human rights of individuals.

The collective name given to such social (non-state) groups or associations is 'civil society', which includes a whole range of voluntary associations ranging from youth groups to political parties and, in its most expansive meaning, including families at one extreme and even multinational corporations (MNCs) at the other. This chapter considers how these constituents of civil society do and should contribute to the institutionalisation of rights.

Do they contribute to making rights a functioning reality, thus forming part of what it means to be a right? Or are they more a force in determining what rights we have in practice? Or should they be seen more as a hindrance, or threat, than a help?

We should note that there is another meaning of 'civil society' in which it has more to do with the general culture or normatively defined way of life in a society. This we have already considered when discussing the existence of societal rights, where the rules that constitute rights are embedded in the social expectations and critical attitudes prevalent in a social group, rather than in law. Societal rights may be viewed as part of a social culture which may contain a variety of inter-related rights, and may be more or less oriented towards the significance of rights as socially valuable entities.

Thus, a society may be said to have a 'rights culture', when its members think of themselves in terms of their rights and interact with each other on the basis of their perceived rights and duties. A 'rights culture', in which people think in terms of rights in their everyday lives and have experience of what it means to be treated as a person with rights, is widely regarded as a pre-condition of the effective promotion of human rights. A social culture is a relatively permanent normatively grounded pattern of human activities, covering all aspects of social life, including economic production, that provides the background and framework for the exercise of political and governmental power. We shall have reason to draw on the idea of a culture of rights, but the prime focus of this chapter is on the voluntary associations that interpose between the individual and the state, including business organisations.

Civil society

The first, and very obvious, point to make is that voluntary associations are themselves dependent on the existence of certain fundamental rights, principally the right to associate, the right to freedom of collective choice, the right to freedom of collective speech and the right to legal personality and hence the rights to enter into contractual agreements and legally enforceable relationships. Civil society is in this sense a concomitant of a rights-conscious society.

Our question is, whether or not as a result of the rights that such associations enjoy in their very existence, voluntary associations have or should have a significant role in the institutions of rights. No doubt much depends here on the sort of voluntary association we have in mind. Certain institutions, such as Amnesty International and Human Rights Watch, were founded to protect and further human rights, while most associations have quite different purposes, although we have noted that a whole range of non-governmental organisations (NGOs) play a role in monitoring, publicising and campaigning on human rights issues.

Indeed, it can be argued that, without the increasing contribution they make in bringing to light human rights abuses and shaming not only states but the United Nations itself into taking some minimal action to combat these, the international human rights régime would be much less effective. Further NGO activity, especially in the case of human rights NGOs, clearly does a great deal to enhance awareness of rights and hence the development of a rights culture generally. NGOs in combination with less organised social movements have a profound impact on the sort of rights institutionalisation that we have considered in the previous two chapters. They play a significant part in the political processes whereby new legal rights are adopted and in contributing to the enforcement process through publicising and monitoring the applications of rights (Freeman 2000: 142–47, Forsythe 2000: 173–37).

This certainly makes civil society an important underpinning for the legal and quasi-legal institutionalisation of rights, but can we say that NGOs play anything more than a supporting role here? Do NGOs have a direct role in giving social reality to manifesto rights? This must be the case where the NGOs act not as pressure groups for legal change, but for the rectification of particular injustices, as in campaigning for the release of persons detained without trial, and in seeking to alleviate the suffering of those whose social and economic rights have been neglected by states and international governmental organisations. Of course, not every activity that reduces unmerited suffering can be classified as an institutionalisation of rights, but where the activity is systematically undertaken for the explicit purposes of dealing with human rights violations and shortcomings, then we may regard the actions of civil society as a constituent part of the institutionalisation that meet the existence criteria for the rights in question. There seems no doubt, therefore, that civil society is a part, perhaps an essential part, of realising rights.

This does raise, however, the question of whether it is morally right that this should be so. Such voluntary associations are, after all, self-appointed groups of individuals who have taken it upon themselves to use human rights discourse to bring about social change. Such bodies are generally not internally democratic and choose to confront governments and international organisations in what may be viewed as a partisan way, at the same time claiming a right to a special voice in domestic and international politics, and in domestic and international courts.

Clearly, such objections are unlikely to succeed within any democratic system of governance in which freedom of speech and association are enshrined as rights that are essential to the proper functioning of a system that is open to debate, persuasion and informed voting. There can be no doubt that there should be a human right for individuals to join together with such peaceful political objectives in mind. Indeed, the operations of NGOs may be seen as even more legitimate in relation to international politics where the government organisations involved, while including some representatives of elected governments, are in fact highly undemocratic in their internal institutions.

If civil society may legitimately engage in the process of institutionalising human rights, this then leads on to the further question as to whether voluntary associations may legitimately be required to protect and promote human rights. We have seen that they are capable of so doing, but does this capacity involve an obligation to use it for such purposes. In general 'can' does not imply 'ought'. Capacity is a necessary but not a sufficient condition of moral obligation. However, in situations where human rights are involved, rights whose correlative duties have high moral import and priority, there may be reason to argue that those who can help have an obligation to do so.

This is a line of argument to which we return when considering the right to be relieved of extreme poverty in Chapter 9. At this point, it can be noted that a voluntary association cannot, by definition, be required to come into or to remain in existence. It may seem odd therefore to require them to pursue externally determined objectives, even if it seems morally legitimate for them to do this sort of thing, since they have no duty to remain in existence. However, for as long as voluntary associations do exist then it is certainly possible to ascribe human rights obligations to them, although it seems questionable to interfere in their internal affairs provided these do not violate existing rights. It is certain that they do have obligations not to violate human rights. The interesting question is whether or not they ought to have positive human rights obligations, including duties to protect and even enforce the human rights obligations of others, duties similar to those of states, such as the duty to control and punish human rights violators within their sphere of influence.

It can certainly be argued that civil society has human rights obligations to remedy the human rights harm they have themselves brought about in the course of their activities, if they have the capacity so to do. But do they have a positive obligation to remedy those human rights violations for which they are not responsible? And should this obligation be adopted as a legal obligation or should it be societal in nature? If such positive obligations are a possibility, then we have the prospect of drawing on the resources of civil society not just to support but to supplement the institutionalised human rights processes of nation states and international organisations.

Looking at civil society in relation to the myriad of social organisations that impact on people's lives, we can see it has enormous potential for good and ill through the enhanced power that derives from social cooperation and the way in which associations enable individuals to pursue their, perhaps illegitimate, self-interest without taking personal responsibility for their actions. This makes it imperative to consider civil society from the point of view of the obligations that are correlative to rights, particularly human rights. These obligations are part of what constitutes rights-relationships, and the means by which these obligations are routinely fulfilled form a decisive part of the rights-mechanisms that must be developed to give moral rights a social reality. Some of these obligations can be enshrined in law, and some of these mechanisms can be given legal support, but a considerable domain remains within which the human rights obligations of civil society are societal, not legal.

It is to this aspect of civil society that the remainder of this chapter is devoted, giving particular attention to the human rights obligations of the business corporation, now the dominant form of human organisation, apart from the state, in the modern world and increasingly the object of attention of international NGOs.

Economic entities and human rights

The state is no longer seen as the only significant danger to the rights of the individual. This is partly because of the decline of the power of individual states with respect to the global economy on which so much of the economic wellbeing of societies depends, and partly because of the rise of corporations as multinational enterprises with enormous resources that often dwarf those of states and the capacity to stave off government restrictions on their activities by removing their activities to a more compliant country.

In so far as they are major contributors to economic development large corporations are actually and potentially enormous contributors to human wellbeing, including, it may be argued, to the positive human freedoms that flow from material prosperity. In addition to their principal role in generating productive activity, their resources can be used to promote the social, economic and cultural rights of people in the countries to which their activities give them access, particularly with respect to working conditions. However, in the single minded pursuit of immediate economic profit corporations are capable of gross rights violations, against which their victims rarely have any recourse. Sweatshops, child labour and inhumane conditions of work are commonplace. Corporations, like governments before them, are the source of much promise and many threats to human rights on a global scale.

Despite the immense wealth of the large MNCs, states retain their formal sovereignty and have the right to regulate corporations that operate within their jurisdiction. And the obligations of the state to protect its citizens against large corporations is no different in principle from its duty to protect its citizens against other sources of power, such as religious institutions, which still exercise major control over people's lives in many countries. To the extent that this is the case, the protection of human rights remains the duty of governments. But there are two limitations that apply to the state's capacities in this regard. One is normative and the other is factual.

The normative limitation derives from the rights of corporations, not as independent moral agents, but as creations of those individuals who have exercised their right of freedom of association to form corporations to act as their agents in the generation of wealth. Individuals have the right to enter into such agreements, and the corporations they create have a right to act as the agents of their creators as long, of course, as they do not violate the rights of others. Indeed, such rights are themselves often protected by constitutions that grant to corporations constitutional rights, such as the right to freedom of speech, and the right not to be deprived of their property without just compensation. Such constitutional rights may limit to powers of states to regulate corporations just as they limit the power of states over their citizens.

The factual limitation of the power of governments to make corporations serve human rights is the economic dependence of states on corporations. Régimes that do not accommodate the demands of large, usually multinational, corporations, do not share in the prosperity that they bring. Whether it be the level of corporate taxation, the rates of pay, the conditions of work, or the protection of traditional ways of life and environmental integrity, governments often lack the effective power to control major corporations.

It is in this context that it is appropriate to raise questions about the moral obligations on corporations with respect to human rights. Indeed, we may raise questions about the moral responsibilities of other elements of civil society in situations where governments are unwilling or unable to act effectively. We have seen the important role that is played by NGOs in bringing pressure to bear in the sphere of international human rights. Such organisations may be viewed as an expression of social and community concern which all citizens have some duty to support. And there may be other ways in which civil society, rather than the state, comes into the human rights picture as a bearer of obligations as well as rights.

A central feature of modern politics is balancing the operation of free enterprise capitalism and concerns for the wellbeing of those who are harmed by, or left out of, these types of economic system. Although, since the demise of the Soviet Union in 1989, there has been no serious rival to the capitalist system, there remains a great deal of controversy about its benefits and drawbacks and how it should be regulated (Braithwaite and Drahos 2000). While the superior productivity of capitalist systems is not in doubt, the quality of life that it generates is vulnerable to criticism, if only because the serious injustices that it brings about by way of domestic and global inequality are increasingly problematic. The inability of capitalist organisations to keep within their own rules with respect to free competition and conformity to law, combined with the failure to exercise their considerable economic power for the benefit of the wider community, raises major moral doubt as to the legitimacy of existing forms of the capitalist system. This is exacerbated by the contemporary phenomenon of globalisation, that is, the growing economic and hence political dominance of the world market, whose rules of operation are currently of disproportionate benefit to economic powerful countries, a phenomenon that undermines the capacity of even substantial world powers to control their own destinies and protect the interests of their own subjects (Sassen 1996).

A counter to this pessimistic picture of global capitalism may be found in that other global phenomenon, human rights. In affirming universal standards of minimum human conduct, human rights can be used, as they have been in the case of states, to both legitimate and limit the activities of corporations (Galligan and Sampford 1997: 2–22). Human rights can be seen as the moral face of globalisation. They may be used to vindicate the economic benefits of liberal capitalism in the production and distribution of desirable goods, while at the same time providing grounds for restricting those economic freedoms that cause unacceptable collateral harm and providing a basis for using the democratic process to channel its activities within acceptable parameters.

Where legal regulation is not politically feasible, human rights can provide a basis for placing the sort of societal obligations on corporations that have come to be referred to as 'corporate social responsibility', a concept that identifies those obligations of corporations that go beyond the distribution of maximal profits to shareholders and conformity to local laws (Donaldson 1989: 163–82). The corporate social responsibility movement has brought about a great deal of institutional development by way of codes of conduct, ethics programmes and even ethical audits, internal to corporations, and external pressures are increasingly brought to bear by consumers, shareholders (including the move to 'ethical investment'), religious groups and NGOs.

Corporate social responsibility is associated with the 'stakeholder' theory of the corporation, according to which the function of the corporation is to protect and further the interests, not only of their shareholders, and not only of those on whom they depend, such as their workforces, their customers and suppliers, but also of all those who are adversely affected by their activities, such as the workers in the factories of their suppliers, the indigenous people displaced by their operations, those who suffer in consequence of the environmental degradation cause by industrial activity and former consumers who have been injured through using their products.

Stakeholder theory has had some success in enlarging the horizons of corporate strategy but it has been less successful in identifying the parameters and priorities of corporate responsibility and suggesting how the diverse and conflicting interests of the various types of stakeholder are to be balanced and reconciled. There is a need to identify those universal standards to which priority should be given in redrawing the boundaries of corporate duty. It is at this point that human rights may be brought into the picture as a basis for identifying those moral consequences of overriding importance that cannot legitimately be ignored by business organisations. Human rights have a global applicability and clearly cannot be excluded from any area of society, be it religious, political, military or economic. They have the moral force to raise corporate social responsibility from the optional extra that it often is, to a permanent imperative of corporate business.

Cynicism as to business ethics is justifiably rife. Much so-called ethical activity is window-dressing and market-oriented, aimed at protecting the reputation on which sales rest and employee satisfaction is increased. Nevertheless, since little moral commitment is entirely altruistic and there are tangible long-term benefits in maintaining a good corporate reputation, corporate social responsibility has the potential to bring about a significant degree of human rights institutionalisation, particularly within the foreign countries in which MNCs operate or from which they source their materials and products (Hutton and Giddens 2000: 215).

Sphere-specific rights

A similar analysis could be applied to other major players within civil society, such as churches, charitable foundations, pressure groups and professional organisations. But the question arises as to whether the human rights obligations of such voluntary associations are equivalent in content and scope to the positive human rights obligations that have been developed with respect to states. Do we, for instance, simply take the current 'international bill of rights' and work out what contribution civil society can make towards their fuller realisation?

This would have the advantage of a ready-made authoritative – if rather indeterminate – list of relevant rights which come with legal and political support deriving from the multifarious international agreements and instruments already in existence. Moreover, it is clearly stated in the Preamble to the Universal Declaration of Human Rights, that the obligations arising from such rights fall on 'all organs of society'. In this way bringing civil society into the picture enables us to draw on a globally institutionalised authority with a palpable presence in the global consciousness.

However, this ignores the fact that existing human rights law is the product of a process designed by states to limit the powers of states. Its content is formed by a consideration, not simply of human values and interests, but of the particular threats and promises presented by coercive political authority.

Further this approach is out of kilter with our analysis, in Part I, of rights as circumscribed and formulated in terms of who, if anyone, can be said to have obligations with respect to the putative rights of those concerned. It is not that we identify rights and then look to see who has, or ought to have, the correlative duties, rather, only when we can be sure that there is a correlative duty can we say that there is, or ought to be, a corresponding right.

Another mistake would be to see the issues as simply a matter of what legal obligations ought to be placed on civil society in order to protect and further human rights. This will no doubt come into the picture in important ways, particularly to secure a measure of freedom of information and a reasonable framework of corporate governance, but to concentrate purely of putative legal obligations is to forget both the difficulty of imposing legal obligations on corporations whose operations can readily be transferred from one jurisdiction to another, and the limitations of law in achieving human rights goals, limitations that highlight the need to see civil society's human rights obligations as including major ethical commitments not, for practical reasons, enforceable by law.

For such reasons, it is important to take a fresh look at the content and application of human rights with respect to the various types of organisation at work in civil society. What we need are sphere-specific human rights which takes seriously the idea that human rights for organisations may differ significantly in form and content from those that prevail in the context of the state.

For a start, some of the international bill of rights is directly aimed at states alone, such as the right to vote. Other of these rights, must vary in content from their normal political application. Thus freedom of speech in the forum of politics is one thing, and freedom of speech in the workplace is quite another. Sphere-specific human rights will vary with the nature of the organisation and the particular opportunities they give rise to in both promoting and harming the sort of major human interests that bear on the concept of equality of human worth. We require different rights for different segments of civil society, all of which have potentialities and problems for which appropriate rights mechanisms need to be developed. Organisations can thus have distinctive human rights duties differing from state-oriented human rights, that relate to the 'standing threats' (Shue 1980: 29–34) to basic human interests on which that type of organisation is most likely to impact, the primary domain of their influence and their distinctive capacities and opportunities. This may lead us to concentrate on the impersonality that is such a degrading element in bureaucratic organisations, or the serious consequences deriving from the commodification of human labour (Ciulla 2000).

Summarising the idea of sphere-specificity in relation to the human rights obligations of the members of civil society, we may identify three strands.

(1) Threat-specificity identifies the characteristic form of evil that is liable to occur in that sphere, e.g. bullying in the workplace, or false advertising of dangerous goods in the market place. These threats vary with the type of activities in question.
(2) Remedy-specificity, which must vary with the institutional mechanisms appropriate for dealing with the sphere-specific threats. Thus, if rights are to be enforced by way of a court-administered bill of rights then this affects what can sensibly be regarded as 'human rights', for this purpose. The same consideration will apply if we deploy rights to justify imposing

sanctions on or using armed intervention against a sovereign state. Depending on the practical consequences of the human rights violation, the content of what constitutes the human rights that are violated must change.

(3) Capacity-specificity comes in with respect to the means that are available to an organisation for achieving human rights goals. We cannot assume a human rights obligation where there is not the capacity to achieve that objective. In this as in other moral spheres, 'ought' implies 'can'.

The implications of a sphere-specific approach to the human rights of civil society organisations are not confined to identifying the characteristic impacts of their traditional activities on human welfare. This would mean that we think of educational organisations being concerned only with rights to education, and religious organisations with the right to belief and to tolerance. It would also lead us to think of the rights furthering mechanisms are those typical of existing practice in the area, such as educational means in the sphere of education and economic means in the case of commercial organisations.

However, it is clear that educational and economic means can be deployed with respect to a variety of human rights objectives other than education and economic wellbeing. Here it has to be emphasised that we are not dealing only with the idea that civil society should further, in both negative and positive ways, human rights goals, but with the idea that civil society may be seen as taking on the secondary human rights role usually confined to the state of preventing human rights abuses by agents other than themselves. Thus the protective role of the state may be shared, having specific reference to areas in which it is difficult for states to make much impression through its characteristic means of imposing legal obligations (see p. 87).

This approach derives in part from our prior analysis of rights as involving a commitment to effective methods for ensuring the protection and furtherance of the identified valued interests. We have explicated this both with respect to the imposition of legal obligations that offer some form of guarantee to those who may thereby be said to have rights, and to the existence of other norms in a society without which there could be little security of expectation with respect to many of the ingredients of a dignified human life.

There are legal and the governmental rationales for confining the implications of human rights to state politics, on the grounds that only states have the legitimacy and authority to achieve such objectives. Some human rights are universal in that they may be violated by any individual or organisation, and states have particular importance through their monopoly of coercive force and access to effective remedies. Yet this does not provide grounds for rejecting specific and positive roles for the organisations of civil society with respect to a number of human rights that are distinctive in content and mechanism.

Human rights responsibilities are not restricted to following the laws that are there to protect human rights. Economic organisations cannot outlaw abuses of human rights, but they can, and perhaps ought to, have a function that goes beyond not violating such rights themselves, a function which requires using the economic means at their disposal to promote human rights objectives by altering the conduct of others, including the conduct of oppressive government towards their people.

Human rights will always require the protection of laws but they remain part of an essentially moral discourse that generates reasons why all organisations should behave in certain ways, reasons connected to such ideas as, human dignity, non-discrimination and distributive justice, that have application far beyond legal and governmental domains. But this does not mean that civil society should simply adopt the form and content of the human rights régimes developed to deal with the conduct of states.

The thesis is that human rights are relative in the sense that they are sphere-specific. The human rights that apply to non-governmental agents will not be the same as those that apply to states. Human rights cannot be seen as a set of self-evident intuitions from which we can work out implications for all areas of social life. The way forward is to accept that human rights, like all rights, are human constructs that serve particular moral aims in ways that will vary in a diversity of social contexts. Human rights are not epistemologically autonomous entities that we uncover by examining the moral fabric of the world independently of the factual circumstances of different forms of human society and social organisations. Human rights are not fixed in content and form independently of the actual problems they are designed to solve.

It may be argued that it is best to stick to a unified content for human rights since only those rights that are incumbent upon states, and which states are required to protect, will be taken seriously. The human rights obligations of civil society may be seen as being, like the organisations themselves, voluntary, and therefore less imperative, less demanding and less significant. But this does not follow. Simply because, for instance, some objectives are not best attained through the enactment and enforcement of coercive laws does not mean that they are of lesser significance. If what matters is the outcome in question then we should adopt the most appropriate means, and that means the most effective, not necessarily the most coercive, approach. It is simply a mistake to equate legality with moral priority. Indeed the moral discourse of human rights is ideally suited to developing a culture in which societal obligations that are taken on voluntarily and realised through educational and economic means, are seen as being equally demanding morally as are the demands of state laws, even when these are human rights laws.

The creative adaptation of human rights in a sphere-specific direction for the various organisations of civil society can serve a variety of functions. Thus, it could legitimate the activities of economically and religiously powerful organisations provided that they stay within the prescribed human rights bounds. Human rights in business corporations may justify both their right to exist and the limits of that right, so that no corporation is legitimate if it violates business human rights in the same way as no government is legitimate if it violates governmental human rights. Corporations have a right to life only to the extent that those who have created them have a right to do so and only then so long as their creators take responsibility for the consequences of their actions (something that fits uneasily with the practice of limited liability).

The rights of association, however, are subject to limitations that require respect for the human rights of others, including sphere-specific human rights, such as hold between employers and employees. In the case of corporations, as well as states, human rights enter into the legitimacy of their existence and their actions while in existence. Given the disproportionate power in the hands of some corporations as against some states, this seems right and proper. The common factor here is that in both cases we are dealing with the protection and furtherance of fundamental human interests. Human rights ought to be based on what is vital to an acceptable rather than a merely desirable human existence. Only in this way can they retain the overriding importance that the discourse of human rights requires. In this regard, a charter of human rights for business must differ from a voluntary code of conduct that serves as part of a merely 'ethical' régime both in its content and force.

This leaves us to consider whether giving such a role to civil society, particularly its large and powerful economic organisations, is capable of generating the sort of assurance and entitlement that the idea of rights, particularly human rights, portends. Arguably this will not be possible unless other aspects of civil society are brought to bear on the otherwise insensitive and inconstant motivations of business corporations. It is here that the role of NGOs, in combination with the ethically motivated choices of investors, employees and consumers, offers the best hope of approaching the degree of certainty that reaches the threshold of effectiveness that warrants the description of entitlement.

Conclusion

Even if we look exclusively to law – domestic and international – as the only effective and fair concretisation of rights, laws will always require popular support in order to work well, and this means more than simply having the support of voters and the approval of media-led public opinion. Most evidently what is required is a deeply rooted cultural commitment, rooted in the beliefs of individuals and fostered by religious groups, educational organisations and the media not just by those individuals and organisations engaged in the overtly political process.

Within this broad context, there is a crucial role for 'civil society' in the sense of voluntary organisations directed to the achievement of specific social and political goals. This is particularly the case in protecting the interests of minority groups and challenging the secrecy and vested interests of governments and public sector organisations. Without these inputs, legal rights become formal entitlements and not the sort of genuine guarantees that are required to realise the full conception of what rights are meant to be. This is all the more so when the rights in question, and this means almost all important rights, are costly demands that require substantial resources and their organised deployment. It is necessary for a right to exist that something can be done to right the wrongs that give rise to rights-claims, but this is not sufficient for the realisation of a right, which requires that this something is in fact done, and done routinely. Only then do a group of people actually have rather than just demand their rights.

However, rights, including human rights, transcend legal rights. Some of the correlative obligations involved either cannot or, for some reason, ought not to be enforced by law. Here we have a role for civil society that goes beyond supporting the state in its protection of rights, or fulfilling its own human rights legal obligations. We have seen that voluntary organisations have such moral obligations to directly meet the needs of those whose suffering they can relieve, as well as to participate in schemes that protect the interests of those directly affected by their operations.

To this extent the institutions of rights include those arrangements that are, or ought to be, put in place by, for instance, corporations, to see that their activities do not unjustifiably impinge upon the human rights of those directly affected by them, and to use their resources to actively promote fundamental human wellbeing, both within and without their own organisation. Establishing the precise parameters of these wider obligations is a difficult community process. If such societal rights are to be effectively established, this process must be taken to the point where it can be said that there is, within that society, a broad acceptance that the rights correlative to societal obligations are indeed rights. This means more than the recurrence of sporadic *ad hoc* demands and media rhetoric. It requires that legitimate human rights claims are routinely made and routinely met in the form of social and economic provisions supplied 'as of right'.

PART III

THREE HUMAN RIGHTS

Thus far we have been concerned principally with the meaning and form of rights and the institutional contexts that give them their life and impact. We have considered what rights are, who can have rights, when we can say that rights exist, and how all this relates to the issue of how we can best promote and protect rights. Only Chapter 4 directly addresses the fourth question: what rights ought we to have? Part III takes up this question again in relation to three illustrative examples of substantive human rights that bring out different sorts of issues. They are: the right to free speech, the right to a subsistence standard of living and a people's right to self-government. These are rights that, it is generally claimed, belong to everyone in that they are rights that everyone ought to have. But what grounds can we give to justify such claims, and precisely what is the form and content of the rights that such grounds can justify?

Raising these normative issues of political philosophy takes us into the high terrain of moral and political justification generally. How can we make well grounded recommendations about any substantive political issue that raises value-laden questions about justice, obligation, equality and democracy? Some extreme right-based theories of political justification hold that rights do not need justification because it is rights themselves that provide the justifications. Rights 'exceptionalism' of this sort assumes that we can have direct intuitive knowledge of what rights are and what rights we ought to have and in some (moral) sense actually do have. On this view, justice, for instance, is a matter of treating people in accordance with their rights. We know what rights we have because we know that we already do have them. All that needs to be done is to apply them to different aspects of social and economic life.

This is not the position adopted here. I assume that even if it is appropriate to think that we can have moral knowledge, this is not available to us through direct intuitions or revelations concerning what rights we ought to have (or actually do have in some universe of moral truths). There is no general agreement on anything so specific as a right, and no 'self-evident' intuitions beyond a degree of consensus as to the moral relevance of certain fundamental values, such as autonomy, altruism, happiness and wellbeing. Nor is there any reason to believe that this lack of agreement is based solely on ignorance or ill-will (Mackie 1977).

We have touched on this matter in our earlier analysis of rights-based approaches to morality and politics (see p. 39). There we explored the idea that the distinctive thing about rights is that they are based on a particular sort of moral consideration, such as human dignity or the equal worth of the individual. This can be interpreted as saying that rights are grounded in giving overriding importance to certain individual interests, perhaps, according to the will theory of rights, the interest of being free to act as one chooses (see p. 43), or according to republican theory, being free of domination (see p. 75). These reflections takes us in a certain direction, opening up lines of normative reflection. Equal worth, human dignity, autonomy, wellbeing and interests, remain broad and indeterminate concepts that need to be developed and applied to concrete circumstances in ways that take into account the contexts of their application and the variety of values that feature in our moral discourse. Philosophy can clarify and explore these questions but philosophers have no more authority than anyone else to claim knowledge as to their correct interpretation and application.

Moreover, once it is accepted that to have a right is to be in possession of a mechanism with which we or others can promote and protect our significant individual and collective interests, it is clear that rights must be justified in part by consequentialist reasons which take us far beyond simple moral intuitions into the complex empirical world of how humans behave and how societies operate. And it is clear that the consequences cited in favour of this or that right are not limited to the future wellbeing of the rights-holder, for granting rights to individuals may be justified either by the benefits that it brings to persons other than the persons whose rights they are or by the public goods that creating such rights generates.[1]

Further, in deciding the necessary detail of the rights we ought to have it is necessary to specify the scope and range of such rights so that they do not have unacceptable consequences for other interests that may (or may not) be candidates for protection by other (perhaps conflicting) rights. Thus the right to liberty, with respect to free speech, may lead to social disorder and religious intolerance, and the right to equality of material goods may lead to widespread poverty and limitations on liberty. The question of what rights we ought to have requires working through these priorities when *prima facie* rights conflict. Approaching these problems by exchanging moral intuitions about rights rather than thinking about the values that underpin our choice of rights and working out how to realise them in practice does not promote clear thinking on these matters. We may all agree that values such as liberty, equality, dignity and creativity are important, but it is another matter to translate this into a set of specific institutionalisable rights and duties.

At this point we might fall back on our accounts of competing ideologies outlined in Chapter 4 in the analyses of Rawls, Nozick, Posner, Marx and Young, and follow this through into their rationales for adopting this or that content and form for particular rights. And we could extend our coverage of normative political philosophies by bringing in others, such as Kant, Dworkin, Finnis, Gewirth and Habermas, all of whom, as we have seen, have important things to say about how we might go about determining what rights we ought to have.

However, despite the efforts of all these major political philosophers, when we seek to go beyond uncontroversial generalities, the proper content and form of particular rights have proved philosophically very elusive. Rawls asks us to consider what basic rights we would choose to have if we had to decide without knowing what sort of person we are or what place we will have in society. Nozick gets us to agree that it can never be justified to take from someone, without their consent, one of their vital organs, and extrapolates from this to a libertarian society of few but powerful negative rights. Dworkin suggests that unpacking the idea of 'equal concern and respect' will enable us to interpret positive laws in a way that best serves moral rights that override all other considerations. Finnis gets us to consider the various ways in which human beings can be said to flourish in the pursuit of a normative ideal as to what is in some way 'natural' to human kind. Gewirth gets us to consider what we must all claim for ourselves by way of support for our existence as rational agents and argues that we cannot deny the similar claims of other moral agents. Habermas holds that an open dialogue on such matters conducted in the right spirit will produce a justified consensus as to what our rights ought to be. None of these simplistic caricatures begin to do the slightest justice to the theorists in question, but they illustrate the enormity of the task of settling on a methodology for the choice of moral rights. Overall, we may say that philosophies provide orientations but not answers to such normative issues.

A critical introduction to rights could very properly seek to demonstrate that all of these theorists have made illuminating suggestions but none have provided a satisfactory method for determining what rights we ought to have. Instead, in Part III, I bring forward some particular arguments as justifications that may be offered in support of particular substantive rights. The object is to bring out the variety of morally relevant considerations that arise when we contemplate how to articulate and defend specific contents for three core human rights, drawing on the broad theories only from time to time. This puts us in a better position to see what we require from overarching political philosophies and to get a feel for how to critically evaluate the arguments that crop up in democratic debate on the basis of which we should exercise our democratic rights of sharing in decision-procedures for determining the rights that we are going to have.

In selecting the specific rights for consideration, I draw on a now familiar distinction that is used to identify three phases of the development of human rights, particularly in the international sphere. Freedom of speech exemplifies 'first generation' rights, the civil and political rights that are identified in the International Covenant on Civil and Political Rights (ICCPR) and the Enlightenment rights current in the formative stage of the modern liberal state. The rights to sustenance is a 'second generation rights', the social, economic and cultural rights that are identified in the International Covenant on Economic, Social and Cultural Rights (ICESCR) and are characteristic of the modern welfare state more akin to a social democrat than a libertarian society. The right to self-determination is a 'third generation right', an example of those group rights that have come into prominence through the claims of peoples and cultural minorities to political self-government, development and cultural recognition. These rights, sometimes called solidarity rights, express aspirations of the developing world, deprived minorities and oppressed groups. Beyond this the choice of these particular rights is largely arbitrary, reflecting my own specific interests.

The distinctions between the three categories of right are crude and in many ways historically inaccurate, but they are nevertheless useful when related to our earlier typologies with their emphasis on correlative obligations and implied remedies. Thus, first generation rights tend to be interpreted as formal liberties or negative claim rights against governments, while second generation rights are seen as positive rights that correlate with the obligations of others to do something active to support the interests identified in such rights. The contrast between negative and positive rights has been demonstrated to be an over-simplification, if only because first generation rights, while requiring no more than inaction from obligation-bearers, are in fact very costly to protect (Shue 1980, Holmes and Sunstein 2000), an issue which is taken up in Chapter 9 where respect to the right to subsistence and its implications for the content of that right. One of the interesting things about third generation rights is how to position them in relation to the distinction between negative and positive rights, an issue that is explored in Chapter 10, where we consider whether collective 'rights' are really rights at all (Alston 2001).

One theme that emerges in these chapters is how first generation rights themselves come to develop the characteristics of later generations, so that there is a development of all rights from a first to a second or third generation mode. In addition, in our responses to critiques of particular rights, other revisionary tendencies are at work, requiring that rights become more specific, that correlative duties become more widely shared and that we find a greater range of mechanisms for implementing rights in a more reliable manner. It should also be noted that all three rights play a part in the sphere of ordinary rights as well as human rights, and apply both in domestic and international systems.

Each of the three rights examined in this part of the book may be seen as an example of the justificatory aspects of rights discourse and how it might be effectively and progressively articulated. This involves an appreciation of the variety of rationales that may be presented to justify and define the rights in question and how these relate to the possible content, form and implementation of these rights.

Chapter 8

Freedom of speech

Article 19 of the Universal Declaration of Human Rights states that 'Everyone has the right to freedom of opinion and expression; this right includes freedom to hold opinions without interference and to seek, receive and impart information and ideas through any media and regardless of frontiers'. This echoes in a broader and less absolute form[1] the famous First Amendment to the Constitution of the United States: 'Congress shall make no law . . . abridging the freedom of speech, or of the press'. Freedom of speech, or expression, is one of the civil rights that is at the core of all Bills of Rights and is claimed as a fundamental right within the common law tradition. Less specifically, it is also in many societies, a deeply embedded societal right, manifest in the wide acceptance of everyone's right to speak their mind and be listened to with respect, especially on matters relating to the general wellbeing.

In practice, freedom of speech is restricted in all countries in ways that vary substantially from state to state, even if we confine our attention to democracies. This diversity relates to the content, form, institutional mechanisms and justifying rationales for freedom of speech, expression and communication.

With respect to the content and scope of the right, many jurisdictions have strict restrictions on such matters as advertising, hate speech, pornography, privacy and defamation. Others are much less restrictive. With respect to form, sometimes the right to freedom of speech is presented as a formal liberty right, a matter of being free from any obligation not to say or publish whatever one wants to say or publish, but nevertheless being liable for the legal consequences of such publications. This means that there is no prior censorship but this does not mean that there are no subsequent legal liabilities. At other times and places the right to free speech is presented as a claim right, either correlating with the negative duty of others not to prevent someone speaking, or the positive duty to enable them to do so, or even to provide them with relevant information to enable them to form and express their views. Then there are rationales that commend, under the rubric of free speech, immunity rights from legal powers that inhibit speech, such as prosecution for sedition or defamation proceedings, particularly where political or other public figures are involved.

With respects to institutions, some jurisdictions protect freedom of speech through constitutional rights, usually by enacting a generalised immunity to legal restrictions on speech. Others depend on the assumption that people are free to say what they like unless there are clear and specific legal limitations in place with respect to such matters as causing offence, revealing secrets or unjustifiably harming the reputation of others. The latter as well as the former may go along with encouraging a culture of tolerating or even welcoming free speech through education and the political process which inhibits hostile criticism of those who speak their mind and express unpopular opinions.

With respect to justifying rationales, some theorists defend their position on freedom of speech by reference to self-expression, others as a means to protect other interests of the rights-holders, and still others by appeal to the good social consequences of free speech, such as the development of knowledge and the furtherance of informed public discussion.

This chapter follows through these themes: first as exemplars of the complexity of determining what rights we ought to have, and then as a domain in which we can test the general critiques of rights that were enunciated in Part I, before passing to some observations as to how freedom of speech régimes and cultures might be constructively reformed.

Free speech rationales

Freedom of speech is often presented as a second order principle, that is, a principle that forbids us (or governments) from intervening in everyday conduct for reasons that would otherwise be appropriate were we not dealing with speech. Speech is taken to be so important that it cannot be restricted merely because there is a good reason to do so (Schauer 1991). Why is speech so special?

Assuming a conception of freedom of speech as the absence of legal restraints on communicative expression (a formal liberty right) plus claim-rights whereby there is an obligation on governments and citizens not to stifle speech in other ways and perhaps also a positive obligation to assist citizens in the expression of their opinions, we may identify a number of distinct types of reason why the special second order status of the principle of free speech is justifiable.

The argument from truth

A fascinating thing about freedom of speech is that a principal argument used in favour of this particularly sacrosanct human right is consequentialist rather than intrinsic. Freedom of speech, it is argued by that doyen of nineteenth century liberals, John Stuart Mill, is the way to promote truth in a society, thus benefiting both people involved in the exercise of free speech and the wider society. For Mill, truth is justified belief and belief is justified only if it has been subjected to unimpeded criticism, something that requires freedom of speech and actual conflict of expressed opinions. To suppress free speech is to make the epistemological mistake of assuming that you know in advance of hearing an opinion that it is false. This is inconsistent with the thesis that belief is only justified once we have heard the arguments on all sides of the issue (Mill 1910).

It may be thought that Mill is corrupted here by his utilitarian enthusiasms, but in the jurisprudence of the Supreme Court of the United States, exemplified by Judge Oliver Wendell Holmes, this argument for freedom of speech is also expounded, this time in terms of 'the marketplace in ideas': 'The best test of truth is the power of the idea to get itself accepted in the competition of the market' (*Abrams v. United States* 1919). According to this market model we choose our beliefs like we choose our purchases and that the best buy is obtained in a free market where anyone can bring forward their products for sale. This means that we cannot deny currency to any expression of opinion without reducing the efficiency of the knowledge market.

The argument from truth is a powerful instrumental rationale against restrictions on free speech (and indeed for encouraging speech) both with respect to the benefits it produces for those rights-holders and for others who desire or will benefit from increased knowledge. However, it does not seem strong enough to justify an absolute prohibition on speech restrictions any more than an actual market is exempt from restrictions that are, for instance, designed to prevent harmful products or false and misleading advertising. An absolute immunity right to free speech would have to be based on the assumption that speech never causes any harm. But this is false. Speaking is an act with foreseeable consequences. Speech may cause pain to others, it may lead to their death or injury, it may corrupt their morals. For this, and other reasons, philosophers often speak of 'speech acts' (Searle 1969).

Precisely for such reasons there are laws that prohibit the public expression of falsehoods that reflect badly on the reputation of other people (defamation), that prohibit the expression of false alarms that cause panic or inconvenience to others (like falsely shouting 'fire' in a crowded place), that prohibit the dissemination of pornographic material to children and so on. If free speech is not to be an absolute right, then its scope may have to be substantially restricted so that only some speech in some circumstances is rightly free from legal restrictions and cultural suppression.

To what extent harmful speech may be justifiably prohibited is hotly debated (Post 1991, Sadurski 1999). It has been successfully argued that 'hate speech', that is speech that incites hatred against a racial, ethnic or gender group, ought to be prohibited because of the insult, social conflict and oppression to which it contributes. On the marketplace analogy, perhaps we ought to be permitted to 'buy' such expressions of opinion, but on the other hand, perhaps 'selling' such dangerous opinions ought to be prohibited.

It may be objected, following Mill's approach, that this assumes that we can know in advance of everyone being exposed to hate speech that it is false. But we do not take this attitude to other types of harmful action. We do not accept that stealing should be permitted because we cannot have sufficient knowledge that it is harmful if we prohibit stealing. We accept that we have sufficient knowledge of the harmfulness of some actions to prohibit them, so why does this not apply to harmful speech acts?

One possible answer is that, although harm can result from speech, it does so only with the voluntary agreement of those who receive the communication in question. We do not have to believe defamatory statements, we may choose not to panic when told we are about to be incinerated, and we may resist the corrupting influence of pornography (MacKinnon 1989: 195–214). Speech does not coerce (Baker 1989). However, this is an unwarranted generalisation, for people do not, for instance, have control over whether or not they feel insulted or demeaned by the speech of another. It also underestimates the harm done to third parties by those who voluntarily accept the opinions or instructions of the original speaker, as the public hysteria sometimes surrounding hate speech illustrates.

There are other considerations that count against using the argument from truth to establish an absolute immunity from restrictions on speech. For instance some speech is only remotely connected with truth and falsity. Indeed it may be argued that moral opinions are neither true nor false, but simply express attitudes or emotions. Similarly giving instructions or issuing threats is not the same as making statements. So it is not clear that the marketplace analogy can be applied to all speech. Further, even if we accept that in the speech market truth will always (or even generally) triumph over falsehood, it needs to be argued that truth is always an overriding consideration. Thus it may be wrong to cause distress to another even if this is done by telling them an unpalatable truth or telling their neighbours about their private lives. All that we can conclude therefore is that, where restriction on speech has an adverse impact on the extension of knowledge there is a strong *prima facie* case against limiting the immunity right to freedom of speech. This does not amount to an overriding second order principle that trumps all first order considerations.

The argument from democracy

Another justifying rationale for freedom of speech is the argument from democracy. The rationale here is that in democratic systems of government, where governments are chosen by voters and are subjected to the constant critical scrutiny of citizens and civil society, freedom of speech is a necessary ingredient of the accountability on which the benefits of democracy are posited (Meiklejohn 1948).

The implications for freedom of speech depend here on what sort of democracy that is being presupposed. The main contenders here are three overlapping but to some extent distinguishable paradigms: the market model, the equal power model and the deliberative model (Held 1993, Campbell 2004: 247–66). According to the market model, derived from James Mill and developed by Jeremy Bentham and Joseph Schumpeter, democracy is a competitive struggle for the people's vote in which rival candidates for government offer manifesto, or policy programmes, designed to maximise support from self-interested voters, and in which those who receive the most votes gain the right to rule for a set period of time after which they are subject to re-election (Schumpeter 1950). Democracy is thus a device for maximising benefit by making it in the self-interest of rulers to please as many constituents as possible. This overtly utilitarian model requires that adequate information as to the performance of governments and the likely success of alternative manifesto can be accurately gauged, otherwise voters will be deceived and not get what they expect. This, it is argued, requires free speech as the best source of reliable information as to government performance and effective critiques of political proposals.

The market model may legitimate absolute immunity rights to freedom of speech, but only to political speech, that is speech that is relevant to informed decision-making by voters. It would justify giving less protection from defamation to public figures, especially those in or aspiring to political office than for the population at large, thus enlarging the scope of that immunity right. It would also justify requiring access to information about government, thus giving special speech rights to those with access to such information, and legitimating a power right on the part of those who have political need of access to information that can be used to compel the speech of officials. It is also arguable that it would justify a positive right to freedom of speech, that is, a right to be assisted in taking part in political debate on an informed basis, including right of access to the media from which people receive the information on the basis of which they vote. The argument from democracy thus provides some powerful rationales for increased and different types of freedom of speech, but only within the domain of political assessment and debate. However, these arguments may be subject to restrictions on harmful speech of the sort we have outlined in relation to the argument from truth. This version of the argument from democracy assumes the market model of free speech.

The equal power, or equal participation, model is an affirmation of democracy as an equal distribution of political power within a society, a model based on the assumption of an equal right to self-determination. What matters, on this model, is not so much the consequences of democracy as its existence, the rationale being that what matters is that people govern themselves, whether or not they do it well or badly. This equal participation model follows from ideals of autonomy where what matters is that people make choices for themselves on the basis of their own freely chosen values, even if those choices are not as good or wise as they might be. This puts less emphasis on the availability of accurate information in general and more on the availability of the information that citizens wish to have, especially information that enables them better exercise their autonomy by controlling their elected representatives. We would expect here free speech rights in the form of option rights (see p. 33) to ask for, receive and debate the issues in relation to which they seek equal rights of self-determination, but with less emphasis on the rights of voters themselves to take part in political debate as long as they can play their part in decision-making. On the whole this provides a rather weaker rationale for free speech in a democracy and therefore one that is more readily overridden by argument arising from harmful speech.

The currently popular deliberative model of democracy, whose roots can be traced to Rousseau, co-opts freedom of speech as a constitutive element of democracy. Democracy is seen as a system in which a decision is made after free and open deliberation amongst those who are affected by that decision (Dryzek 2000: 1–7). This model seeks to counter the criticism of the market model for overweighting the preferences of the majority and the criticism of the equal participation model for underplaying the need to obtain good outcomes from the democratic process.

The object of deliberation, on this model, is to produce a reasoned consensus as to what is in the general interest, a consensus that is based on the best available evidence and the most thorough consideration of alternatives. To some extent this is a political version of the argument for truth, but it requires that those who take part in the deliberation are, in good faith, seeking to arrive at an impartial judgment as to what is in the general interest of all equally. It is a public discussion in terms not of contending private interests but diverse views on what arrangements are in the public interest. This approach is a development of the epistemology of achieving truth (or justified belief) through debate. It is also associated with the political philosophy that obtaining through dialogue the agreement of all affected by a decision renders that decision is justified because it maximises consent, and thus autonomy, which is deemed to be a good thing whether or not what is consented to is actually right or true.

The deliberative model of democracy puts the greatest emphasis on free speech rights, including immunity rights against legal restriction, positive rights for access to the deliberative process and power rights to take part in the debate that produces the determinative political decision. Since the deliberative model is often associated with the move to local democracy in which as many decisions as possible are relegated to the jurisdiction of the smaller groups that are most affected by the decisions in question, the scope of the free speech which it requires is wide ranging and open ended. It is still the case, however, that the speech which matters is the speech that is undertaken in *bona fide* efforts to reach a consensus on matters of public concern. It is perfectly compatible therefore with extensive restrictions on speech outside this context where the speech in question is seen as harmful or even disruptive of the community's needs for reasonable communicative interaction. Indeed it may be used to justify restrictions on hate speech on the ground that such speech tends to exclude those who are the object of hatred from the political dialogue.

The argument from autonomy

Both the argument from truth and the argument from democracy may appear far too instrumental or consequentialist for some advocates of human rights. Thus some rights-based theories stress the significance of speech as a basic human faculty which is inseparable from the distinctively valuable features of human life: rationality and freedom of choice. Thus, the argument from freedom of expression is that without exercising our faculties of speech in interaction with each other we cannot fulfill our nature as communicative beings. On this view freedom of speech is an intrinsic not an instrumental right. It values speech for its own sake, not for the indirect results that flow from it. It is part of what it means to be an autonomous being (Scanlon 1972, Richards 1986, Baker 1989, Nagel 2002).

Self-expression of this intrinsic type may take place in a political context, but is not confined to politics. It features in any human activity that involves thought, choice and expression: in music, art, authorship, worship, education, sport, entertainment and, yes, politics as well. It flows seamlessly into all human activities that are regarded as fulfilling our natures, and enables us to take part in worthwhile activities, especially those that involve communicative interaction between people. This may be seen as a true human rights argument in that the justification for the right is firmly directed at the fundamental wellbeing of persons living a creative and dignified life. Speech is an intrinsic part of a genuinely worthwhile human life. The denial of freedom of speech on this view is an affront to the equal worth of humanity as we admire and treasure it.

The self-expression rationale is powerful in its scope, for it can take in all forms and types of speech, and it is powerful in its foundations, for it finds its justification in the flourishing of distinctively human capacities. To this extent it may be considered a stronger bastion against rationales that seek to limit freedom of speech in that it can present all speech, even that which is defamatory and pornographic, as exemplifications of desirable human self-expression. In this way it is liberating and pluralistic. But it gives no special protection to political speech and can be excessively self-centred and insular in its neglect of the broader consequentialist functions of freedom of speech. Indeed, once we detach free speech from the benefits that flow to it for the speaker's future interests or the improvement of society, free speech may seem a much less important human right than, for instance, the right to a decent standard of living, and may not readily be given the sort of over-riding significance human rights are thought to have the sort of restrictions that feature in current anti-terrorist legislation.

This brief survey of some of the justifications for free speech in a variety of forms demonstrates the complexity and depth of moral debate in this area. It illustrates that the determination of what rights we ought to have is a difficult business far removed from the exchange of clear intuitions about what these rights should be. Moreover, they are not all arguments that play down the sort of utilitarian considerations that some rights theorists seek to exclude. It shows also that a lot depends in these debates on what form of rights we have in mind: formal liberty rights, negative or positive claim rights, immunity rights or power rights.

Critiques

Our travels through the debates on freedom of speech enable us to consider in more detail the general criticisms of rights outlined in Chapter 2. How far does rights skepticism apply to the right to speak your mind and convey your thoughts?

Egoism

Are free speech rights egoistic? They can certainly be presented as such. The routine denial of the harm that speech can do to others, the constant use of speech to promote the self-interest of the speaker, the self-indulgence of those who constantly demand to be heard, and the clamour of the crowd seeking to promote its will on others, can all readily be seen as manifestations of extreme human self-interest. This is evident in the version of the argument for democracy which depends on the market analogy in which the object of the exercise is to give rights to individuals so that they are able to maximise their individual welfare (although this must be mitigated by the assumption that everyone has an equal right to do this, so there is no assumption that one person's interests will dominate another person's).

However, a moment's reflection reveals that speech is largely a neutral vessel as far as the dichotomy between selfishness and unselfishness is concerned. Speech is a vehicle for altruism as well as egoism. Indeed, speech is an inherently inter-personal activity as it is aimed at communication and hence at increasing and developing the contacts between people, contacts that are a necessary condition of a communal and cooperative society. Speech is an activity of individuals, it requires us to pay attention to the speaker, but it is not inherently selfish if this means giving unwarranted emphasis to the individual's interests.

In fact most of the arguments for freedom of expression appeal to the good consequences for society as a whole, in particular the argument for truth, while it does not exclude the benefits that accrue to the individual speaker, is largely concerned with the wider social benefits of increased communication. Similarly democracy, especially in its deliberative aspects, is a public good that benefits all those who are members of such societies. And even on the market model it can be argued that what is involved is legitimate self-defence against the possibility of oppression, and there is nothing egoistic about combating threatened injustice to oneself.

Even self-expression or autonomy need not be considered egoistic, since the self that is expressed and the autonomy that is exercised can involve activities that are directed to the benefit of others. Communication in general is viewed as a win-win exchange that profits all those involved. It is simply a mistake to hold that my speech must be directed to my own interests, or that I can be moved to speak only out of self-regard. Any failure here is a failure of human nature not of speech as such, and giving equal rights to speak may be seen as a curb on our unbridled natures.

Nonetheless, some arguments for unrestricted speech do assume the predominance of self-interest. Why else, for instance, would it be argued that individuals' interests are best protected by a system that enables each to speak for themselves? And points about the potential for altruism and mutuality in free speech do assume that there will be something like an equal distribution of speaking and listening, which means that only altruistic speech should not be regulated except to ensure an orderly debate. Even unselfish speech needs regulation if it is to be effective, so it might be argued that free speech is compatible with limitations being applied to everyone so that equality of speech may be achieved, and perhaps also an equality of duty to listen. But this points to the fair regulation of speech rather than its absolute freedom. In fact there is a considerable modification of free speech as a pure liberty right if it is said to require taking part in mutual communication. This involves both a right to only an equal share, and also a right to be listened to with respect and attention.

Nevertheless, 'interest' is not the same as 'self-interest' and can be given an altruistic or communal reading in which the interest is to communicate desirable information or opinions to others for their sake, or just to participate in a dialogue that is for the common good. This fits well with the deliberative model of democracy in which freedom of (no doubt orderly) speech is a constituent element.

I conclude that the communitarian critique of the egotism of rights has force in this context if the concept of speech is abstracted from social relationships in the same way in which the unencumbered individual is extricated from his or her social context, but the idea of non-social speech is evidently so lacking in importance as to make a purely individualistic rationale for freedom of speech unsupportable. It is another matter, however, to develop a conception of free speech that takes the social character of speech properly into account, without transgressing into the suppression of disorderly and disruptive speech. The dangers of communal conformity may be greater than those of individual irresponsibility.

Legalism

Legalism seems the least likely reason for criticising the right to freedom of speech, especially if this is taken to be the rejection of any laws limiting speech. This fits the idea that what is important about speech is that it be spontaneous and free flowing not confined by rules and pedantic distinctions.

However, this may be itself a form of legalism if the implication is that it is only legal restrictions on freedom of speech that matter, when in fact speech can be stifled by public opinion, by religious intolerance, by employer dictates and by lack of access to education and the means of communication. It is an important matter to investigate, if we are concerned about free speech rationales, whether there are significant social forces that inhibit speech. Being legally permitted to say what you like is much less important if the community in which you live is intolerant and closed-minded. It may be noted, for instance, that there is so little free speech in the work place, where people spend so much of their waking time. The absence of legal restrictions on speech is of little import in the work place if the employer forbids criticism and dismisses those who speak against management policies or other employees simply refuse to listen. More generally the alleged advantages of free speech do seem to require that the bundle of free speech rights include the negative claim right to be listened to and to be subjected to no ill consequences as a result of the speech in question.

Of course, things change if freedom of speech is thought of as a right that correlates with duties on government to intervene to protect social speech, including workplace speech. Dismissal or demotion for speaking out could be made illegal and subject to sanctions. Indeed whistle-blowing legislation does exist to impose sanctions on employers who victimise those who publicise internal wrongdoing outside the workplace. If the right to free speech is a claim right against society which the state is obliged to enforce, then law becomes directly involved in freedom of speech, and legalism in the ordinary sense of the word emerges as a possibility for there must be rules that specify the content and scope of the correlative duties. And it should be noted that the law of defamation is one of the most complex and obscure areas of law in all jurisdictions.

This may not be considered too much of a worry until we consider attempts to protect freedom of speech by entrenching the right within a constitution or international charter of rights. This then involves courts in tortuous debates as to what counts as 'speech' and must therefore be free, and what does not count as speech, and can therefore be restricted. Thus the protection of women against pornography may depend on whether we see pornographic pictures as a form of speech, which it may in some sense be, or rather as an act that demeans women, which it also certainly is (MacKinnon 1989: 130, Langton 1994). It also turns moral questions about such issues as pornography, into matters that fall to be decided by courts, a form of legalism that usurps the right of self-government and the contribution of speech to that process. This may be considered no more than an institutionalisation of the rights required by the argument for democracy, since we cannot have majorities taking away the right of minorities to speak for themselves, but the inevitable result is the legalisation of moral discourse.

I conclude that when we consider the sort of mechanism that are needed to protect and further freedom of expression it is clear that a great deal of legal regulation is required. Human rights legislation should include free speech legislation. However, what must be avoided if the moral debates about free speech are not to be diverted into the sphere of legal argument is that the legalisation of free speech should be done in the moral debate of political process and not in the technical language of the courts as they seek to give concrete form to vaguely worded expressions of speech rights.

Dogmatism

Does freedom of speech present complex problems in oversimplified ways and give rise to irrationally blinkered demands? This could be claimed with respect to the absolute nature of many statements of the right and the stubborn refusal of some advocates of freedom of speech to consider that they might be mistaken on this count, when in fact any supportable conception of free speech must be highly qualified and complex to understand and articulate. It is difficult not to find ideological explanations for the way in which rather flimsy and overly dogmatic distinctions such as that between speech and action are used by those who are advantaged by the absence of legal regulations on speech.

Yet even here there is cause to be cautious. It seems paradoxical to say that free speech is dogmatic, since dogmatism is normally the basis for restricting speech, and free speech is often presented on the basis that our knowledge is fallible and our legitimate certainties are few. Speech is the inherent enemy of dogmatism. Moreover, because free speech is constantly endangered, there is reason to have in place a few 'dogmatic' rules that are not easily modified or overridden by the deployment of specious arguments against free speech by those, like governments, who benefit from its suppression. While the process of deciding on these rights is complex there is a need to draw some clear lines as to what we may and what we may not say. The arguments might be complex but the outcome may be fiercely held 'dogmatic' applications of the few rules that we allow for the purposes of limiting speech.

Here we have to be aware of the enormous opportunities for abuse that arise when we permit restrictions on speech, perhaps on the grounds of commercial competitiveness, national security or police investigation. Any limitation on speech, however reasonable in theory, can readily be abused by those in power. Exemptions introduced for good reasons can readily be deployed for bad reasons and, as a result of the restrictions on speech, we may not even know about this. Rule dogmatism, in this sense, may not be a bad thing when we are dealing with talk.

Of some considerable concern with respect to dogmatism is the increasing importance of mass media in the dissemination of opinions and information. Such media have a tendency to be highly selective in what they include and very compressed in what they permit to be said, thus exhibiting and encouraging 'sound bite' dogmatism, especially in the context of elections. This indicates that in some context the freedom to speak combined with control over the means of communication can turn ordinary speakers into passive recipients of dogmatic and therefore misleading speech. If some of the alleged objectives of freedom of speech, such as self-expression, and legitimate protection of interests, are brought in to assess the free speech benefits of mass media communication, then there may be a significant free speech argument in favour of considerable media regulation, contrary to the normal assumptions of free speech advocates. Yet the caveats outlined above about abuse of such restrictions have particular relevance here.

Elitism

The charge of elitism is the one most likely to be laid against free speech rights. Free speech rights may be seen to unfairly advantage the educated and articulate. Indeed, on the argument from truth, it is possible to hold that freedom of speech is of special importance to intellectuals and even that intellectuals should have special free speech rights. What a right to freedom of speech gives is an opportunity to compete in the persuasion game in which the majority are losers and particular minorities are winners. Thus in the world modelled by Robert Nozick, all own their bodies and all may freely exercise their faculties as long as they do not infringe the similar rights of others (Nozick 1974). Anything they can persuade others to agree to produces outcomes that cannot be criticized as illegitimate. But we vary in our powers of persuasion, on the basis of natural talent, educational opportunity and social position. Free speech therefore inevitably enhances ('justified') inequality.

This may be thought to be only right, as the differences that emerge are the result of the exercise of choice and effort by those who succeed in the persuasion game. As long as everyone is entitled to compete, in other words as long as there is formal equality of opportunity (the law treats everyone equally), there is nothing wrong here. This can be countered by pointing out that we are not to be congratulated on our superior natural talents, for these come to us by chance, and the social and economic advantages that contribute to our success are equally as much a matter of good luck as good judgment and praiseworthy application. This sort of point led Rawls, for instance, to commend 'fair', not merely formal, equality of opportunity whereby people are given the means to develop their talents to the point at which they can compete with others, at least those of similar natural talents (Rawls 1972: 83–89). However, this again is no more than an ameliorating factor in a process that tends to inequality. Even so, it suggests that the most defensible form of freedom of speech makes powerful demands on state and society to achieve equalities of education and of access to the means of communication that take us far from the simple world of allowing no legal intervention in matters affecting freedom of speech.

So far we have focused on intellectual elites, but these are inseparable from economic and political elites. In particular a major problem about 'free speech' is that it is not free at all, but costs a great deal of money, particularly if it is to be heard by more than a few people. This means that the major obstacle to actual freedom of communication is private power, which can be intelligence and ability as well as air time (Schauer 1994: 1–16).

This form of the elitist critique is that the minority whose interests are unjustly advantaged is the wealthy elite who control the means of communication, especially mass media. The absence of laws constraining speech gives enormous power to those who can hire and fire editors, journalists and broadcasters. Even without such interference from proprietors, the impact of advertising revenue on media conduct is such that no mass media outlet is willing to criticise vigorously the major advertisers on which its profits depend, even if they be tobacco or pharmaceutical companies marketing unsafe products. Inevitably, they self-censor their material and choose their content to improve circulation rather than provided reliable information thus making speech subservient to commercial not intellectual and moral interests. Private market power greatly inhibits communicative freedom.

A particular version of this elitist critique is that free speech rights open the way for business to control politics through the use of their superior wealth to buy votes through media manipulation. Attempts to restrict the amount that can be spent on media advertising to support political causes tend to founder on the grounds that freedom of speech must involve freedom to spend money on speech. While there may be some controls on what may be given to political parties, and some countries do have restrictions on commercial spending on political speech in election periods, there is seldom much of an attempt to counter the influence of money on politics by providing funds to enable poor minorities to make themselves heard.

Yet without such interventions, what is left of the arguments for democracy and the arguments for truth or the argument from self-expression that feature in the core rationales for free speech rights?

The answer has to be: not much. And the implications for those who accept these rationales is that freedom of speech does not exclude controlling expenditure on and control over the mass media. Indeed, it requires extensive distribution of access. But this is not in itself a critique of free speech rights *per se*. Rather, it is an argument for developing new free speech rights, rights which involve positive claim rights that reduce the power of government and business over the media and ensure the provision of adequate universal education. The critique applies not to free speech rights as such, but to the free speech rights we have. This is a prime example of a 'first generation' negative claim right ('no law limiting freedom of speech') being turned into a second generation positive claim right ('equal access to the means of communication').

Implications and institutions

Exciting as it may be to contemplate the prospect of extending free speech rights in more positive or affirmative forms and into a wider range of social contexts, there must be some anxiety that, in the process, something of the fierce simplicity of fundamental human rights is lost and the imperative force of rights is diminished by the introduction of more aspirational elements into what was a straightforward matter of demanding that there be no laws abridging freedom of speech. Not only may our conception of freedom of speech become unhelpfully diffuse, but the range of institutional mechanisms for implementing the correlative duties may become so diverse and dispersed as to be in effect unenforceable and hence optional.

Such anxieties can be met in a number of ways. One is to insist at every stage that what we are talking about are minimally acceptable levels of implementation not the full realisation of the rationales that underpin the justification of these minimum standards. It must be the case that it is more than just an enhancement of free speech goals that some equality of media access is institutionalised. It must be the case that we cannot reasonably speak of freedom of speech to the degree that reaches a minimal threshold for the realisation of the goals identified in the principal free speech rationales. The limitation of financial domination of the mass media with respect to political speech has to be seen as a necessary condition of effective freedom of speech in this sphere and not simply as a further improvement on an already satisfactory arrangement.

More fundamentally, it is vital to be clear about the use to which human rights are to be put, and here we must be able to contemplate that there be different content and form to human rights depending on the use in question. Thus, we must bear in mind our earlier distinctions between using human rights

(1) to legitimate governments (and perhaps other organisations, such as corporations) and hence ground political obligation
(2) to give courts power to override democratically enacted legislation on the basis of rights violations
(3) to justify the use of coercion against and within states that fail to meet the relevant human rights standards
(4) to implement a system of international criminal law for the trial and punishment of individuals who violate the specified human rights.

The variations here relate not only to the type of institutional arrangement that is licensed to enforce human rights obligations, particularly whether the use of force, and specifically military force is involved, but also to the objective that is being sought. In fact the two aspects – means and ends – are closely inter-related, since more coercive means, for instance, are justified only in the pursuit of proportionately more important ends. The minimal standard of free speech for warding off armed intervention and bringing people to trial in criminal courts must clearly be lower than that justifying political disobedience, which must be lower than that which might be enforced through a judicially administered bill of rights. It does not follow, however, that the most basic standards are those involving only correlative negative obligations. A failure, particularly on the part of government, to intervene to protect free speech violations by third parties or to provide the minimum resources and information necessary to participate in political speech, for instance, is, dependent on the consequences, just as culpable in principle as positive acts to prohibit or prevent free speech.

Conclusion

In responding to critical evaluations of free speech rights we have constantly had recourse to developments of free speech rights that take in more positive or affirmative claim rights whereby the correlative obligations in question are aimed at enhancing all individuals' capacities to take part in discursive activities. This is an awesome task that suggests an explosion of free speech law to the detriment of the glorious simplicities of the idea (but not in fact the practice) of an absolute right to free speech, conceived as a formal liberty right. It also casts doubt on the desirability of leaving the articulation of free speech rights to courts in the process of interpreting bills of rights, for what is required is a major social reconstruction that needs to be planned with the resources of government and endorsed by the approval of the people if it is to prove effective and legitimate. If this is what is involved then it may be thought that we are going to lose at least some of the benefits on which the high reputation of rights depends. In particular, we stand to lose those simple, powerful weapons to prevent the intervention of others in our own lives. For some that will be too high a price to pay for a system of rights that is developed to meet the criticism of rights sceptics. For others it serves as a good example of maturing political systems that take rights really seriously.

Chapter 9

Sustenance

Article 25.1 of the Universal Declaration of Human Rights states that 'Everyone has the right to a standard of living adequate for the health and wellbeing of himself and his family, including food, clothing, housing and medical and necessary social services, and the right to security in the event of unemployment, sickness, disability, widowhood, old age or other lack of livelihood in circumstances beyond his control'.[1] Here, and more so in the more developed version in the International Covenant on Economic, Social and Cultural Rights (ICESCR), there is a coming together of ideas about 'social security' provided within each state through its welfare policies and a more international vision of efforts to redistribute resources towards the poorest people in the poorest countries. Some progress has been made in the fifty or so years since the foundation of the United Nations towards state provision of welfare within developed states, very little if anything has been achieved in relation to the reduction of poverty internationally. One-fifth of the world's population live in extreme poverty, with insufficient food and no access to the basic health care they need as a result of their deprived conditions. None of this is due to a lack of total global resources.

The right to food, or adequate sustenance, can be considered the most basic of the economic or social rights that have been developed to identify what is required for people to survive and live in a tolerable and dignified manner, and to participate in a minimal way in the life of their society (Unger 1999, Stiglitz 2002). These rights seek to identify needs for a basic income, health care, housing, recreation and tolerable conditions of work, including protection against arbitrary and inhumane treatment in the workplace. This chapter puts to one side the aspirational aspects of some of these rights and concentrates on what are uncontrovertibly the basic material needs of any and every human being. This enables us to focus on the nature of the correlative obligations, if any, to which such basic needs give rise, on whom such obligations fall, what their content might be, and how they might be reliably and effectively enforced.

This done, it will be apparent that some of the principal critiques of rights do not have much purchase in relation to the right to sustenance. It is not a right that is readily construed as selfish, or elitist, nor does it seem to rest on arbitrary dogma. Moreover, relieving world hunger is not seen primarily as a goal to be achieved by legalistic tinkering with laws and giving responsibility for economic policy to courts. Perhaps, however, this relates to the fact that many economic and social 'rights' have a disputed status within the cannon of human rights. Certainly, it used to be argued that, if there can indeed be such rights, then they should be clearly distinguished from civil and political rights, the 'real' rights that set the paradigm for human rights. The critiques of rights may not readily apply to economic and social rights because they are not, in fact, really rights at all, as seems to be borne out by low priority that is given to their implementation. This is a thesis that is carefully examined, and largely dismissed, early in the chapter.

When we turn to the most basic philosophical issues concerning the right to sustenance it is natural to turn to interest rather than will theories of rights (see Chapter 3) for the principal consideration involved is the relief of severe suffering. Whether or not the right to sustenance is an option right would seem to be a secondary matter to be dealt with when we come to consider how best to secure the right to a decent standard of living.

However, deontological considerations do come into the picture when we debate who might have the obligations correlative to a right to sustenance. Here there is a sharp division between those who give prominence to the idea that only those who are to blame for causing poverty should be required to alleviate it. The other view is that what matters most is the capacity of people to give help, so that the obligations in question should fall proportionately with the wealth of those concerned. On this basis developed countries, and wealthy corporations come high on the list of those with an obligation to provide sustenance to the very poor.

This comes out in the discussion of whether the correlative duties are based on a principle of humanity, or of justice. The distinction here is between responding to the suffering of hunger and malnutrition simply for the purpose of relieving that pain and suffering, and responding in order to rectify an injustice on the part of those who are responsible for bringing about extreme poverty. This has a profound impact on precisely who it is that might be thought to have an obligation to do whatever they can to alleviate the poverty of others: either any person or group with the capacity to do so, or those individuals or groups that are to blame for the lack of sustenance in question. Normally the second approach is favoured because it is thought that the relief of poverty should not be an act of 'mere charity'. It will be argued that this ignores the possibility that the principle of humanity can provide a moral basis for ascribing and enforcing obligations.

The chapter concludes with a consideration of how the need for food can be the basis for a right in the full sense of a justified claim to a secured entitlement. This takes us to a further consideration of the human rights obligations of civil society, in particular its economic dimensions and the ways in which legal and societal obligations can work together to instantiate a global right to sustenance.

Economic and social rights

There can be no dispute that there are many rights with economic and social content: legal rights for creditors, rights within marriage, rights to receive non-negligent medical care and such. All these relate to rules whose purpose is to locate and define obligations to the person concerned that can be claimed and enforced at law. Some civil and political rights, such as those relating to slavery and freedom of association are of direct economic and social relevance. Then there are a whole series of economic and social rights that are implemented through laws that establish clear and justifiable obligations to provide certain welfare benefits in certain defined situations. Why, then, is there any doubt about the concept of economic and social rights?

One objection is that economic and social rights typically correlate with positive rather than negative obligations. They are claims to be given something, not to be left alone. Even if this were true, this would only mean that economic and social rights have a distinctive form, but in fact these rights are not always positive ones. Here I am thinking not just about slavery and laws prohibiting freedom of association in economic matters, but also about legally enforced non-discrimination on grounds such as race and gender with respect to access to employment, health services and education. Negative economic and social rights feature here.

Moreover, as we have seen in relation to freedom of speech, civil and political rights can have positive correlative duties as well as negative ones. Indeed negative rights are generally of limited use if the persons protected from interference do not have the capacity to do or have what they have the formal freedom to do or have. This is why it is argued that economic and social rights are more basic than civil and political ones. And, once we add the activities and resources required to protect, police and remedy violations of negative rights, it becomes clear that the cost of negative rights can be extremely high.

Nevertheless, it may be argued that the objectives of negative rights are definable, realisable and delimitable. They are not open-ended aspirations but identifiable and in principle attainable freedoms. The problem which affects the status of economic and social rights is that they place in principle and in practice unlimited demands for the use and creation of resources to achieve ever greater levels of health care, welfare provisions, educational standards and recreational facilities (Griffin 2001).

If economic and social rights place such boundless demands on others it becomes difficult to conceive of such rights in terms of the sort of rules that can enable us intelligibly to speak of entitlements. Rather, such 'rights' serve to provide a set of desirable goals which have to be pursued through government policies for economic prosperity, zero unemployment, ever improving health, welfare and education services. Societies ought to have economic and social policies that promote prosperity and a measure of economic equality and social justice, but these are not policies that can be implemented by passing laws and making up rules.

There are various strategies that can be deployed to answer these sorts of points. One is to develop a concept, such as that of 'basic needs', to identify those interests that require to be protected at least by certain core economic and social rights, such as health, education and welfare (Plant, Lesser and Taylor-Gooby 1980, Shue 1996). This may help to circumscribe the range of interests to which such rights are directed and suggest what specific content may be given to these rights and their correlative positive duties.

An analyses of the human condition based on the concept of need involves identifying those things that are required to live a minimally tolerable human life. It pinpoints survival, absence of distress, tolerable health and the wherewithal to utilise distinctively human capacities including participation in a measure of social and family relationships (Nussbaum 2000). Positively, this may be seen as a conception of minimal wellbeing; negatively, it may be seen as the absence of suffering and deprivation.

All this cannot, of course, be deduced from the concept of being 'in need'. In purely formal terms, 'need' may mean no more than that which is required to achieve a specified goal, however trivial that goal may be. A person may need a screwdriver to tighten a screw or need a loan to buy a Ferrari. However, the discourse of need does point us in the direction of something more than a mere wish or want, and the idea of being 'in need' is standardly used to identify what is required to reach a condition that has an imperatival status, in that the goal in question is mandatory rather than optional. The imperatives in question derive from the fact that we are dealing with something that any human being must have to live any sort of acceptable life rather than what is required to follow this or that desirable but not in this sense necessary path.

Again, this conceptual approach does not by itself enable us to pick out what these needs are, but it does indicate the sort of things we are looking for. If we then add to the conceptual analysis some uncontroversial data about the human organism, then we can soon provide it with a certain amount of straightforward content, such as the need for shelter, for clothing, for health, for company and above all for food and water. Such needs may be said to be 'basic' as they are the necessary pre-requisites for the existence which then enables us to pursue an infinite variety of other objectives.

So articulated, the concept of being in need has just as much specific content as other concepts, such as agency and autonomy and individuality, on which so many other human rights are said to be founded. The fact that, when it comes to specifying what economic and social rights we are going to have, we put something more precise into the idea in order to identify the obligations to be involved in these rights is a standard feature in the process by which we come to articulate all rights claims in a manner that can be effectively institutionalised. There is also no more difficulty in drawing boundaries in determining the content of economic and social rights than there is, for instance, in determining what should count as necessary for having a fair trial or protecting privacy.

As we shall see, there is a crucial role for the formulation of rules that establish justiciable entitlements in economic and social life, even if these rules only make sense in the context of a society that has reached a certain stage of economic development and administrative competence. Even if the principal means for doing away with poverty is by improving economic policy and the efficient use of available resources, there can be no actual right to economic security if this does not include a legal right to a certain minimum income relative to family needs.

Sometimes the objection to economic and social rights as human rights is that the level of minimum income will clearly vary from society to society, thus introducing a relativity that is thought to be out of place with respect to human rights. Universality, however, takes many forms. If the objection is that welfare provisions are episodic in that they kick in only when someone is in need, then this is a type of relativity that is common to many rights, such as the right to a fair trial (which applies only when someone is accused of an offence) and more broadly to whole categories of human rights, such as children's human rights. If the objection is that other episodic rights apply to everyone in a certain phase of life, such as childhood or old age, then this allows into the human rights' fold most economic and social rights, such as the right to education. And, of course, not everyone at any stage in their life does have need for a fair trial.

The point may be, however, that economic and social rights are relative to the stage of economic development and the type of economic system. It is certainly the case that in a truly successful economy there would be no need for a right to a minimum income, since no one would be in poverty. Rights are only of significance when the interest in question is threatened. But this is true of all rights, even though it is difficult to envisage that any society will be able to dispense with, for instance, the need for the right to life or equality of opportunity. If the point is that some economies are too underdeveloped to be able to feed their hungry members (which is rarely the case), then this does mean that there can be no correlative obligations to meet such needs within the resources and hence no right to have such needs met domestically (leaving open the possibility of international obligations). However, the same human need is there for all human beings, a universality so basic that it is impossible to deny.

What is likely to be meant by the alleged cultural relativity of economic and social rights, however, is that the level of welfare representing a minimum income will vary according to the resources and expectations of different societies. This is not a significant point if all it means is that different amounts of money are needed to purchase the same foodstuffs or health care in different economies. It is a more substantial issue if it is argued that the idea of what constitutes a minimal level of, for instance, health care, will vary according to the cultural values and expectations of those involved. Yet there is as much objectivity, probably more, in determining what nutrition and what medical treatment is necessary to sustain a level of health functionality in a human being, as there is in determining how much privacy or freedom of speech is required to meet minimal standards for civil and political rights. The variations that come into the picture with the possibility of new treatments, longer life and more demanding standards of health do nothing to diminish the objectivity and universality involved in identifying existing nutritional deficits that are a threat to life and the absence of cheap treatments for treatable serious illnesses. If poverty is thought of in terms of lacking the resources to take part in the life of the society in which the poor person lives, then this is relative to the nature and costliness of the activities that are considered constitutive of the life of that society. But this is a weaker and less basic interpretation of 'poverty'. Social exclusion is a distinct problem with its own set of rights and duties.

The relative ease of successfully responding to these attempts to exclude or diminish economic and social rights from or in the discourse of rights, particularly human rights, may lead us to conclude that the real objections to economic and social rights are not based on the logic of rights but on the ideologies of those who oppose them. The difficulty many people have is in accepting that states and civil society have obligations, particularly obligations that ought to be enforced in law, to provide individuals with welfare benefits. The provision of the material necessities of life and health is seen essentially as a duty that people have to themselves and their families. Not everyone will be able to fulfil their duties in this respect, in which case it is accepted that charitable provision should be made through voluntary contributions to help those who are undeservedly 'in need'. This is not something that states should be involved in and certainly not something to which recipients of welfare benefits have 'a right'. Welfare is not something to be demanded, it is something to be grateful for. Such a position is concisely and clearly articulated in the philosophy of Robert Nozick (see p. 69).

To say that something is ideological is not to say that it is thereby wrong. An ideology is a fundamental moral stance within a world view of how things are and how they ought to be that affects a person's whole outlook on social justice and human rights. To identify the criticism of economic and social rights as lesser rights, or no rights at all, as 'ideological' does mean, however, that we are free to oppose such views with counter arguments based on a different set of values. With this in mind we can turn to one of the major debates within contemporary international justice, namely the moral basis, if any, for obligations on those who are well off to assist those who are very badly off, as we may almost euphemistically describe the contrast in today's world between the haves and the have nots. Is our obligation to the world's hungry a matter of justice, or of humanity? And what difference does it make if we opt for one or other moral basis for the human right to sustenance?

Institutionalising a right to sustenance

The idea of a human right to sustenance is scarcely a novel one. It can be traced back beyond the Universal Declaration of Human Rights to the pioneering tracts of Thomas Paine in the late eighteenth century who proposed the introduction of graduated income tax, maternity allowances, benefits for poor families and retirement pensions (Paine 1969) (see p. 7), ideas that were immensely popular in the period after the French Revolution, and which continued to inspire left-wing movements right up until the introduction of the welfare state post 1945.

Although economic and social rights owe their presence in the Universal Declaration of Human Rights historically to the need to secure the participation of socialist countries in the foundation of the UN, a pressure that has greatly decreased since the collapse of the USSR in 1991, there is currently something of a resurgence of interest in these 'Cinderella' rights, due to an increasing awareness of the gross inequalities within developed and developing countries and between developed countries and the rest of the world. The downside of global capitalism is its failure to meet the basic needs of a substantial minority of the world's population. Just occasionally these pressures surface in constitutional law cases. Thus Article 21 of the Indian Constitution that concerns the 'right to liberty and security' has been interpreted to require the state to ensure the provision of such shelter, food, water education and health care as are required to support life (Jain 2001: 205). The Constitution of South Africa has social and economic provisions that have been used to facilitate the supply of cheap medicine for the treatment of HIV/AIDS. There is renewed interest in the European Social Charter in the context of constitutional debates within the European Union and in a proposed Declaration of Fundamental Rights and Freedoms with a strong economic and social content.

Other examples of a developing interest in economic and social rights relate to the work of international NGOs, such as Amnesty International, on the failure not only of states but also of multinational corporations to address world hunger, an issue that raises questions about the moral legitimacy of capitalism and the causes and cures of global terrorism. This has provoked developments within the UN, such as the Secretary-General's 'Global Compact' which seeks to gain the commitment of global corporations to a programme of social responsibility. Another example is the proposal, emanating from the United Nations Economic and Social Council

(UNESCO), that extreme poverty be regarded as a violation of human rights. It is argued that:

> If . . . poverty were declared to be abolished, as it should with regard to its status as a massive, systematic and continuous violation of human rights, its persistence would no longer be a regrettable feature of the nature of things. It would become a denial of justice. The burden of proof would shift. The poor, once recognized as the injured party, would acquire a right to reparation for which government, the international community, and ultimately each citizen would be jointly liable. A strong interest would thus be established in eliminating as a matter of urgency, the grounds of liability, which might be expected to unleash much stronger forces than compassion, charity, or even concern for one's own security, are likely to mobilize for the benefit of others
>
> (Sane 2003: 4).

There is, however, some controversy concerning the implications of regarding poverty as a violation of human rights, and the moral assumptions underlying the thesis that justice rather than compassion (or, as I prefer to call it, 'humanity') is what legitimates such a move. Considerable clarification is required on these points if we are to identify where about to ascribe the correlative duties on which the existence of the right depends.

The implications of regarding poverty as a violation of human rights takes us back to the ways in which manifesto rights can be institutionalised according to the objectives that are sought and the means of implementation that are to hand (see p. 81). At the very least, the object must be to give the elimination of poverty a higher priority but that is of little significance if there are no implementation mechanisms. The UN has always said that economic and social rights have equal priority with civil and political rights.[2] A minimal mechanism would be to extend monitoring and surveillance of economic and social performance to give publicity to failures of governments to direct available resources to then eliminate poverty, a process to which international NGOs could be expected to contribute. In itself this can scarcely count as implementing a right, although it could have some impact at the margins.

What legal remedies might be introduced to implement the right to sustenance? The idea that poverty can be 'abolished' like slavery seems far fetched as slavery is a legal status while poverty is not. It would perhaps be possible to make the legal debts of impoverished people unenforceable at law, but that is likely to exacerbate rather than reduce poverty by drying up sources of credit for poor people and poor nations. Another possibility is to make it possible for those in poverty to sue their governments if they have negligently failed in their duty of care to use available resources to alleviate their condition. Finally, it may be proposed to constitutionalise such economic and social rights as the right to sustenance so that courts, not governments, determine the level of subsistence payment and to whom they must be paid.

Transferring our focus from domestic to international remedies, if poverty is adopted as a violation of human rights, we might expect to see this used as grounds for the implementation of sanctions against delinquent régimes such as those which distribute massive state oil revenues to private individuals rather than to those in desperate need. Or it might serve to legitimate armed intervention, perhaps only under UN auspices, where failed states are incapable of dealing with famine and poverty related diseases. This could be extended to make it an international crime to be a member of a government that intentionally reduces to, or keep in, poverty a section of their population, a crime that some consider equivalent to genocide.

If we see the failure to feed the starving as a moral criticism not just of governments but of corporations and affluent citizens around the world, then we might think of other means of implementation. For instance, one proposal, put forward by James Tobin (1978), is for a small tax on international financial transactions. Another is Thomas Pogge's 'Global Resources Dividend' (Pogge 2002), designed to take a percentage of profits from extractive industries operating around the world. My own proposal is for a 'Global Humanitarian Levy' paid by all individuals and corporations who are sufficiently well-off to easily make a small contribution to poverty relief. With some such global taxation scheme we can see the possibility of a genuine right to sustenance that makes significant steps towards an entitlement not to go to bed hungry.

Determining which method of implementation to adopt is a difficult and complicated matter that brings in issues of political practicality (how could we ever get such a system going?), economic capacity (who has the resources to contribute?) and controversial opinions as to how extreme poverty is best eradicated (through the efforts of economists, government or courts?). It also depends on what we regard as the moral basis for ensuring that those with the capacity and opportunity to 'abolish' poverty (and there are certainly sufficient resources available to do just that) actually do so. In the next section I will consider two lines of thought about this, one that emphasises the injustice of extreme poverty and the other which stresses its inhumanity.

Justice or humanity

We are dealing here with the question of responsibility for eradicating extreme poverty. On whom should the duties correlative to the right to sustenance fall? The 'justice' answer is that it should fall on those who have culpably brought about the poverty in question. The 'humanity' answer is that it should fall on all those who are able to help and can do so without significant diminution in their standard of living. The first looks to blaming, the second to the simple imperative for one human being in comfortable circumstances to help another in distress.

We can approach this disagreement or debate by trying to identify what constitutes the violation of the right to sustenance. We may say that it occurs when the poverty is caused or brought about by the culpable behaviour of other people or of the victims themselves. Or we may say that the violation occurs when those who are able to alleviate that poverty fail to do so. This would mean that the violation occurs through the omissions of others.

There are several reasons why the justice approach is more immediately appealing. First, it is more common to blame people for what they do than for what they do not do. There seems all the moral difference in the world between killing someone and letting someone die. It is in general our acts for which we are held responsible not our omissions. Exceptions apply mainly when we are in a special relationship to other people, such as a parent, or treating medical practitioner. It is therefore more convincing to place the obligations correlative to the right to sustenance on those to whose actions we can attribute inexcusable causal responsibility for extreme poverty.

Also, founding the right to sustenance on the faults of others readily gives rise to a sense on the part of recipients of assistance that they are entitled to this assistance. It is a matter of reparation, not a manifestation of supererogatory kindness or charity. It gives it the feel of a 'real' right, an entitlement that can be demanded with moral propriety and received with dignity.

Further, it can be argued that there is a happy coincidence between those who are morally responsible for causing poverty and those who have the resources to do something about it. Thus Thomas Pogge argues that the cause of global poverty is the system of international trade which is unfairly structured in a way that benefits the governments, citizens and corporations of the most developed countries. Poverty is an evil because it is brought about by some human beings to their own benefit. Thus, the primary produce of developing countries is extensively excluded from markets in wealthy democracies who use tariff barriers to protect their own, subsidised, producers. Hugely wealthy global corporations pay large revenues to corrupt governments in developing countries that are not used to benefit those in need in those countries. While it is subsidised primary producers and large multinational corporations, and the governments who support them (and whom they support), who are the primary beneficiaries of this unfair system, everyone in developed countries to some extent benefits from this unfairness and is thus complicit in the violation of human rights involved.

On these grounds, Pogge recommends as a matter of justice his Global Resources Dividend through taxation of the extraction and sale of non-renewable resources, and argues, on the same basis that 'the continuing imposition of this global order, essentially unmodified, constitutes a massive violation of the human right to basic necessities – a violation for which the government and electorates of the more powerful countries bear the primary responsibility' (Pogge 2006).

This is an impressive case and provides powerful moral reasons for remedies of the sort he proposes. However, there are several worries to be raised about its adequacy as a total approach to global poverty. Its main disadvantage is that it can take account only of that extreme poverty that can be traced to such culpable conduct. What of natural disasters, inefficient governments, bad luck in the distribution of natural resources and cultural problems that make it difficult for traditional societies to adapt to a global market economy? Does the poverty that arises from these sources provide no basis for a right to sustenance?

Within the parameters of its own approach it is vulnerable also to difficult disputes about who actually is responsible for the existence of an unfair trading system. It is difficult to ascribe much in the way of blame to individuals who are powerless to affect government policies and corporate conduct and who themselves may be exploited by those with economic and political power. Moreover, experts disagree about which alternative trading and governmental systems would produce better results. Further, it is not clear that we should look solely or even primarily to states and corporations to remedy global problems beyond their duties to their own citizens and shareholders.

It may, therefore, be worth looking again at the alleged disadvantages of basing the right to sustenance on the principle of humanity, that is, on the suggestion that it ought to be obligatory for any comfortably-off human being to do something to help others in extreme distress. Pain, suffering and death are the great evils. It seems impossible to disagree with the proposition that it is an immense moral advance for these evils to be reduced to a minimum. This moral foundation is an essential ingredient in the belief that human beings have a duty not to cause such evils to other people, and some would say to other sentient creatures. It can also serve as an independent foundation of the duty to render aid to those in such extreme circumstances, especially if this is at little cost to the contributor.

If we accept this moral insight, then there is no reason why it should not form the basis of a moral duty to render such aid. In which case providing this aid ceases to be 'mere charity', an optional extra for which we may be praised but whose omission calls for no blame. It makes perfect sense to say that such duties are owed to those in poverty and that they ought to have an entitlement to such aid. There is no logical reason why omissions should not be culpable (Singer 1993). This would be in practice a difficult principle to serve as the basis for more than a very limited number of obligations, but there is no practical or moral objection to identifying certain omissions as violations of specific duties. This is a matter on which we can come to a moral view according to the circumstances in question. If this is accepted then, of course, it is an injustice if these humanitarian obligations are not fulfilled. Those who fail in their positive duties are culpable and those who go unaided have suffered a wrong. This means that remedies such as reparation become appropriate. But the justice here is not dependent on actually harmful acts and does not serve as the grounding of the underlying obligation to feed the starving.

It follows that there is also no reason why such obligations should not be enforceable at law, as it is arguable they already are with respect to that part of revenue raised by taxation that is distributed to those unable to earn their own living who have no other means of support. There may be practical reasons that make it difficult to implement such a system on a global scale, but this is no more so than is the case with institutionalising a system that seeks to make accountable all those who are believed to be complicit in producing global poverty. Both require a considerable degree of coordinated action to turn relatively small contributions from a multitude of sources into an outcome that can effectively target world poverty.

It may be argued that neither approach is feasible without the emergence of a minimal form of world government, but this ignores the possibility of involving international civil society, and international governmental and non-governmental institutions, in the development of a voluntary scheme to coordinate the contributions of substantial numbers of people, corporations and governments in a way that makes it possible for each to fulfil their moral obligations to the poor. Currently no-one, such as the United Nations or the World Bank, has the legitimacy or capacity for undertaking such a task, especially where it involves operating for the benefit of those living under governments that do not prioritise the elimination of hunger within their own country. Yet it remains possible to envisage the emergence of such an agency and even to contemplate a transition from a voluntary to a compulsory scheme, at least in terms of internal legal obligations. That such developments are not currently feasible does not in itself demonstrate that humanity could not serve as the moral foundation for an effective human right to subsistence. Currently what we have with respect to extreme poverty is little more than a manifesto right to domestic and international relief, but it is a manifesto right the contours of whose implementation it is possible to envisage and not impossible to achieve. These, at any rate, are the logical and practical consequences of adopting the eradication of poverty as a human right.

All this may seem too speculative to be taken seriously. Currently there is no widespread sentiment in any affluent society that it is seriously blameworthy for not contributing to the relief of poverty. Although such acts are considered praiseworthy, they are regarded as acts of supererogation, showing a generosity that goes beyond duty. Yet it is not difficult to be persuaded that everyone with even modest means ought to make a small contribution toward the relief of poverty in proportion to their means. Even so, this would make such measures of poverty relief a matter of right, not of rights. However, on the same moral basis of humanity, it is not difficult to be persuaded that we should encourage the emergence of a social conscience that accepts the morally blameworthiness of failing to make appropriate voluntary contributions. This takes us into the realm of societal rights in that, given the emergence of such social rules, it does seem appropriate to say that those in hunger have a right to receive such assistance.

There is, however, a problem here in that there is no evident way in which those in poverty can have their legitimate expectations of relief supported by the expression of social disapproval against those who fail to contribute. What is lacking is a mechanism for relating the violation (failure to contribute) to the harm done (lack of food). Given this situation positive societal rights to the relief of poverty are unrealisable in the absence of coordinated action. On my analysis of rights, raising expectations would not amount in itself to creating a right to sustenance, for there would be nothing to guarantee an effective entitlement to all those suffering extreme poverty. That is not to say that the spasmodic and irregular contributions that are made do not help in the relief of poverty. But it does mean that in such a disorganised situation there is no actual right to poverty relief.

However, on the same (humanitarian) moral basis, this very situation generates a moral duty to work for the adoption of a comprehensive system that can offer appropriate guarantees to those living in hunger. This is not something that individuals can achieve singly, but it can be construed as a collective obligation, since it is an objective that requires joint action for its success. This is sufficient to legitimate a manifesto argument along the lines that it is morally justified to establish legal obligations to contribute (in taxation) a specified share of what is necessary to eradicate poverty in that society, thereby establishing a régime in which it is possible to say that there is a positive right to subsistence, as is actually the case in well-ordered welfare states. A similar chain of arguments can be used to vindicate a similar system at the global level, but there is not room here to articulate this extension of the argument.

The point of this attempt to legitimate the creation of a legal right to subsistence on the basis of the principle of humanity is not simply to commend that this be done, although that is in itself important. Rather it serves to illustrate what it is for there to be a right of this sort, how it is possible to justify such rights, and what is distinctive about the concept of a right, namely the creation of a certain sort of social mechanism that ensures the protection of those interests identified in the expression of the right. Republicans might be prepared to adopt this as an example of securing non-domination for the very poor (see p. 75).

Conclusion

The main purpose of this chapter is to examine the sort of complex moral arguments that are required in deciding what economic and social rights people ought to have, and how these arguments draw on our analysis of rights in terms of the existence of social rules, that we either do have, or ought to have.

The right to sustenance also serves as an example of a substantive right that is clearly not excessively self-centred, dogmatically simplistic, narrowly focused on legal niceties and mainly of interest to elites. Any problems there may be with establishing a right to sustenance lie in the difficulties that arise in relating a morally imperative goal to a do-able set of duties whose fulfilment can be achieved and whose results would meet that threshold at which it makes sense to say that there is indeed a globally comprehensive right to sustenance. The challenges here are organisational, not conceptual issues. They are not about what it means to call something a (human) right, and they are not moral issues about finding an appropriate moral basis for the obligations in question.

The problems in actualising the right to sustenance on a global scale are ones of political will, governmental structures and, at base, a general moral failure to accept that there is a humanitarian obligation to render aid. One residual advantage of likening the proposal to abolish poverty to the campaign to abolish slavery is that both objectives require a widespread development of moral consciousness. The development of world opinion from acceptance of slavery to universal condemnation of the practice, may one day be matched by a similar moral development with respect to collectively preventable extreme poverty.

Chapter 10

Self-determination

According to Article 1 of both the International Covenant on Civil and Political Rights and the International Covenant on Economic, Social and Cultural Rights: 'All peoples have the right to self-determination.'[1] This chapter considers this right of peoples, partly in terms of its role in international law, but mainly as a human right (or bundle of rights) that call for philosophical clarification and justification.

A people's right to self-determination is a collective or group right, characteristic of the controversial third generation rights that have come into prominence over the last few decades (Baker 1994, Kymlica 1995, Shapiro and Kymlica 1997). Assessing competing analyses and justifications of self-determination rights extends our critical examination of rights to contemporary developments and takes us back to the question introduced in Part I of who it is that can be said to have rights.

Self-determination is another word for autonomy or freedom, both in the negative sense of being free of restrictions imposed by others and in the empirical or 'positive' sense of having the normative and actual capacity to control things that matter to them (Berlin 1969). As applied to individuals, self-determination is a central constitutive and justificatory ideal in the panoply of human rights. Indeed, on some views, it is a summation of the very idea of human rights, with all other rights being either specific aspects of self-determination, as in the case of freedom of speech, or preconditions of self-determination, as is the case with the right to sustenance (Gewirth 1982).

Moreover, the right to make your own decisions and control your own destiny is at the core of substantive forms of the will theory of rights and forms part of any scheme of rights that claims to protect and promote human preferences. Even utilitarians, who subject all other values to the test of their contribution to human happiness, identify self-determination, or autonomy, as a fundamental right, both intrinsically as a constituent of wellbeing and instrumentally, because rights give normative power over others that can be used in pursuit of individual and group wellbeing.

The self-determination under consideration in this chapter applies to collectives (or groups or 'peoples'), not individuals. As with all collective rights it is not clear how an idea that has been developed in relation to individuals can be applied to groups. How can a collective be free or autonomous if it has no mind, will or emotions, and no interests apart from those of its members? Such questions are particularly pertinent with respect to collective self-determination with its assumptions of the exercise of choice, will and purpose. The coherence and justification of the idea of collective rights is therefore the first main issue dealt with in this chapter.

The second main issue is the analysis of 'self-determination' itself as applied to collectives such as 'peoples'. On one interpretation, collective self-determination is just another term for democracy, and the idea that states should operate democratically is of course as old as the philosophy and practice of the small city states of Ancient Greece. However, 'self-determination' in a more limited sense is often taken to mean no more than political sovereignty in the sense of independence from other states, a foundational assumption of the modern conception of the sovereign state. A people may be said to be self-determining if they have a government of their own, whether or not that government is democratically accountable. More recently, 'self-determination' is also used to refer to political and social arrangements that involve only a measure of autonomy within a larger political unit, a form of political devolution with special protections for the culture and way of life of those involved. Careful attention must be given to these distinctions, between democracy, independence and devolution, before we are in a position to take a considered view on whether or not there is, or ought to be, a people's right to self-determination.

Finally, the third part of the chapter looks at the right to self-determination in the light of the sceptical critiques directed at the theory and practice of rights. There it is argued that a people's right of self-determination, in its various forms as a collective right, can illustrate that the discourse of rights is flexible enough to escape the charge of being inherently individualistic and egoistic. This may lead, however, to a reduction of its utility as a bulwark against oppression of individuals by collectives and, by increasing its complexity, diminish its rhetorical power as a form of political debate and decision-making.

Collective rights

Can peoples be self-determining in anything like the way in which individuals can be self-determining? Do collective rights not fallaciously personify groups and erroneously assume that collectives are super-individuals with all the attributes of mind, emotion, will and interests that have literal application only to individual people. Are not 'peoples' simply collections of individual persons? Does it, on any theory of rights, make sense to ascribe rights to collectives?

Such questions cannot be answered without distinguishing between various types of 'collective' – the general term used here to cover all the many ways in which a number of individual human beings can be related to each other for social and political purposes. Within the generality of collectives we may distinguish between 'aggregates', 'associations' and 'groups'. This simplified classification, based loosely on Max Weber's 'ideal types of social relationships' (Weber 1964), enables us to clarify some of the conceptual and moral questions that arise in relation to collective rights.

'Aggregates' are statistical collectives based simply on some real or imputed shared characteristics of the individuals involved, such as the same middle name or having a particular blood type. Aggregates are used to categorise individuals for many scientific, social and legal purposes. For instance, all those individuals with a particular disease, such as haemophilia, may be selected as subjects for a particular medical study, or be individually objects of sympathy, or qualify for free medicines or a disability pension. Such people may not know or interact with each other and therefore do not constitute or operate as a social group. In total they may be described as a 'minority', but only as an accumulation of individual people whose interests require protection against the apathy or hostility of another statistical collective, the 'majority'. Aggregates are a collection of individuals classified together purely in virtue of some actual or ascribed common characteristic they possess individually.

'Associations' are voluntary social organisations whose members have joined together, perhaps informally but usually by adopting articles of agreement or a constitution, for some specific purpose or purposes, such as recreation, politics, business or worship. Here the institutional relationship is such that it makes sense to speak in terms of joint actions that belong to the association (Miller 2001: 24–5). Characteristically individuals may join or leave such associations at will but may be subject to their rules while they are members of the association in question. Like aggregates, associations comprise individuals, but unlike aggregates, these individuals not only interact with each other but do so in a structured way that may enable the collective to have some of the attributes and capacities of individuals, such as making choices, owning property and employing people.

'Groups', on the other hand, are collectives in virtue of the regular pattern of social interaction between the either small or large number of individuals involved in ways that create emotional bonds and cooperative conduct based on their overlapping interests and objectives. These relationships may be voluntary but they are not governed by consciously adopted rules. In the case of large groups we may speak in terms of 'communities', although these actually involve a complex mix of associations and groups covering a wide range of economic, social and political interests and activities in what can be regarded as a common 'way of life'. 'Peoples' I take to be large scale combinations of communities in which there is a widespread sense of identity or belonging together based on a belief in shared kinship, history, culture and the existence of continuing emotional solidarity and functional interdependence.

Collectives of this sort (groups, communities, peoples) are made up of people who have characteristics in common that enable participation in shared patterns of action. This goes with a subjective awareness of belonging together and a belief in their possession of shared characteristics (real or imaginary). Those involved identify themselves with the group, seeing themselves as co-members by virtue, for instance of their ethnicity, locality, culture, religion or nationality. With this may come a sense of commitment to other members of the group and the wellbeing of the group as a whole. This involves a sense of solidarity that may include strong attachment to a shared history, culture and destiny.

Aggregates, associations and groups may regarded simply as different types of collective, or they may be viewed as a progression from less to more collective entities. It can be argued that aggregates are not really collective entities at all, and that associations and groups represent two different types of social relationship, identified by Ferdinand Tonnies as *gesellschaft* (associational or contractual) and *gemeinschaft* (organic social groups). Interestingly Tonnies's classification goes with the assumption that the former but not the latter involves the concept of rights (Kamenka and Tay 1978: 6).

Does it make sense to ascribe rights to any type of collective, be it an aggregate, an association or a group/community/people? The short answer is that it depends on what the form and content of the rights in question happen to be. In the case of aggregates for instance, there is no difficulty in conceiving of a duty to benefit all individuals with a particular characteristic and having rules and institutions in place to ensure that such benefits are secured, perhaps making this subject to the option of those with the correlative rights. These are, however, clearly individual rights. There is no right of the aggregate as such, only the sum of the rights that belong to the individuals who make up the aggregate. More specifically, it makes no sense to think of an aggregate having a right to self-determination because an aggregate, by definition, does not have the capacity to make choices and cannot, therefore, be self-determining. Aggregate rights are collective only in a very weak sense and may be regarded as another way of expressing individual rights.

Of course individuals who are classified as members of the aggregate may choose to become an association and an association may adopt decision-making procedures that enable us to identify choices made by the association. In this case it makes sense to conceive of the collective in question having a measure of self-determination so that, for instance, it may run its own internal affairs, be protected from external interference and seek to achieve chosen objectives through the joint action of its members. This means that we can properly speak of (but not necessarily justify) an association's right to self-determination and its right to freedom of speech. This does not mean, however, that we can intelligibly ascribe to associations all the rights that apply to persons, such as the right to sustenance. And some rights may be given to associations that cannot be given to persons. Individuals have the right to join and leave associations, but associations themselves can have rights that are not reducible to the rights of their individual members, such as the right to restrict its membership.

But what of group rights, such as the right of a group to its own religion, language or culture? Groups, as defined, do not have the capacity to make choices and enter into legal relationships but they do have a real social existence above and beyond the characteristics of the individuals who are members of the group. Group members can, of course, have aggregate rights in virtue of their being members of the group. Thus all supporters of a football team might have the societal right to wear the team colours. But most group rights cannot be divided up into individual parcels in this way. For instance, a large kinship or ethnic group might have the right to a school, and perhaps a right that the teaching in that school be done in a particular language. These are not benefits just for those individuals who attend the school but for the group as a whole. It is a group good, not the sum of individual goods, that is the basis of such rights. There are genuine or distinctively 'group' rights that are irreducible to a set of individual rights (McDonald 1991: 218).

There is nothing unintelligible or incoherent in this idea of a group right. The correlative duties can be clearly formulated, the appropriate rules and institutional backing can be envisaged and the group interest identified. True, in the absence of an association founded on the basis of group membership, group rights cannot be option rights since a group, as defined, has no decision-making procedures to make the requisite choices involved in waiving or demanding rights. This is no conceptual barrier to the recognition of group rights since many individual rights are not option rights. As was concluded in Chapter 2, optionality is not a necessary characteristic of a right.

Nevertheless, there are those who have qualms about accepting that there are any group rights that are not reducible to individual rights. Can we really say, for instance, that groups have interests in the same way as individuals have interests, and is it not the case that a right must be directed toward the furtherance or protection of an interest? Well, we can easily point to what a group as distinct from an individual interest is. For instance it might be to maintain a certain type and quality of interaction between members of the group, something that we normally speak of in terms of the culture of a group, its way of doing things together, as distinct from the nature and quality of the interactions that constitute those involved as members of that social group or community.

Disquiet may remain about this answer. This may be due to a confusion between analysing the nature of group rights and giving reasons why we should have such rights. It is one thing to agree that it makes sense to talk of group rights and quite another to decide whether we ought (or ought not) to create them. When we look for a justifying reason for having a group right it is appropriate to take into account the benefits that derive to individuals and to disregard the interests of the group *per se*. It may be only because of the benefits that eventuate for the individuals who experience the social relationships involved that we are persuaded that it is a good thing to have a certain group right. So, while there can be no doubt that groups can have non-reducible collective rights, it is not clear that they ought to have these rights unless this is to the benefit of the individuals actually or prospectively involved in the group (Hartney 1991: 300).

This is a moral argument to the effect that all justifiable distinctive group rights are instrumental rights, instrumental, that is, in relation to the benefits that transpire to individuals, even although it is not always possible to precisely identify which individuals will benefit. Instrumental rights are a type of right (indeed we have seen that many human rights are largely instrumental), so it must be conceded that groups can have rights, including human rights, even if these rights cannot be morally justified except in terms of their beneficial consequences for individuals.

Major problems arise if we want to speak of and adopt intrinsic group rights, where the group interest defined in the right is taken to be the moral basis of the right. If we take the moral view that the sort of interest that can justify a right must be a conscious interest, an interest in something expressed by a being that is capable of knowing what it/he/she wants or is concerned about, then it is not possible to attribute intrinsic rights to groups. This remains true even when groups adopt associational forms, for the decision-making process (let us say debate and then voting) does not involve any consciousnesses beyond that of the individuals taking part. If we cannot bring ourselves ontologically to say that groups have minds and wills distinct from the organised sum of the minds and wills of its members, then we must take the moral position that groups cannot have intrinsic rights.

This would be the standard position of liberal individualists. Liberalism, in its purest forms, attributes moral significance only to the individual persons. Individual persons are the sole loci of the action, experience and reason that gives them high and equal worth. All collectives are ultimately dependent on individuals for their existence and are there to serve individuals' ends. Nothing is lost or gained if a collective ceases to exist as long as the individuals that comprise that collective survive and are not harmed or benefited by the collective ceasing to exist *qua* collective. Collectives have no independent value in themselves and no ultimate morally significance beyond their utility to the members who constitute the collective.

Liberal individualism does not, however, rule out valuing and rewarding the sort of individual minds and wills that have a concern for and commitment to other people (perhaps other group members) and are engaged in interactive processes that serve to integrate and promote the type of social relationships that lead us to identify persons as members of a group. If the 'group mind' is a certain form and content of individual mind-set that we can value for its own sake, then we may be prepared to think in terms of intrinsic group rights as the rights that people have in virtue of this sort of other-regarding attitude, without committing ourselves to the idea of a group mind and will be quite distinct from aspects of the minds and wills of individuals. Such group rights may be a way of recognising the intrinsic moral significance of mutually caring social relationships.

Here we may draw on the idea of 'participatory goods'. Participatory goods are similar to public goods because they cannot be enjoyed by individuals acting alone (Waldron 1993: 339). Joint action is involved, as in a team game. The communal good involved here is something that does not relate to a selfish individual interest since it cannot be enjoyed without the exercise of unselfishness, but it is an interest that we may consider sufficiently valuable to give rise to a justifying rationale to have a right (such as to take part in a team game). Indeed it is easy to conceive of a society in which there is such a respect for such participatory goods that preference is given to them in the allocation of rights.

Generalising this argument, we can argue that just because rights are based on justified prioritising of certain interests this does not mean prioritising self-interest or selfishness. Nor does it need to involve being able to individuate the interest involved so that they are reducible to the discreet interests of separate individuals going their own way. And this does not apply only to collective rights. We can conceive of the rights of parents, for instance, being based at least in large part on the approval we have for the selfless commitment of parents to their children. In this case at least some rights, collective or otherwise, can escape the principal critiques of the institution of rights.

There is danger that the discourse related to this sort of group rights may get out of hand and be understood as involving a literal personification of groups that gives them the properties of personhood independent not only of any but of all members of the group, so that groups in the form of communities, peoples and nations are thought of as having an existence that is valuable in itself. Historically this tendency has led to demands that individuals devote themselves to the group as a superior being over and above the life of its members. This is understandable in that membership of a group, with its normative patterns of interaction, inevitably gives rise to obligations that impinge on individual liberty even if they do also have benefits for the individuals who conform to group mores. But there is no need to understand these obligations as being owed to the collective in a way that transcends its past, present and future members. There is therefore no pervasive irreconcilability between individual and group rights (McDonald 1998, *contra* Hutchinson 1995: 47).

It may be concluded, therefore, that collectives of all types may have rights of one sort or another, but that it is an open (moral) question whether or not we should ascribe rights to collectives except for instrumental purposes that are ultimately justified by the benefits that accrue to individual persons, including those benefits that further their interests as social persons who have an interest in and concern about other members of their association or social group. This we have already discussed in relation to communitarianism (see p. 72).

Collective self-determination

We have already examined the individualistic basis of liberal thought and the theories of rights that derive from liberalism. In this tradition it is the individual human being that is of equal worth and, as such, intrinsically valuable. Collective self-determination can be approached through an analysis of individual self-determination to see how far this concept can be applied to collective self-determination.

Individual self-determination has at least three aspects: moral, developmental and utilitarian. Each generates rather different contents and justifications for self-determination, whether individual or collective.

The moral thesis, associated with Immanuel Kant (see p. 55), is that human beings are moral agents, which means that they are able to work out the difference between moral right and wrong and to make up their own mind about whether to act morally or immorally. As we saw in Chapter 3, moral obligation, according to Kant, is a matter of following universal maxims of conduct that establish what every rational being ought to do in specified circumstances. In this sense morality is like legislation. But it differs from legislation in that each individual person, as a rational agent, must decide for themselves which maxims they are able to endorse as universal maxims not only for their own but for everyone else's conduct. The right act is the one the maxim of which they can commit themselves to universalising, that is which they are able to will that everyone follow. Universalisibility is what makes morality rational. In Kant's terminology, the moral duty of an individual person is to act on that maxim that they can at the same time 'will as a universal law' (Kant 1948).

Moral autonomy may not be thought of as a property that can be attributed to collectives, yet this would be surprising, since Kant's test for individual morality is the ability to will that the maxim of your action be adopted as a universal law, that is, a law that everyone in the same situation could follow. If the collective in question is an association then it has the capacity to make such 'universal' laws, at least in relation to its own members. Further, there is no difficulty in conceiving of an assembly of associational members deciding to adopt a maxim of conduct as a 'law' after debating whether or not it is one which they as individual members, are prepared to see, in this case literally, 'universalised'. Indeed the concept of legislation, used by Kant, makes more sense in the collective than in the individual case.

This model does not require us to posit the collective as a moral person since the morality of the situation can be cashed out in terms of the attitudes and conduct of those engaged in making the collective decision. We are not therefore required to ascribe 'dignity' and 'respect' to the group as such, although we may approve of a social arrangement which enables individuals to fulfil their moral role in a collective setting.

The developmental aspect of individual self-determination is similar to the moral aspect in that it has to do with individual agency, but it is much broader in scope with respect to the range of ways that human beings can develop their manifold capacities. Human beings are capable of moral development and of much else besides. In their work, their creativity, their artistic capacities, their physical and mental achievements, in literature, science, wealth creation, politics, religion, management, communications, human relations, theatre, parenthood and education, people have the potential to achieve worthwhile things and live meaningful lives. In a whole range of different activities individuals can develop their talents and determine what sort of person they are going to be and what they are going to make of their lives.

This romantic ideal of self-determination, associated with the nineteenth century philosopher G. W. F. Hegel, has a strong element of personal vocation. Each person should decide for themselves what they are to be and how they are to develop themselves. It has room for individuality, diversity and eccentricity. It can be varied to the particular capacities and potentials of the diversity of different human beings. However, the developmental aspect of self-determination is not a normless individualism in which each individual simply does what they want, but a process in which the individual realises herself, perhaps her 'true' self, that involves overcoming those internal aspects of her inherited and socially conditioned personality with which she chooses not to identify herself (Knowles 2002: 221–40).

The developmental rationale for self-determination has ready application to collectives with respect to those collective rights that are instrumental for the development of individuals, as when an association provides the opportunity to its members to engage in individual or collective action that contributes to the development of their personal abilities. More distinctively collective developmental rights are directed towards increasing and improving the relationships between members of the group that help to constitute their existence as a group, such as those which foster patterns of conduct in which individuals develop the quality of their relationships with each other.

The utilitarian aspect of self-determination sees it as a device that fosters and protects the happiness of the self in question. This approach is based on the observed fact that, throughout human history, people have wanted to be in control of their own lives, to make their own destiny, to develop their talents and do what they want, not what other people want them to do. This may not be universally true but has sufficient basis in fact to say that self-determination is a human desire. When people have positive freedom of this sort, they enjoy it and want to keep it. It is enjoyable in itself and it enables them to satisfy their other needs. No one cares so much about their own pain as they do themselves. No one knows better than they what they do not want to happen to them. Autonomy provides some protection against disaster and disappointment because it puts people in a position to look after themselves. Self-determination may not always contribute to human happiness, since people make mistakes and their choices may turn out to be unlucky ones but, by and large, it is argued, autonomous people are the happier for their autonomy (Mill 1910: 6–11).

The utilitarian rational for self-development is also applicable to collectives, certainly associational ones, but also social groups and communities. Some hedonic objectives can be achieved by individual actions but most require social action, that is the joint activities of a number of people that are directed towards a common objective that is attainable by joint but not by individual action. Such patterns of activity are the common feature of groups as well as the organised feature of associations of all types. It is particularly characteristic of joint actions to produce 'public goods', that is, outcomes that benefit all individuals affected but which cannot be experienced as individual goods since they are either available to all or to none (such as clean air and defence against armed invasion) (Raz 1986: 198, Green 1991: 316). Again, this does not have to be expressed in terms of the collective itself being made happier as a result of its self-determination, for it can be analysed in terms of the pleasure that is involved for the individual both in taking part in successful joint action and in enjoying the benefits of such public goods as are produced by such action.

Self-protection as a utilitarian device also applies to collectives in so far as we can envisage associations being formed for the purpose of protecting their members against the intrusion of other individually or collectively more powerful non-members. This is something that relates not only to the preservation and wellbeing of individual members at the time but in a more long-term way the protection of a form of life that they see as benefiting themselves and those whom they care about. The self-determination of collectives can thus be seen in part as a means for protecting its group rights that identify for protection and furtherance the nature of the social relationships that exist within that collective.

This analysis indicates that, while self-determination may be an individualistic ideal, achieving that ideal requires cooperative activity. This is not only because the resources required for individual self-determination can only be created and distributed through social organisation, but also because most of the avenues to self-determination that people choose themselves involve developing and using social relationships. Even the most intensely personal forms of creativity draws on the ideas and reactions of like-minded persons and most life plans cannot be visualised without a social setting in which they are realised. Self-determination is as much a collective as an individual process.

Varieties of self-determination

Within this analytical framework we can locate a range of meanings given to the idea of collective self-determination in the discourse of international law as part of a broad set of 'solidarity rights' that feature the needs of developing nations (Alston 2001: 1–6, Crawford 1991).

The recognition of 'the self-determination of peoples' as featured in the Charter of the U.N. has developed in a variety of ways. One is in relation to democracy. Article 21 of the Universal Declaration of Human Rights states that 'Everyone has the right to take part in the government of his country, directly or through freely chosen representatives, and that 'The will of the people shall be the basis of the authority of government; this will shall be expressed in periodic and genuine elections which shall be by universal and equal suffrage and shall be held by secret vote or by equivalent free voting procedures'. In principle the U.N. is committed to the idea of universal democracy within nation states but this has not historically been a major U.N. priority.

The more immediate use of the idea of self-determination has been in relation to achieving independence for colonies. Self-determination has been significant in declarations of the U.N. General Assembly and judgments of the International Court of Justice in relation to such issues as the withdrawal in 1972 of the mandate granted to South Africa over South West Africa (now Namibia) under the League of Nations, and the imposition of sanctions against Rhodesia when it had declared independence from the United Kingdom under a white minority government. It has also been used to bring strong pressure on Portugal, Spain and France to grant independence to their former colonies.

Self-determination has also occasionally featured in the efforts to protect minority groups within existing states, particularly indigenous peoples, and in making claims for a degree of self-government for such groups within a larger sovereign state. This requires some devolution of political power in specific areas with special protections for minority cultures. The idea of 'peoples' within states having a general right of secession has not been accepted as a principle of international law outside of de-colonisation, although it underpins continuing political demands for the dismantling of existing states and the creation of new ones. This has led to the idea of self-determination as devolution.

As there are three very different conceptions of self-determination – internal democracy, external independence and devolution – which are associated with the rights of peoples it is clear that there is no one collective right to self-determination and, *a fortiori*, no simple set of arguments and moral intuitions from which to read off a definite set of particular self-determination rights. Looking at each in turn, we may take a brief look at what sort of collective rights are involved and the different ways in which they may be justified.

Self-determination as internal democracy

The concept of self-determination has been developed most fully with respect to internal democracy and the rights that go with democratic governance. Democratic rights of citizens and elected officials are individual rights in that they can be ascribed to and activated by individuals but are collective in that they cannot be enjoyed or exercised in isolation but presuppose the existence of an association that facilitates joint activity, such as voting in an election, and passing legislation. The rights of a democratic state are collectivist in an associational sense along the same lines as any other form of state in that the state has the right to make decisions that are decisions of the association.

The wide ranging and diverse justifications given in favour of democratic rights cannot be explored adequately here. It can be noted however that many of the arguments deployed in favour of democracy are thoroughly individualist, resting on the benefits that accrue directly to individuals living in a democratic system of government. This sort of democratic rationale features in both utilitarian theories, which stress that democracy is a device for maximising the happiness of the greatest number, and contract theories which concentrate more on the objective of securing equal rights and obligations for all individuals within a state. Both approaches emphasise the concept of the state as a political association which enables them to interpret democratic rights as a combination of individual intrinsic rights and associational rights possessed by the state, such as the right to make laws and have them obeyed. Such rights, as we have seen, are collective rights in that they cannot be analyses entirely individualistically, but their justification can be tied to the benefits that derive to actual and future individual members of the society in question.

Other arguments for democratic rights stress the intrinsic value of the forms of social and political relationship that involve a commitment to the general wellbeing. In the tradition of Rousseau, the individual's right to democratic participation is conceived as promoting, not the aggregate benefit of individuals but the welfare of the society as a whole. A vote should be cast, therefore, not on the basis of calculated self-interest but as an expression of an opinion about what is just for all and in the common good. Modern developments of this participatory approach stress the significance of pre-vote political processes that involves everyone affected by a decision in a deliberative exchange aimed at coming to a consensus as to what is right and good for the group. Consensual decision-making after debate is a joint activity the value of which resides as much in the shared activity in which people jointly determine their future as in the consequences that follow from it.

Participatory theories of deliberative democracy can be fitted within an individualistic model for justifying rights provided that it is recognised that individual interests involved in the justification relate to the other-directed interests of social beings which can only be articulated in terms of seeking to benefit the collectivity. Also involved is a positive evaluation of the indivisible benefits of participation in joint activities motivated by a common concern for the wellbeing of all those involved, including the quality of their social relationships.

We have, in consequence, a very complex set of democratic rationales that serve to commend a variety of democratic rights, in which are embodied a range of collective concepts but in which all the justifying arguments are still, at base, individualistic in that they relate to the intrinsic or instrumental benefits that accrue to the persons involved.

Self-determination as sovereign independence

One of the reasons why democratic self-determination is a relatively neglected principle of international law and politics is the difficulty of determining the boundaries and membership of the nation states whose existence is a foundational assumption of global governance, whether or not these states are democratic. At this point the concept of group collectives, particularly the idea of 'peoples', comes into the picture as a basis for establishing the borders within which internal self-determination takes place.

The concept of a people carries on the nineteenth-century notion that there are cultural groupings, then called 'nations', that are the proper basis for determining the territorial boundaries of independent or 'nation' states. Criteria of nationhood are notoriously difficult to agree on but they usually include elements of cultural homogeneity (such as language, ethnicity and common history), political viability (such as size, economic capacity and defensible geographical boundaries) and emotional attachment (such as a strong belief in a common identity and destiny).

The idea of self-determination as sovereign independence for peoples has a particular history. Political struggles for independence are a constant feature of human history, and the idea that 'nations' or 'peoples' are entitled to have their own state dominated nineteenth century international relations. The current principle of sovereign independence for peoples in international law emerged from a number of more recent historical situations. One was dealing with the remnants of the Austro-Hungarian empire after World War I and the proposal embodied in the Treaty of Versailles, emanating from the US President Woodrow Wilson, that the constituent parts of that empire be permitted to choose in a plebiscite what arrangements should be put in place for their future as independent states or parts of other states. At the same time, under the League of Nations, 'mandates' to govern former colonial or conquered territories were given with the express intention that they should be brought to the point of determining their own future. However, states do not look kindly on the idea that groups within their boundaries have, for instance, the right to secede. In consequence, the self-determination of peoples came to be interpreted more as a reason for preserving existing states than creating new ones.

It is only in the process of decolonisation that the sovereign independence concept of 'self-determination' has been successfully deployed in recent times, and this has assumed a concept of 'nationality' that almost entirely reflects the pre-existing colonial boundaries. The justification for decolonisation does draw on collectivist assumptions about the common interests of those who suffered under colonial exploitation, with an important aspect of that suffering being the suppression of traditional ways of life. Included in this was a rejection of those racially based groups that derived from the colonial régimes. But no serious attempt was made to redraw state boundaries to better reflect the distribution of peoples, although subsequent civil wars have brought about such results.

Despite this historical retreat, the philosophical question remains. Which collective of persons have a legitimate claim to have a state for themselves? These may be peoples within a particular state, like the Quebecois in Canada or the Chechnians in Russia. Or it may be cultural groups, large enough to constitute peoples, who live in a number of existing states, like the Kurds in Iraq and Turkey. Or it may consist of all those who live in a particularly well defined territorial area within a larger state. Ought such 'peoples' have rights to this sort of self-determination? This is a question that requires some consideration of the nature and justification of the state, the doctrine of sovereignty, and the possibility that in a globalising world, the state is a form of governance that can no longer be taken for granted as the preferred primary political unit.

Tough-minded sceptics can readily dismiss the notion that the world is divided into a certain number of nations that can be fitted into the sort of geographical areas that could conceivably be placed under separate governments. Such extreme forms of nationalism could only be justified on the assumption of a sociologically indefensible reification of 'nations' that takes literally the idea of a collective reality, over and above the shared consciousnesses and activities of individuals, to which it makes sense to attribute moral value in and for itself. In reality, it is clear that the idea of a nation is an historically relative social construct that serves to enhance social cohesion and shared commitments within existing states as much as to justify the creation of new ones. From this it can be deduced no more than that a sense of shared identity and a commitment to a common culture are morally relevant factors to be taken into consideration when the territorial boundaries of states are in question, but only as one factor amidst many other considerations.

Self-determination as devolution

The particular context of the contemporary right of self-determination in international law is as an ingredient of the 'Law of Peoples': a collection of associated 'solidarity rights' including rights to development, peace and environment, as well as the right to existence, minority rights and indigenous peoples' rights, all of which feature in the African Charter of Human and Peoples' Rights (Organisation of African Unity 1981). This mode of self-determination is therefore part of a wider movement to redress the economic and political imbalance between developed and developing nations.

In fact, the Charter of the UN and the International Bill of Rights take a basically individualistic view of the self-determination of minorities which is concerned less with the rights of groups than with the rights of individuals who are discriminated against because of their group membership. The Charter calls for granting human rights to all individuals, so that human rights are denied to no one by virtue of their gender, race, language, religion and culture. This does not involve giving minorities a right to their own state or to special group privileges within existing states. Indeed it seems to presuppose a degree of assimilation within existing states that are bound by their Charter obligations to treat all citizens equally. Nevertheless, third generation rights are reintroducing in a weaker form of sovereign independence rights in the shape of a plan for devolved political and cultural rights for minority groups.

This is particularly directed at indigenous peoples who have a long traditional association with land that has been incorporated in larger states mainly populated by people from very different ethnic and cultural backgrounds. There is a growing movement to secure greater recognition and autonomy within the confines of the existing state for such indigenous collectives. The suggestion is that those living in the territory in question consisted of groups, communities and even peoples whose distinctive way of life would be protected and enhanced by a government made up of those who are part of these collective cultures. This programme of devolving power to indigenous and other minority collectives is also seen as in accordance with the alleged dilution of the concept of the sovereign state in the face of economic globalisation. The demand is not for sovereign independence, but for land in which to carry on their traditional and evolving way of life and for constitutions that enable them to have a measure of self-government in relation to the cultural practices that feature in the inherited nature of their relationships to each other and to the land.

The issues that arise when this is attempted are complex and various. One is the difficulty of giving significant political power to indigenous peoples without this resulting in practices within the group that conflict with the rights that members of that group have as citizens of the larger state. The traditional culture may not only be undemocratic, it may involve significant gender inequalities and disadvantages. Liberal theorists like Will Kymlica are prepared to go along with this to some extent provided that individual members of the indigenous group can opt out of the devolved community, but this may be difficult, particularly if the individual cannot opt out without losing the benefits that come from the resources regained or transferred to those who are continuing within the revived traditional community (Kymlica 1995).

Here we have a clash between individual and group rights in that there is a practical incompatibility between fostering traditional collective communities and allowing access to the sort of individual rights that are taken for granted in régimes that seek to implement a wider range of human rights based on the idea of individual autonomy. The devolution conception of self-determination appears to be an unstable compromise between the bolder conceptions of sovereign independence and the associated goal of internal democracy on the one hand, and the desire to permit the protection and revival of distinct and valuable socially-oriented forms of community life. This raises in a stark form the issues of cultural relativism discussed in Chapter 6.

Many arguments can be put forward in favour of devolution, not only for indigenous but for other group collectives that share a different set of values, practices and beliefs. Crucially, these include reasons that make reference to the existence of a group rather than a mere aggregate or associational collectivity. Thus it may be argued that those who have and cherish a distinctive and developed social group or community existence have a right that this shared interest be furthered and protected by institutional arrangements that promote the sustenance of the relationships that constitute their existence as a community or people.

There are many arguments against granting such rights. For instance, they may lead to a loss of individual liberty for some members of the group and it may generate unfairnesses because of the special rights granted to some groups but not to others. But there is no question that a case can be made for limited group autonomy on similar grounds to those used to argue for other forms of self-determination. Only some of these arguments come close to abandoning individualistic justifications in favour of ones in which there is an assumption of the intrinsic value of groups as such.

With these three different conceptions of self-determination and the plethora of arguments with more or less collectivist overtones that can be deployed for and against each of them, it is evident that the idea of individual self-determination does not translate neatly to the collective sphere. However, provided we are careful to distinguish the different types of self-determination, it makes perfect sense to ascribe a whole range of self-determination rights to social groups called 'peoples', particularly where they have the potential to become associations. Whether it is desirable to do so is a complex moral and empirical question that cannot be solved by an appeal to any pre-existing concept of an intuited moral right to self-determination.

Answering the critics

If we agree that it not only makes analytical but perhaps also moral sense to speak in terms of distinctively collective rights to self-determination on the part of those who constitute a people, then we have an example of rights that can be used to disprove the contention that rights are necessarily individualistic and potentially selfish normative instruments. The attitudes that are necessary for the existence of a group and the successful workings of an association have significant elements of altruism. The people involved care about other members of the group and are concerned about the continuation and development of their common culture for reasons that transcend their own happiness and wellbeing.

This need not involve attributing a separate personality to a group and taking it literally when we speak of the group as having a mind and will of its own. Rather we can be identifying an aspect of the individual consciousness of members of a group that is directed towards the furtherance of relationships and shared outcomes in which they may participate, but do not and cannot dominate in a way that renders them analysable as self-interested or selfish.

A shared interest in the pursuit of the public interest or of shared public goods is a clear example of an interest that can generate a right without favouring one individual over another. Indeed such rights may be inseparable from a duty on the part of the individual to sacrifice their interest to the wellbeing of the form of life that they perceive as being for the benefit of other members of the group and their successors. This can take the form of a duty to stay within the group, or to contribute to the group life in ways that clearly benefit others more than themselves. It is not of course the duty that generates the right, but the capacity and willingness to contribute to furthering the group interest can be the basis for a right to have a group within which a community life is possible, and this means a life in which those involved have a commitment to and care for each other.

We do not, however, thereby escape the difficult problem of sorting out the very different rationales and values that are used to justify such a diversity of kinds of rights with different contents. Here, little can be derived from the concept of a right itself or the analysis of different sorts of rights. Rather rights are the forms in which we set out the decisions that call to be made by deploying an open-ended number of morally relevant considerations to the determination of what sort of societies we consider morally preferable. In this deliberative process rights are conclusions more than premises. In this sphere, at any rate, rights cannot be thought of as essentially dogmatic any more than they can be condemned as essentially selfish.

PART IV

A THEORY OF RIGHTS

Rights, and theories of rights, feature more prominently in some political philosophies that in others. Rights-based philosophies, like those of Nozick and Dworkin, make rights central, consequentialist philosophies, and like utilitarianism, give rights an important but derivative place. But all theories of rights have to be seen as part of a wider context of political theorising. Ideally, a theory of rights will provide a working analysis of the concept of rights, elucidate a preferred justification for having rights and a set of values for determining the proper content of rights, and identify the empirical assumptions that underpin such recommendations. This cannot be done without relating rights to other basic political concepts, such as equality and justice, and bringing in a normative model of decision-making in a political system. A philosophy of rights requires a philosophy of politics.

Evidently, a wide range of theories on rights and politics are available, many of which have been considered in previous chapters. At the end of our journey, rather than undertaking a retrospective survey of all these approaches, I present an illustrative theory which outlines one particular set of interlocking ideas about rights and the sort of answers that this theory suggests for the four questions that are raised and very partially answered in this book. I call this theory 'Democratic Positivism'. It includes a positivist theory of what rights are, and a political theory about how we should go about deciding what rights we ought to have.

'Democratic positivism' is 'positivist' in the technical sense used with respect to 'legal positivism', a type of legal theory that conceives of laws as social phenomena identifiable through their origin in certain empirically observable social 'sources', such as an act of parliament or a judicial decision. Legal positivism is standardly contrasted with natural law theory, which holds that what counts as law is determined in part by certain fundamental moral values that lie beyond the opinions of any particular human beings. Legal positivism makes a sharp conceptual distinction between what law is, and what law ought to be, while natural law holds that law is, in part, constituted by what it ought to be. Legal positivism is also 'positivist' in an epistemological sense, in giving central place to experience as a source of knowledge. Some, in this sense, 'positivist' epistemologies claim that all knowledge is based on sensory observation, but this is not the normal position within legal positivism, which stresses only that we can discover what law is (but not what it ought to be) by generalising from our empirical knowledge of observable social institutions.

Legal positivism is currently conceived of as primarily an analytical theory about the meaning of law and associated with an empirical approach to the study of law. However, traditionally, legal positivism is closely associated with an evaluative approach to law, in that it gives (largely utilitarian) reasons for adopting a positivist theory. For this 'normative' or 'prescriptive' form of legal positivism, it is considered politically important that citizens and courts should be able to know what the law that binds them is without having to make moral judgments in order to do so. This involves separating the making of law and its application. The moral choices about what the law ought to be should, in this view, give rise to the making or 'positing' of laws, by law-makers, which can then be understood and applied by looking to see whether a particular piece of conduct conforms with the posited law. This positivist vision of a good political system is expressed constitutionally in terms of the separation of powers between legislatures, courts and executives. Prescriptive legal positivism presents moral and political reasons in support of governance via clear and specific rules that can be understood, followed and applied without those involved having to make moral judgments to determine the content of that law. Normative or 'prescriptive legal positivists' argue for the social benefits that accrue from this type of political system, both in terms of efficiency and justice. The same sort of analysis is applied to legal rights, as effective mechanisms within a positivist system for enabling cooperation and protecting liberty in a potentially fair manner that can be subjected to democratic control. A similar line is also taken with societal rights as a less formal method of obtaining similar objectives.

The democratic element of 'democratic positivism' derives from the conceptual distinction between 'is' and 'ought' when it is applied to the division of labour in a political system between the making of law and its application. While recommending the benefits of having positive (as distinct from 'moral' or 'manifesto') rights, democratic positivism stresses the epistemological and political difficulty of deciding what form and content rights ought to have. While there are clearly better and worse answers to these questions, we simply do not have sufficient agreement on the crucial specific issues that arise when we seek to determine what rights are best. Democratic positivists accept the importance of autonomy and creativity, but also value such things as human happiness, fair distribution, beauty and truth, all of which makes choosing a particular set of rights a difficult and complex matter for any group of people. It is at this point that democracy enters as the preferred way of making such decisions. Of course, democracy itself involves a view of the significance of certain rights (democratic ones such as freedom of speech and the right to vote), about which, it is hoped, there is sufficient consensus to get an effective system of democratic decision-making under way. It is easier to get agreement on how to decide a political question than on the correct decision to make.

As will become clear, it is suggested that there is much to be learned here from the currently favoured theory of deliberative democracy that stresses the vital importance of dialogue and debate amongst all those affected by a decision. However, it is also suggested that we need to retain a substantial element of the sort of democratic theory that emphasises the importance of the distribution of power, in particular the use of voting in a representative system to provide citizens with an effective means to actually control the elites who tend to dominate actual dialogue and human relationships generally. Democratic positivism is not to be identified with deliberative democracy, although it requires a major deliberative ingredient if actual democracies are not to descend into a competition for power between purely self-interested individuals.

It is apparent that the ideas brought together in the theory of democratic positivism have been at work throughout the book so that the final chapter is, to that extent, something of an overview of lines of argument that have already been presented. The opportunity is also taken to run over the implications of this theory for the central issues addressed throughout. The idea is that this concluding part will make clear what is involved in working through to the adoption of a theory of rights as part of a general political philosophy and the sort of implications that can follow from the theory that is adopted. It is, however, only one of many possible end-points to the journey outlined in the Preface. The analytical techniques, historical interpretations and moral argumentation explored throughout the book should serve the reader to make up their own mind on law, rights and democracy, and to find or create their own theory of rights.

Chapter 11

Democratic positivism

This closing chapter draws together the themes running through this critical introduction to rights and presents them in the framework of a specific theory of politics and law that combines two theses. The first (positivist) thesis is that the meaning and value of rights requires them to be established in legal, social and political institutions. The second (democratic) thesis is that the complex business of determining the precise form and content of rights ought to be a matter for democratic debate and decision-making. As outlined in the introduction to Part IV, the two theses are brought together under the label 'democratic positivism', a prescriptive version of legal positivism according to which rule governance is seen as an essential ingredient of any social and political organisation that effectively promotes the human rights values of wellbeing, equality and respect for persons (Campbell 2004). Democratic positivism is a social and political theory that focuses on the value of rules, their impartial administration and their democratic legitimation. Rights feature in democratic positivism both in the formulation of what constitutes democracy (such as the right to vote and freedom of speech) and in the emphasis on having rules that are designed to promote wellbeing in ways that respect the equal worth of human beings.

The prime analytic recommendation in the articulation of democratic positivism is that we confront directly the ambiguity of such statements as 'you have a right to life' which may be taken to be either an 'is' or an 'ought' statement. Statements that this or that person has this or that right may be taken as factual assertions that there is in place in a specific community/society/law an effective entitlement, or as prescriptive assertions that there ought to be such an effective entitlement in place. Ambiguous talk of moral or human rights that run the 'is' and the 'ought' together in ways that suggest that people in some mysterious way do have rights that they do not in practice have, although perhaps they ought to have, is an impediment both to clear thinking about rights and to their effective articulation and implementation. This was discussed in Chapter 2.

Once we make these moves, and distinguish the question of what it is to have a right from the question of what rights people ought to have, then the principal critiques of rights (their egoism, their dogmatism, their elitism and their legalism) can be turned into strategies for reforming and redirecting those aspect of rights discourse that are targeted in these critiques, and to do so in ways that better serve the core values, such as autonomy and wellbeing, that justify having the institution of rights in the first place. This does not produce neat answers but it does provide a conceptual framework for fruitful democratic debate and decision-making.

The positivism

Positivists insist on the analytical distinction between 'is' and 'ought', particularly the distinction between what law is and what law ought to be (Austin 1954: 184). These are two quite distinct question that require quite distinct sorts of answer. In determining what law is, positivism requires that this be settled in terms of some social event, such as the order of a monarch, or the decision of a court, that is recognised as an authoritative source of law. In determining what law ought to be, positivism has historically relied mainly on an appeal to the consequences of enacting and enforcing a law for the wellbeing of those affected. This utilitarian approach to determining the content of binding rules is capable of accommodating a wide range of moral values, including happiness and autonomy, but it rejects the thesis that the rightness of social rules can be determined by inspecting their content in abstraction from their outcomes.

Legal positivism is not currently regarded as an attractive theory. It seems to suggest that law should not be concerned with morality and that judges should concentrate on legal technicalities rather than on doing what is morally right in individual cases. The term 'positivism' also has associations with strictly empiricist approaches to society, which confines our political attention to what can be observed and counted and is unreasonably dismissive of the subjective meaningfulness of human conduct and social interactions.

The assumptions underlying these criticisms are not entirely misleading. In particular, legal positivism, at least in the prescriptive form, does hold that judges should apply existing rules and only rarely depart from these rules or introduce modifications to them, and it does suggest that this requires us to have rules that can be routinely understood and applied to situations on the basis of factual evidence derived from observation of behaviour that can be readily obtained and verified. Legislatures should enact laws that can be understood and applied without recourse to moral judgments on the part of citizens or courts. Courts should apply the law without introducing the moral or other controversial opinions of members of the judiciary, either individually or collectively (Campbell 1996: 125–59).

Nevertheless, this system of law is designed to promote, not to evade, morality. Morality comes into the picture in the selection of the rules we are going to have as authoritative and binding within a society, and in the freedom and fairness that is involved in treating people in accordance with rules of which they have prior notice and which are applied consistently to everyone in similar circumstances. Governments must control and guide conduct through rules, and administrators and courts must follow these rules. These constraints on political power prohibit officials from letting their own moral opinions intrude into the processes of rule-application, but the system of which they are a part of is designed to foster a way of life in which moral individuals can live together in a manner that respects their autonomy and fosters their cooperative and coordinated activity.

I have emphasised here the prescriptive aspects of legal positivism, evident in its founding father, Jeremy Bentham (1970), according to which what we have is a model of a formally good legal system in which rules are clear and comprehensive and adjudication is faithful to the meaning of laws as established by the legitimate authority. It has to be said that most contemporary forms of positivism confine themselves to conceptual and empirical versions of the theory. While entirely endorsing the need for developing objective ways of describing and explaining the operations of social and legal rules and acknowledging the contribution that legal positivists have made to this type of legal science, I am less than enthusiastic about the significance of many of the purely conceptual debates that go on about the concept of law in abstraction from either empirical or prescriptive debates about law's actual or commended purposes and methods.

It may be that prescriptive legal positivism is better described as a theory of the rule of law, and this is indeed how it is presented in Chapter 5 (Legal rights) where the benefits and drawback of rule-governance are discussed in some detail. However, it was pointed out there that the 'rule of law' has come to have a very broad or 'thick' meaning defined in terms that include substantive moral considerations that should be used to justify rather than define the law that is applied by officials and courts. For instance, contemporary ideals of 'legality' have been developed incorporating substantive human rights that are then used by courts to disallow interpretations of positive law with which they have a moral disagreement.

This concept of legality tends to turn the idea of the rule of law into something like the rule of lawyers where judicial officials seek to control the content as well as the application of the law. To distinguish the legalism of prescriptive legal positivism from the thicker, more directly moralised, concept of legality, we may speak in terms of the rule of rules rather than the more nebulous terminology of the rule of law. This makes the point that only a certain type of legal system will do, one that is dominated by the formulation and application of clear and specific requirements and permissions that can be understood and followed without recourse to moral and other speculative or controversial judgments.

The advantages of a system of positive law conforming to the ideal of clear, comprehensive and specific rule-governance are ones which are very much associated with rights. Thus, the guaranteed protection and furtherance of the interests of individuals in situations where those interests are at risk from the conduct of others, or other factors outside the control of the individual, is inconceivable without enforceable rules that make clear the conduct that is prohibited or required if those interests are to be secured. The additional arguments for the rule of rules, outlined in Chapter 5, include the benefits that generally accepted and effectively enforced rules bring in terms of fostering social cooperation, and avoiding the feelings of outraged injustice that arise when officials treat people in arbitrary and haphazard ways so that citizens are unable to know in advance how the coercive power of the state will be used against them.

For these sorts of reasons the analysis favoured in this book commends a concept of rights that ties the existence of rights to identifiable and effective social rules, albeit only those rules that have as their justifying rationale the protection and furtherance of the interests of those involved. These rules may be either legal or societal norms, the latter being those norms that are generally accepted and followed without legal formalities and sanctions. Once we say that there are moral rights which somehow or other exist whatever the social and legal realities of life for those who are said to have these moral rights, then we are on the way to destroying the distinctive usefulness of the idea of rights and leaving ourselves at the mercy of whoever, be it courts, priests or neighbours, determines what these moral rights are to be in practice. Hence the positivist thesis that moral rights talk should be viewed either as statements about existing societal rights or as prescriptive assertions about what our societal or legal rights ought to be.

Where this analysis goes beyond the bulk of the positivist tradition is in arguing that the existence of rights requires that the entitlements promised by the relevant social and legal rules are backed by the necessary resources and administration to provide, not only remedies when these expectations are not met in individual cases, but an overall success rate which is such that we can say that the specified interests are in general effectively protected by systems in which rules play an essential part. This is not to deny that there are many other ways of implementing the goal of maximising human wellbeing in an egalitarian way. The claim is that the positivist analysis identifies the distinctive contribution that the discourse of rights can make in this enterprise.

The democracy

The second strand of democratic positivism is its democratic ingredient. Oddly this may be considered paradoxical for a theory that presents itself as a framework for the development and deployment of rights. The contemporary commonplace is that we need rights to limit and control democracy, a system that will otherwise entrench the power of ignorant and selfish majorities (Dworkin 1977, 1990). The democracy of democratic positivism harks back to the earlier belief that law and rights are part of a system that is designed to limit and channel the activities of governments that tend to act in the interests of powerful elites in opposition to the interests of the general population.

Nevertheless, the same democratic positivists who have an uphill struggle in convincing others of the virtues of rule-governance, have an equally hard time as apologists for a system of government that generates as much cynicism and apathy as admiration and enthusiasm. To comfort those who feel aggrieved by the rules that have been applied unfeelingly to their plight by saying that they have themselves chosen those rules might seem to add insult to injury. What power does the ordinary individual have to change the rules that have emerged from a process as complicated and indirect as a modern democracy? Even if we discount the disproportionate influence of commercially based media and powerful economic organisations, the equal distribution of rule-making power produces a minute influence on such outcomes for one individual in a large state.

The beginnings of a response to democratic disillusionment is to emphasise the significant symbolism of each individual having the right to stand for election, the right to be heard on matters of public policy and the right to an equal share in choosing who will govern. All this is a palpable affirmation of the equal worth of human beings. In rhetorical terms, it is an insult to the dignity and moral status of any human being to exclude them from an equal share in political power.

A more material approach is to chide democratic detractors for their hyper individualism. Concentrating on the powerlessness of the individual is to miss the power of joint action and the immense difference that individuals can make through acting together, even in the fragmented way facilitated by the ballot box. To expect more than an equal share in the processes of a vast association such as a state is arrogant. To underestimate the possibilities of collective action is a mistake. This is to assume, of course, that there is sufficient reliable information available to citizens to engage in relevant and useful discussion of political issues and make an intelligent estimate of the consequences of voting one way or another. That is an issue to which a number of democratic rights, such as freedom of speech, freedom of association and access to education, are addressed.

It is argued that, even if we can be assured that citizens are able to make informed political choices, this exacerbates rather than diminishes the problem of selfish majorities exploiting their morally irrelevant statistical advantage to the detriment of various minorities, the problem to which rights theory is currently most frequently addressed. Does this not suggest that there is a need for some counter-majoritarian devices if the interests of all citizens are to be given equal weight in the political process, and if certain vital interests of all citizens are not to be vulnerable to despotic governments (Bickel 1962)?

Partial answers to minority disadvantage are available within those versions of democratic theory that see voting in a representative system of government as a means of protecting individual self-interest and hence maximising the greatest wellbeing for the greatest number. The theory is that contending political parties will seek to attract votes from as many sections of the public as possible thereby seeking to please everyone to some extent, in which case there should be something for everyone that emerges from such a process (Held 1996). This has some merit in relatively homogenous populations where there are weak class, religious and ethnic divisions (thus providing some basis for the idea that the boundaries of states should coincide with the locations of 'peoples'). However, it is clearly inadequate where there are group-based minorities with interests and values in conflict with those of homogeneous majorities.

At this point we can shift attention to a less individualist model of democracy and embrace at least some of the assumptions, or ideals, of participatory theory which suggests the possibility and desirability of citizens debating and voting in their own self-interest only to the point where they believe that it is compatible with an ideal of a fair and just society in which everyone's interests are given equal weight (Nino 1996, Habermas 1996, Bohman and Rehg 1997, Dryzek 2000). If political disagreements can be approached with a measure of impartiality in that those involved are able to consider issues from the point of view of all those affected by collective decisions, then there is reason to hope that problems of minority exclusion will be reduced. One way in which this can be promoted is to develop in a society certain types of moral belief, including those that are exemplified by the concept of equal worth and the importance of embodying this ideal in a system of rights that produces fairness as well as prosperity. This makes the major impediment to majoritarian selfishness the awareness by majorities of the danger that they will make determinations that are unfair to those who are persistently in the minority, particularly when this is due to their distinctive ethnic and economic circumstances.

Why not, then, formalise the suggested solution to this problem by entrenching minority rights in a constitution that can be used by judiciaries to protect minorities when majorities fail to act impartially? Democratic positivism does not rule out this approach entirely. If it is possible to reach agreement about what these specially protected rights should be then there could well be merit in an institutional arrangement that takes these rights outside the democratic political process in which short-sighted populism can readily endanger minorities, especially in times of crisis. However, a principal theme of this book is that there are few rights on which there is agreement at a level of specificity at which actual legal and administrative decisions have to be made. Everyone can agree that there ought to be freedom of speech for minorities, but disagreement emerges as soon as we come to debate issues such as hate speech and campaign finance.

Moreover, once we go down that path, it is difficult to prevent rights constitutionalism eating away at the basic democratic right of everyone to take an equal part in determining the outcome of the moral and political issues that divide them. In short, there is no fail-safe device for protecting minorities. Making courts into guardians to supervise elected legislatures only takes us on to the problem of how to guard against the failures of the guardians. The tragic paradox of politics is that we have need for states and also reason to fear them. This paradox cannot be avoided by pretending that we have agreement on the content of fundamental rights and can safely hand over their administration to a non-elected minority.

These issues have been engaged with in Chapter 5 and the partially complementary market and deliberative theories of democracy have been explored briefly in Chapter 10 and cannot be more fully discussed here. This section acts mainly as a reminder that a positivist theory of rights, being concerned with the formal features of rights, must be supplemented by a model that provides a satisfactory means for determining the content of rights. The model I suggest is a democratic one, although a positivist theory of rights could, of course, be combined with more authoritarian ways of deciding what rights we ought to have.

The critiques

Four lines of critical thought have been followed through this study of rights. These are outlined in Chapter 1. There I indicated that the discourse and institutions of rights are sufficiently flexible to allow responses to be made to these critiques without denying that some of them are well grounded and that rights have their disadvantages as well as their more considerable advantages. Here I outline the responses developed to meet the standards reservations about rights drawing on the interest theory of rights and the theory of democratic positivism.

Egoism

The central critique of rights is the opportunities they give to selfish and self-centred egoists and the way in which they encourage the development of such personality traits. The easy answer is that this all depends on the content of the rights that are in operation, and that is a major point that merits frequent repetition. Egoism is a feature of human nature (albeit one that varies from person to person and society to society) and this cannot be blamed on rights. Indeed rights may be seen as mechanisms for protecting ourselves against each other and encouraging the more cooperative aspects of our nature.

Nevertheless, the very form of rights, associated as it is with talk of entitlements, justified demands, claims and counter claims appears to encourage competitive individualism rather than harmonious coordination. Again, it can be responded that claims do not have to be selfish claims, either in that they give too much emphasis to the interests of the persons making the claims or because they cannot be claims directed to the protection of other people or the interests of the group. Moreover, we do not need to accept strong versions of the will theory of rights according to which it is an essential feature of a right that the rights-holders can demand their rights. At the same time those who hold to the will theory may point to the other-regarding potential of the idea that we can always waive our rights.

The communitarian version of the egoist critique is that societies do not comprise the sum of individual interests but are organic wholes that serve as the source of our ideas about what constitutes a legitimate individual interest and requires a robust concept of the common good which cannot be broken down into the sum of individual interests. That critique may in part be met by bringing in the concept of collective rights, as discussed in Chapter 10, but there we see that much of the talk about collective rights can equally be stated in terms of valuing the interest that individuals take in the wellbeing of others and their commitment to the public goods that serve the collective as a whole. Interest theorists, it must be remembered, do not ascribe rights on the basis of any or all interests, but use the idea that rights are for the protection and furtherance of interests as a mould into which they can pour their moral views about which interests (self or other directed) are worthy of the special protections that rights bring.

More broadly, a great deal depends on whether is it negative or positive rights that dominate in a social and legal system. The egoist critique fastens on systems where the law enforces prohibitions on 'interfering' with the lives of other people, thereby leaving people free, within their 'private' sphere to pursue their own narrow self-interest in isolation from the wider group. While there are difficult balances to be established between increasing negative liberty and minimising harm to others, there is nothing in the discourse of rights to prevent the balance being established on the harm minimisation side of the equation, and nothing to prevent a change of emphasis towards the enforcement of positive duties that encourage a more caring and communal society.

Legalism

It may be thought that the positivist aspect of democratic positivism offers no contest to the legalism critique. In emphasising that rights exist only when they are recognised in law or public opinion, it would appear that legal answers are being given to moral questions as to how we ought to behave towards each other in our social relationships. However, it has to be noted that the significance of having positivistically good rules, and hence making possible positivistically good rights, is a moral significance that depends both on the beneficial consequences of rule-governance and the way in which it treats autonomous individuals with respect. Moreover, the legalism to which objection is strongest is that which encourages moral questions to be answered in legalistic ways. Yet positivism, by clearly separating questions of what the law is from questions of what the law ought to be, ensures precisely that this is not the case. Prescriptive legal positivism insists that we do take a moral approach to determining the content of law and that we do not forego the advantages of this by reopening the same moral questions at the point where these laws are implemented by administrators and courts.

Further, when it comes to analysing the nature of the moral reasoning employed in determining what ought to be the form and content of rights, democratic positivism does not commend the sort of quasi-legal moral reasoning which takes place when we regard morality as the application of a set of easily grasped moral rules, as some deontologists contend. By taking a broadly consequentialist approach to the debates that ought to take place when our rights are being decided, this particular theory of rights ensures that there is a sharp contrast between the rule-based reasoning of law and the consequence-based reasoning of critical morality.

It should also be noted that this theory of rights does not contend that all actual rights are legal rights. Full acknowledgment is given to the importance of having settled social norms that underpin, and go beyond legal rights and duties, some of which are used to judge the performance of governments and multinational corporations as well as friends, enemies and neighbours.

But, yes, if legalism means taking law seriously and applying societal and legal rules faithfully and consistently, then rights, as conceived in this book, do involve a strong dose of legalism. And that can have drawbacks. We may not want to give judges the power to apply their own opinions in the place of clear and settled law, for reasons that range from democratic principles to the risk of judiciaries abusing such discretionary powers, but this does mean that we will have to endorse outcomes in individual cases that we consider morally unsatisfactory. Giving more scope to adjudicators and less emphasis to rules is in itself no guarantee of substantively just outcomes in individual cases.

Dogmatism

A central purpose of Part II of the book is to illustrate that the form and content of those rights that we ought to have, are controversial and unclear. Whatever benefits rights discourse may provide, it is not clear, definitive answers to complex moral questions. The dogmatism critique is not, therefore, well directed at my account of rights.

This does not mean that a positivist line on rights assumes that there are no correct answers to normative issues about the best form and content of rights. Positivists may not be quite as prone to adopt objectivist theories of morality as natural law theorists, but they are as likely to take this line as anyone else. The foremost prescriptive positivist, Jeremy Bentham, had very firm ideas that the right answer to moral questions lay in the greatest happiness of the greatest number, a calculation to be made on the basis of each person counting for one and no more than one. However, it is the case that this sort of moral realism goes with the belief that in practice moral decisions remain controversial in that it is often difficult to work out what will maximise happiness, and utilitarians, like anyone else, cannot require that others use their preferred method for making up their minds on matters of morality. Whether or not we believe that there is such a thing as moral truth, we can be sure that there is no way that we can avoid a measure of disagreement as to what that truth is. Whether or not we believe that there is such a thing as moral truth, we can be sure that there is no way that we can avoid a measure of disagreement on moral matters. Indeed that is one of the reasons why we need to have a system of rights in place by which we can govern our conduct while we continue to debate the rights and wrongs of having these particular rights.

Yet there is an aspect of dogmatism that remains with respect to rights. One function of rights is to enable us to interact, cooperatively and competitively, in conditions of moral disagreement and practical conflicts. They give us rules by which we can settle our disagreement, make our arrangements, and get on with life. This is a general aspect of law, and one which is contributed to by the clarification of norms of conduct by spelling out the correlative duties that go along with the formulation of rights. It has been called the 'exclusionary' force of law (but it applies to societal rules as well) because authoritative rules require to be followed to the exclusion of considerations that would otherwise be relevant. All law, all good law, is in this sense dogmatic. It provides an answer, an answer that may not be morally the best one, but it is definitive and resolves the matter in question one way or another without having to re-open all the issues that went into the making of that law. This is not, however, a moral dogmatism and does not become so as long as we hold in our minds that the question of what the law is does not settle the matter of what the law ought to be.

Elitism

Our answer to the legalism critique may encourage the idea that rights are the specialist province of the legal elite. However, this is considerably mitigated by the way in which democratic positivism limits the role of lawyers and courts to utilising and applying laws, not manipulating, ignoring or changing them. There does remain considerable anxiety about a system in which our access to rights, as precious possessions, requires technical knowledge, expense, time and considerable persistence and courage. A rule-governed system does seem to favour the educated, the pushy and the wealthy.

Some answers here point to the fact that law is primarily aimed at administrators and organisations whose duty it is to see that people get their rights and do not require special skills, knowledge and experience to do so. Court activity and professional legal activity are relatively small parts of the law-governed administrative state. But it remains the case that the value of rights is greatly diminished by the costs involved in gaining remedies and defending threatened rights in both criminal and civil cases. Effective rights require fair access to the formal justice that courts are meant to provide.

We have seen that this is not the only cost of rights. By insisting that rights be effective entitlements, and that positive rights be recognised as a crucial part of any system that aims at creating a remotely fair society, we have admitted massive costs into the realisation of the potential of rights for human wellbeing. Securing rights is not just a matter of passing laws, nor is it a matter of simply enforcing them, it requires in addition the availability of resources to make it possible to have a range of rights that guarantee the fulfilment of extensive positive obligations to protect and further the interests that are necessary for people to live a tolerably decent life. How far this is possible is a matter of circumstances and will, but it is nevertheless the implicit commitment involved in having a rights-based society.

Here the obstacles are not from legal elites so much as from economic ones. The consequences of redistributive rights are such that they are fiercely resisted by those whose relative affluence is put at risk and they may indeed sometimes undermine the prime sources of prosperity. The ideological counter is for economic elites to insist on the centrality of a relatively small number of negative rights that protect their substance but otherwise enable them to further their economic goals. Given that rights cannot serve good purposes without economic resources, no objection can be made to the creation of wealth as such, and it is important that whatever system of rights is adopted it is conducive to the efficient production of goods for which there is a legitimate demand. But this must also be consistent with the availability of this created wealth to serve the morally imperative objectives of securing a society in which there are human rights that are respected.

So, yes, systems of rights may disproportionately benefit legal and economic elites, but any hope of attaining a more egalitarian society requires a system of rights that, for all its undoubted elitist elements, can be framed so as to diminish the inevitable inequities of actual societies. Similar points can be made at the global level in relation to the ambivalent role of international political elites.

The questions

At the beginning of the book we set out to answer four key questions, while at the same time warning that the benefits of the exercise are to be found more in the journey undertaken than the answers reached.

The conceptual elements of our answers to these questions are not based on claims that there are deep truths to be mined from careful study of the discourse of rights or any one correct concept of rights to be found there. Moral, legal and political discourse is what we have to work on, but they are all in many ways untidy and inconclusive. These discourses are conflicting and contain ill-defined ingredients variously expressed. Actual discourse cannot be systematically defined as a clear and coherent system. Choices have to be made about how we will participate in this jungle of words. My preference has been for fastening on specific rather than general or vague uses of the terminology. Otherwise I have been concerned to commend conceptual clarifications that best serve the elucidation of the moral choices that call to be made in and about political life.

What are rights?

Rights are legitimate expectations, arising from the adoption of authoritative rules and the institutions that support them, that identify the interests to be protected and furthered by the acts and forbearances of others. Characteristically but not universally they are mechanisms for protecting and furthering interests through fostering mutually beneficial cooperation, and by giving to rights-holders the normative power to exercise control over the conduct of others in ways specified in the right.

Effective rights-governance is not simply a matter of making rules that aim to protect interests, it is also a matter of making them effective in relation to their objectives, and that means institutionalisation, including, but going far beyond, administrative arrangements to the generation of the capacity to fulfil the obligations that correlate with rights.

What rights do we have?

To answer this question we have to consult the rules and normative social practices that apply to our polity and community group, but these do not include the paper rules to be found in statutes and social platitudes, unless they are actually generally followed and, where they are violated, there is an effective response to remedy the harm caused by the violation.

Who can have rights?

The bedrock prerequisite here is that rights can be ascribed to any entity that can be said to have interests and that acquires the capacity to have a conscious interest in something of value. This must certainly include higher animals and collectivities that are made up of individuals related in one way or another.

In order that this does not become merely a semantic matter of what we mean by 'interests' we might want to focus on interests of the sort which it makes sense to describe as having intrinsic value. This is where it becomes appropriate to think of rights as particularly germane to human beings, to whom we may ascribe high and equal worth. Without confining this to the moral qualities of persons, such as the capacity to make and follow autonomous moral judgments, it makes sense to explicate interests in terms of those aspects of human life that we particularly treasure, along with the material and social prerequisites of realising these capacities. However, the threshold for having rights must not be placed so high that it effectively excludes the lesser values of other beings.

This applies, however, only to what I have called intrinsic rights, that is, rights that exist to protect the intrinsically valuable interests of the right-bearer or joint rights-bearers. In the case of instrumental rights, that are justified in relation to wider public goods and further individual interests, the prerequisites of having a right include only what is required to enjoy or exercise that right. Thus the rights of associations to own property and bind their members require that these bodies have the capacities to administer property and make biding rules, something that can be satisfied by an artificial structure of legal personality.

What rights ought they to have?

This is the huge question that no theory of rights can answer without being embedded in a wider social and political philosophy. The interest theory of rights points us towards ways of identifying and evaluating significant interests, while the will theory suggests that we may confine ourselves to a more limited range of personal qualities, such as the capacities for choice, action and moral evaluation.

The interest theory of rights propounded in this book has the advantage of being compatible with a diverse range of normative political philosophies. Some may think it particularly favourable to utilitarian theory, others may associate it more with contractual theories. In either case it may be thought to have liberal leanings, if only because of its recurrent efforts to interpret collective rights in largely individualistic terms, at least when it comes to justifying there being collective rights.

Yet there is much in communitarian theory that is echoed in democratic positivism. In particular there is a suspicion of abstract rights talk that is not directed at erecting, sustaining and applying sets of positive norms than are embedded in the legal and social practice of particular communities, including global ones. Democratic positivism departs from communitarianism in so far as this, rather amorphous, tradition tends to acquiesce in a form of cultural relativism that sees rights as inevitably the product of particular communities in a particular historical situation. The anti-communitarian assumption is that our inherited rights can be critiqued, changed and improved, and that it is legitimate to do so through a process of democratic deliberation and choice.

Beyond that, the conclusion is that the rights we (or others) ought to have are those that emanate from appropriate real life democratic procedures. When participating in these procedures we would do well to draw upon the immense range of considerations made explicit and available to us in the history of human politics and in the writings of leading political philosophers.

How are these rights best secured?

To some extent we have pre-empted this question by insisting that rights do not exist until they are routinely secured. But the more relevant question is how we can best turn manifesto rights which express demands or proposals as to what rights ought to exist into rights that actually do exist.

Given that the aim is to secure effective protection for selected interests, no dogmatic view is in order as to the preferred method of securing those interests. There is no automatic preference, for instance, for legal rights over societal rights, or for special rights over universal rights. Indeed it may be that the interests in question can be secured without drawing on the mechanisms of rights at all. In a world of economic wealth and complete altruism, much of the need for rights would not exist.

In the real world in which there are ever-present threats to human welfare and the need for fair social cooperation to secure the material and social needs for a tolerable existence, we have simply to look to the most effective social mechanisms for attaining those moral goals that we set ourselves. If we can remove the threat to valued interests without affecting other valued interests then this should be done. If we can further values or interests through appropriate social arrangements, these should be put in place. Always a preference must be given to ways of achieving these goals that maximise consent and can be implemented without coercion. This makes for a case for giving priority to societal over legal rights and encouraging the workings of civil society over government officialdom.

Where there is pervasive disagreement, recurrent and significant non-compliance or particularly harmful consequences from rare violations of societal rights, or just a need for more sophisticated sets of inter-personal arrangements, then there is a need for legal rights. Increasingly there is an effort to combine societal and legal rights and obligations within theories of regulation that seek to gain the best of both worlds by providing a legal framework that encourages voluntary compliance with voluntary codes that are adopted internally after consultation with those involved. It is a matter for social scientists to determine what works best here, as long as their investigations do not ignore the morally relevant factors that arise in such arrangements beyond the attainment of the specific goals that the regulation is intended to achieve.

That then leaves the issue of whether or not there is a place for the protection of highly important rights, or of those rights that cannot be trusted to a democratic system, by a system of judicial review whereby judiciaries draw on bills of rights to annul contravening legislation. There are many compromise positions here. The bills of rights in question may be statutory rather than constitutionally entrenched. They may allow judges to reinterpret legislation but not to overrule it. They may give parliaments the right to override judicial annulments of their legislation. Or they may encourage judiciaries to interpret statutory change narrowly when it appears to conflict with long standing legal principles.

It is often said that the choice here should depend on the practical outcomes of the alternative systems. That must in part be right. But who is to judge which outcomes are best? And how are we to know if other systems might not produce results more to our liking? Whatever approach we adopt here, must take into account the fact that judicial annulment of democratically approved legislation is always, by definition, a violation of rights – the democratic rights that we ought to have. The question then is whether this is outweighed by the greater benefits that may result from the undemocratic methods adopted.

Conclusion

This chapter serves as a conclusion to the book, outlining a general theory of rights within a philosophy of law and politics, and indicating the sort of answers it might generate to the sceptical questions that have been raised about rights. The hope is that this will help to demonstrate how a theory of rights can combine analysis, explanation and prescription in a way that provides a coherent, plausible and, perhaps, attractive overview on rights. This may seem a rather partisan way to conclude an introductory book on a contentious political concept but it has the advantage of challenging the reader to respond in a critical manner that stimulates reflection and opens the way for the development of alternative theories.

What was promised in the Preface was an exploratory journey that would introduce the analytical work that has to be undertaken to make progress in theorising about rights and which would be useful whatever particular theory of rights is ultimately adopted. I hope that this promise has been at least partly fulfilled and that those who have got this far, even if they do not go along with the theory of democratic positivism or its suggested application to the discourses of rights, will nevertheless find the experience has better prepared them for setting out towards their own preferred destination.

Appendix

A literature map

Using the simile of the expedition adopted in the Preface, this appendix provides some bibliographical signposts that readers might like to follow in planning their own intellectual (and moral) journeys.

The literature on rights is simply huge. Any work on political philosophy and most works in the history of social and political thought has something to say about rights and the associated concepts of equality, justice, law and democracy. Treatments of the institutions of rights feature in diverse legal, social and political texts and there is a vast literature on particular rights, international and domestic, legal and social. What follows is therefore highly selective and arises from the debates to which this book contributes, and the author's particular interests, with an eye on works that are readily available and widely read, as well as some more advanced items.

Introductory

The two best simple introductions to political philosophy both deal briefly with the analysis and theories of rights: Wolff (1996) and Swift (2001). Young (1990) gives a distinctive feminist perspective with a revisionary conceptual approach. Of the introductory books dealing solely with rights I would commend, for a philosophical approach: Jones (1994), together with Freeden (1991), and Freeman (2000) for a more social science based account. All of these are lucid, comprehensive and succinct. Edmundson (2004) is more historical and selective, but excellent. The most systematic and impressive work that comes closest to my own views is Sumner (1987). The best collections of philosophy essays dealing with rights are Waldron (1984) Paul, Miller and Paul (1984) and Shute and Hurley (1993).

Analytical

Some of the most important analytical work on rights was done some time ago by Berlin (1969), Feinberg (1970, 1973, 1980), Flathman (1976), Lyons (1969, 1970) and Raz (1986). Most of these draw significantly on Hohfeld

(1919). Raz is currently the most influential. More recent systematic works include Martin (1993) and Wellman (1995), who defend the will theory, as does Steiner (1994). The most detailed and effective recent discussions of this and the interest theory is Kramer, Simmonds and Steiner (1998) and Kramer (2001). For more traditional views on moral rights, see Gewirth (1982), Thomson (1990), Griffin (2001) and Kamm (2002). Also on the will and interest theories, see MacCormick (1982), Jones (1994), Lyons (1994), Raz (1994) and Hirschman (1997).

Critical

The best general introduction to recent critiques of rights is Glendon (1991). Douzinas (2000) gives a wider theoretical and political perspective. The main critical reading on rights stems from Marx (1977), some of which is followed through by Critical Legal Studies scholars: Tushnet (1984), Horowitz (1988), and Hutchinson (1995). Feminist scholarship has been important in its critique of rules as well as rights: Gilligan (1982) and Kingdom (1991). Shklar (1986) is the classic on legalism. Wellman (1998) deals with the proliferation of rights.

Historical

If you can get hold of it, Waldron (1987) is a must, with text and commentary on Bentham, Burke and Marx. Most collections of Marx's writings include his influential critique of rights, including Marx (1977). Of crucial important for the natural law background is Aquinas, which is probably best approached through Finnis (1980). For historical accounts of the origin of rights: Tuck (1979), Brett (1997) and Tierney (1997). Mill's 'Essay on Utilitarianism' (Mill 1910) is invaluable for those interested in consequentialist approaches to rights.

Moral and political theory

For introductory works on ethics see Mackie (1977), Hare (1981), Singer (1993). Also O'Neill (1996). On preference utilitarianism see Griffin (1986) and Parfit (1986). On capabilities, Sen (2000) and Alkire (2002). Putting theories of rights in the context of contemporary political theory requires reading of Rawls (1972, 1993), Nozick (1994), Dworkin (1977, 1986), Sandel (1982), Habermas (1996) and Kymlica (1995). Of these, by far the most important is Rawls (1972), on which for commentary read Pogge (1989). For a great survey see Mulhall and Swift (1996). On communitarianism: Taylor (1985), Sandel (1982), and MacIntyre (1981). On Republicanism: Pettit (1997).

Law

For introductory material on law, with a philosophical twist: Waldron (1990), Atiyah (1983) and, more theoretical: Hart (1961). Following from Hohfeld (1919) on legal rights, a crucial essay is Raz (1984). More accessible, and more on the rule of law, are Fuller (1969) and Waldron (1989). An acute and very readable discussion of rules may be found in Schauer (1991). On the issue of judicial review, concentrating on mainly critical North American literature: Freeman (1990), Ely (1980), Waldron (1999), Mandel (1989) and Beatty (1994).

International human rights

Steiner and Alston (1996) is the best text in this field. See also Donnelly (1998). After reading Forsythe (2000), try Falk (2000) and Beitz (2001). For cultural relativism, there is an excellent general treatment in Levy (2002), which can be followed with Donnelly (1982) and Okin (1999). Harman and Thomson (1996) is quite difficult. For humanitarian intervention see Moore (1997), Ignatieff (2001) and Chatterjee and Scheid (2003). On the International Criminal Court, I recommend the impressive collection put together in Simpson (2004).

Civil society

For an introduction to the idea of civil society: Fukuyama (1995), followed by the more complex Gellner (1994). Risse, Ropp and Sikkink (1999) has a variety of relevant material. On business corporations, highly recommended: Donaldson (1989) and McBarnet (2004). For background material on globalisation: Stiglitz (2002) and Sassen (1996).

Free speech

Accessible classic works include Mill (1910) and Meiklejohn (1948). More recent philosophical treatments are: Schauer (1982), Baker (1989) and Sadurski (1999). Also Raz (1994), Scanlon (2003) and Nagel (2002).

Social and economic rights

Hunt (1996) serves as a good introduction. The most influential book in this area is Shue (1996) which presents the concept of basic rights. For a utilitarian approach: Singer (1993). On justice and human rights in relation to global poverty: Pogge (2002).

Self-determination

A wide range of excellent essays are available in Alston (2001), McCorquodale (1994) and Crawford (1991). For philosophical background: Kymlica (1995) and Baker (1994).

Democratic positivism

For Positivism, the modern classic is Hart (1961) and the most authoritative current authority is Raz (1979). More prescriptive forms are present in MacCormick (1982) and Waldron (1999). My own position is set out in Campbell (1996, 2004). For democratic theory, the best survey is Held (1993). For deliberative democracy see Dryzek (2000), Gutman and Thompson (1998) and Williams (2000). Also recommended are Nino (1996) and Louglin (2000). Habermas (1996) is immensely important but heavy going.

Notes

Preface: Exploring rights

1 I gratefully acknowledge the helpful comments and advice of Dr Craig Taylor and Professor Leif Wenar who read and commented on drafts of the book.

2 In this case the re-focusing is from justice as economic distribution to justice as having to do with domination and oppression: 'instead of focusing on distribution, a conception of justice should begin with the concept of domination and oppression. Such a shift brings out the issues of decision-making, division of labour, and culture that bear on social justice but are often ignored in philosophical discussions (Young 1990: 4).

3 For West re-imagining relates to seeing justice in a more progressive and caring way: 'We need and do not have a progressive jurisprudence – a conception of the point of the Rule of Law, of Rights, and of the meaning of Formal Equality – that is respectful of the needs, ambitions aspirations and, yes, the natures of heretofore not terribly well-respected women, men, children and animals' (West 2003: 11).

Part I: THE DISCOURSES OF RIGHTS

1 The reputation of rights

1 Douzinas 2000: 1:

> A new idea has triumphed on the world stage: human rights. It unites left and right, the pulpit and the state, the minister and the rebel, the developed world and the liberals of Hampstead and Manhattan. Human rights have become the principle of liberation from oppression and domination, the rallying cry of the homeless and the dispossessed, the political programme of revolutionaries and dissidents. But their appeal is not confined to the wretched of the earth. Alternative lifestyles, greedy consumers of goods and culture, the pleasure-seekers and playboys of the Western world, the owner of Harrods, the former managing director of Guiness Plc as well as the former King of Greece have all glossed their claims in the language of human rights.

2 Dworkin 1977: 269: 'if someone has a right to something, then it is wrong for the government to deny it to him even though it would be in the general interest to do so'.

3 Rawls 1972: 43: Lexical order 'requires us to satisfy the first principle in the ordering before we can move on to the second'; 280: 'The principles of justice are to be ranked in lexical order and therefore liberty can be restricted only for the sake of liberty'.

4 Griffin 2001: 2–3:

> A term with our modern sense of a 'right' emerged in late medieval or early modern times, perhaps with the later Glossators in Bologna, whose characteristic literary products were glosses on central texts of Roman law. In any case, sometime between the thirteenth and seventeenth centuries, between Thomas Aquinas and Francisco Suarez, the word *ius* shifted from meaning a law defining what is fair to roughly our modern sense of 'right' that is a power that a person possesses to control or claim something.

5 The general acceptance of the UDHR may now be regarded as part of international customary law, thus joining the subsequent International Covenant on Civil and Political Rights (1966) and the International Covenant on Economic, Social and Cultural Rights (1966) to constitute what is now regarded as the 'International Bill of Rights'.

6 As epitomised by Thomas Hobbes, who sees rights as a sort of compromise agreement between self-interested individuals:

> . . . a man be willing, when others are too, as farre-forth as for peace and defence of himselfe he shall think it necessary, to lay down his right to all things: and be content with so much liberty against other men as he would allow to other men against himselfe
>
> (Hobbes 1957, Part I, chapter 14, pp. 104f.).

7 Glendon (1991):

> Absoluteness is an illusion, and hardly a harmless one. When we assert our rights to life, liberty and property, we are expressing the reasonable hope that such things can make more secure by law and politics. When we assert these rights in an absolute form, however, we are expressing infinite and impossible desires to be completely free, to possess things totally, to be captains of our fate, and masters of our souls. There is pathos as well as bravado in these attempts to deny the fragility and contingency of human existence, personal freedom and the possession of worldly goods.

8 The situation is more complex than that if only because it is clear that in the case of some rights there are no correlative duties implied in the affirmation of that right. Sometimes, having a right means no more than that the rights-holder has herself no duty not to do the act in question. In this limited sense of a right it means the absence of an obligation on the part of the rights-holder. Such rights are freedoms or liberties in the purest form of those terms, meaning simply that the person with the right is under no obligation to refrain from the conduct in question. There are no correlative obligations here. Thus, in a competition everyone has the right to win but others have no duty to allow them to win. Or, if a person's spouse dies they are free to remarry in a way that was not true before, but no one has a duty to marry them or a duty to refrain from persuading anyone else from marrying them. So there are rights, liberty-rights, where there are no correlative duties. However, standardly it is assumed that rights are what are usually called 'claim rights', where the right to do something entails that others have at least the duty not to prevent them so doing (often called negative rights), and, maybe, have a duty to assist them in the activity in question (often called positive rights).

9 The correlativity of rights does not mean that a person's right is necessarily conditional on the fulfilment of their duties with respect to the same right in others, although this may be the case (as when my contractual rights lapse if I do not fulfil my side of the bargain). Indeed there are 'absolute' rights, such as the right to a fair trial, or, maybe, not to be tortured, that are arguably never conditional on the fulfilment of any duties on the part of the rights-holder. Nevertheless, overall people have as many duties to respect the rights of others as they have right.

2 Varieties of rights

1 Sumner 1987: 1:

> Like the arms race the escalation of rights rhetoric is out of control. In the liberal democracies of the West, and especially in the United States, public issues are now routinely phrased in the language of rights . . . there is virtually no area of public controversy in which rights are not to be found on at least one side of the question – and generally on both.

2 It is particularly important to keep this distinction in mind when we come to consider political morality, for it is sometimes mistakenly assumed that deciding what is right and wrong in politics always comes down to a consideration of the rights of the relevant persons. This is a serious oversimplification as a matter of political morality (which deals with how we ought to make political decisions) and totally inadequate when it comes to individual people deciding how they ought to behave.

3 An exclusionary reason is a type of 'second order' reason that requires us to ignore the 'first order' reasons, that is the reasons that normally guide our conduct in everyday life. It is claimed, for instance, that we have good (second order) reason to follow socially accepted or enforced rules rather than our own judgment as to what would otherwise be the best thing to do.

4 Schauer talks of the 'entrenchment' and 'stickiness' of rules rather than their exclusionary force, to distinguish authoritative rules from rules of thumb, but points out that the special weight we give to such rules is usually 'presumptive' only, in that they may be modified or amended in exceptional circumstances.

5 Hohfeld (1919) set out to formulate a coherent and logical system of 'jural relations' that would cover all legal relationships not only rights. His scheme involved a matrix of correlative obligations and opposites which enabled him to say, for instance, that the opposite of a right is a 'no-right' and its correlative is an obligation. Hohfeld uses legal labels for his various relationships because he hoped to encourage more clarity in actual legal discourse. His scheme has been criticised for failing to capture all actual legal relationships although it can be argued that he was in fact seeking to improve rather than merely describe existing laws. In general his approach applies equally well to moral as to legal rights and obligations.

6 The term 'positive rights' is plagued by a radical ambiguity between rights which have been 'posited' and are actually embodied in a social or legal system, on the one hand, and claim rights whose correlative duties involve positive actions rather than mere omissions, on the other hand.

7 Perhaps the issue here is more to do with identifying who has the obligations correlative to human rights. The immediate answer must be 'everyone', at least with respect to negative rights, but with respect to protecting negative right and

promoting affirmative rights, the question of the capacity to fulfil the relevant obligations is at least one relevant factor in determining who has such duties. Further if no person or group has such obligations can it be said that there is or could be a correlative right?

8 Dworkin applies his analysis of right-based theories only to what he calls basic or 'background rights' rather than ordinary positive rights (Dworkin 1977: 269).

9 Consequentialists attempt to meet the force of right-based theories in two different ways. Indirect consequentialists argue that, given human nature and limited information, the general happiness is best served by having rights and duties that do not aim directly at the general good although they eventually do maximise the aggregate welfare of all (Hare 1981). Rule consequentialists suggest that the test of maximising the good be applied to rules not to individual acts (see Lyons 1969).

3 Theories of rights

1 A powerful argument for human rights based on agency is given in Gewirth (1982) who points out that if we enter into any sort of purposive action, such as defending the idea of human rights, we are thereby committed to endorsing the elements of agency that make this possible and cannot without inconsistency deny that all others capable of agency have an equal claim to be able to act. This means that all the elements and preconditions of agency can be justified as human rights. This 'Kantian' argument does provide a powerful basis for the importance of respecting agency but does not justify confining the scope of human rights to agency alone.

2 Finnis does not claim that these goods can be deduced from facts about human nature, otherwise he would come up against that established dogma of modern thought that it is not possible to deduce and 'ought' (or value) from an 'is' (or fact) and so commit the 'naturalistic fallacy'. But even so it is hard to see how controversial question about the content of rights can be settled by making nature rather than our response to natural things the standard of right and of rights. Clearly many empirical realities are essential to working out what rights are best, matters such as what it is that makes for happiness, what encourages creativity, how to promote longevity, and so on. Here the social and psychological sciences have important contributions to make. But these sciences cannot tell us what values to adopt; they cannot establish the 'ends' that Aristotle hoped to discern in nature.

Part II: THE INSTITUTIONS OF RIGHTS

6 International human rights

1 'The term 'speciesism' as defined by Peter Singer in *Animal Liberation* (Singer 1976) refers to the morally unjustified attitude of favouring one's own species merely because it is one's own species somewhat analogously to similarly unjustified attitudes towards one's own sex (sexism) or race (racism).

2 Thus the International Court of Justice deals with disputes between states under Charter of the United Nations under which it is set up. Regional human rights courts, such as the European Court of Human Rights do deal with individuals but although member states are bound to give effect to its decisions they do not directly override the decisions of national courts.

Part III: THREE HUMAN RIGHTS

1 This is obliquely recognised in modern statements of rights, although normally by saying that rights are 'limited' by other considerations rather than that these considerations determine what rights we ought to have. Thus:

> The State Parties to the present Covenant recognize that, in the enjoyment of those rights provided by the State in conformity with the Present Covenant, the State may subject such rights only to such limitations as a determined by law only in so far as this may be compatible with the nature of these rights and solely for the purpose of promoting the general welfare in a democratic society.
>
> ICESCR, Article 4 (United Nations 1996b)

8 Freedom of speech

1 This is expanded in Article 19 of the International Covenant on Civil and Political Rights to permit 'certain restriction, but these shall only be such as are provided by law and are necessary: (a) for respect of the rights or reputations of other; (b) for the protection of national security or of public order (ordre public), or, of public health or morals'.

9 Sustenance

1 Also Article 11.1 of the ICESCR:

> The State Parties to the present Covenant recognize the right of everyone to an adequate standard of living for himself and his family, including adequate food, clothing, housing, and to the continuous improvement of living conditions . . .; 2. The States parties to the present Covenant recognizing the fundamental right of everyone to be free from hunger, shall take individually and through international co-operation, the measures, including specific programs, which are needed: (a) To improve methods of production, conservation and distribution of food . . . ; (b) Taking into account the problems of both food-importing and food-exporting countries, to ensure an equitable distribution of world food supplies in relation to need.

2 Preamble to the ICESCR: 'the ideal of free human beings enjoying freedom from fear and want can only be achieved if conditions are created whereby everyone can enjoy his economic, social and cultural rights as well as his civil and political rights' (United Nations 1996b).

10 Self-determination

1 ICCPR, Article 1:

> 1. All peoples have the right of self-determination. By virtue of that right they freely determine their political status and freely pursue their economic, social and cultural development. 2. All peoples may, for their own ends, freely dispose of their natural wealth and resources without prejudice to any obligations arising out of international economic co-operation, based on the principle of mutual benefit, and international law. In no case may a people be deprived of its own means of subsistence.

Bibliography

Abrams v. United States (1919) 250 US 616.

Alexander, L. and Sherwin, E. (2001) *The Rule of Rules*, Durham: Duke University Press.

Alkire, S. (2002) *Valuing Freedoms: Sen's Capability Approach and Poverty Reduction*, Oxford: Oxford University Press.

Alston, P. (ed) (2001) *Peoples' Rights*, Oxford: Oxford University Press.

Aquinas, T. (1979) *Selected Political Writings*, ed. D'Entreves, A. P., Oxford: Blackwell.

Aristotle (1948) *Politics*, Oxford: Clarendon.

Atiyah, P. S. (1983) *Law and Modern Society*, Oxford: Oxford University Press.

Austin, J. (1954) *The Province of Jurisprudence Determined*, ed. H. L. A. Hart, London: Weidenfeld & Nicolson.

Bagger, R. (1989) 'Rights' in ed. Ball, T. Farn, J. and Hanson, R. L., *Political Innovation and Conceptual Change*, Cambridge: Cambridge University Press.

Baker, E. (1989) *Human Liberty and Freedom of Speech*, New York: Oxford University Press.

Baker, J. (ed.) (1994) *Group Rights*, Toronto: University of Toronto Press.

Barry, B. (1973) *The Liberal Theory of Justice*, Oxford: Clarendon.

Beatty, D. (ed.) (1994) *Human Rights and Judicial Review: A Comparative Perspective*, Dordrecht: Martinus Nijhoff.

Beitz, C. (2001) 'Human Rights as a Common Concern', 95 *American Political Science Review*, 269–282.

Bentham, J. (1970) *Of Laws in General*, London: Athlone.

Bentham, J. (1982) *An Introduction to the Principles of Morals and Legislation*, London: Methuen.

Berlin, I. (1969) *Four Essays on Liberty*, Oxford: Clarendon.

Bickel, A. (1962) *The Least Dangerous Branch: The Supreme Court at the Bar of Politics*, 2nd edn, New Haven: Yale University Press.

Bobbio, N. (1996) *The Age of Rights*, Cambridge: Polity.

Bohman, J. and Rehg, W. (1997) *Deliberative Democracy: Essays on Reason and Politics*, Cambridge MA: MIT Press.

Bork, R. (1990) *The Tempting of America: The Political Seduction of the Law*, New York: Free Press.

Braithwaite, J. and Drahos, P. (2000) *Global Business Regulation*, Cambridge: Cambridge University Press.

Brett, A. (1997) *Liberty, Right and Nature*, Cambridge: Cambridge University Press.

Burke, E. (1969) *Reflections on the Revolution in France*, Harmondsworth: Penguin.

Campbell, T. (1996) *The Legal Theory of Ethical Positivism*, Aldershot: Dartmouth.

Campbell, T., Ewing, K. and Tomkins, A. (2000), *Sceptical Essays on Human Rights*, Oxford: Oxford University Press.

Campbell, T. (2001) *Justice*, 2nd edn, London: Palgrave.

Campbell, T. (2004) *Prescriptive Legal Positivism: Law, Rights and Democracy*, London: UCL Press.

Chatterjee D. K. and Scheid, D. E. (eds) (2003) *Ethics and Foreign Intervention*, Cambridge: Cambridge University Press.

Ciulla, J. B. (2000) *The Working Life: The Promise and Betrayal of Modern Work*, New York: Three Rivers Press.

Cranston, Maurice (1973) *What are Human Rights?*, London: Bodley Head.

Crawford, J (ed.) (1991) *The Rights of Peoples*, Oxford: Oxford University Press.

Davis, M. (1986) 'Harm and Retribution', *Philosophy and Public Affairs* 15: 236–266.

Dicey, A. V. (1964) *Introduction to the Study of the Law of The Constitution*, London: Macmillan.

Donaldson, T. (1989) 'Moral Minimums for Multinationals', *Ethics and International Affairs* 3: 163–82.

Donnelly, J. (1982) 'Human Rights and Human ignity: An Analytic Critique of Non-Western Conceptions of Human Rights', *American Political Science Review* 76: 303–16.

Donnelly, J. (1998) *International Human Rights*, Denver: Westview Press.

Douzinas, C. (2000) *The End of Human Rights: Critical Legal Thought at the Turn of the Century*, Oxford: Hart.

Dryzek, J. (1996) *Democracy in Capitalist Times: Ideals, Limits and Struggles*, Oxford: Oxford University Press.

Dryzek, J. (2000) *Deliberative Democracy and beyond: Liberals, Critics and Contestations*, Oxford: Oxford University Press.

Dworkin, R. M. (1977) *Taking Rights Seriously*, London: Duckworth.

Dworkin, R. M. (1986) *Law's Empire*, London: Fontana.

Dworkin, R. M. (1990) *A Bill of Rights for Britain*, London: Chatto.

Edmundson, W. A. (2004) *Introduction to Rights*, Cambridge: Cambridge University Press.

Ely, J. H. (1980) *Democracy and Distrust: a Theory of Judicial Review*, Cambridge MA: Harvard University Press.

Falk, R. A. (2000) *Human Rights Horizons: the Pursuit of Justice in a Globalizing World*, New York: Routledge.

Feinberg, J. (1970) 'The Nature and Value of Rights', *Journal of Value Inquiry* 4: 63–267.

Feinberg, J. (1973) *Social Philosophy*, Englewood Cliffs: Prentice Hall.

Feinberg, J. (1980) *Rights, Justice and the Bounds of Liberty*, Princeton: Princeton University Press.

Finnis, J. (1980) *Natural Law and Natural Rights*, Oxford: Oxford University Press.

Flathman, R. E. (1976) *The Practice of Rights*, Cambridge: Cambridge University Press.

Forsythe, D. P. (2000) *Human Rights in International Relations*, Cambridge: Cambridge University Press.

Freeden, M. (1991) *Rights*, Milton Keynes: Open University Press.

Freeman, M. (2000) *Human Rights*, Cambridge: Polity.

Freeman, S. (1990) 'Constitutional Democracy and the Legitimacy of Judicial Review', *Law and Philosophy* 9: 327–370.

Frey, R. G. (1980) *Interests and Rights: The Case Against Animals*, Oxford: Clarendon Press.

Fukuyama, F. F. (1995) *Trust: The Social Virtues and the Creation of Prosperity*, London: Hamish Hamilton.

Fuller, L. L. (1969) *The Morality of Law*, New Haven: Yale University Press.

Galligan, B. and Sampford C. (1997) *Rethinking Human Rights*, Sydney: Federation Press.

Gauthier, D. (1986) *Morals By Agreement*, Oxford: Oxford University Press.

Gellner, E. (1994) *Encounters with Nationalism*, Oxford: Blackwell.

Gewirth, A. (1982) *Human Rights*, Chicago: Chicago University Press.

Ghai, Y. (1994) 'Human Rights and Governance: The Asia Debate', *Australian Year Book of International Law* 15: 1–34.

Gilligan, C. (1982) *In a Different Voice: Psychological Theory and Women's Development*, Cambridge MA: Harvard University Press.

Glendon, M. A. (1991) *Rights Talk: The Impoverishment of Political Discourse*, New York: Free Press.

Golding, M. (1984) 'The Primacy of Welfare Rights', *Social Philosophy & Policy* 1: 119–136.

Green, L. (1991) 'Two View of Collective Rights' *Canadian Journal of Law and Jurisprudence* 4: 315–27.

Griffin, J. (1986) *Well-Being: Its Meaning, Measurement and Moral Importance*, Oxford: Clarendon Press.

Griffin, J. (2001) 'Discrepancies Between the Best Philosophical Account of Human Rights and the International Law of Human Rights', *Proceedings of the Aristotelian Society* 101: 1–26.

Gutman, A. and Thompson, D. (eds) (1998) *Democracy and Disagreement*, Cambridge MA: Harvard University Press.

Habermas, J. (1996) *Between Facts and Norms*, Cambridge: Polity Press.

Hare, R. M. (1981) *Moral Thinking: Its Level, Methods and Point*, Oxford: Oxford University Press.

Harman, G. and Thomson, J. J. (1996) *Moral Relativism and Moral Objectivity*, Oxford: Blackwell.

Harrison, R. (1993) *Democracy*, London: Routledge.

Hart, H. L. A. (1957–58) 'The Separation of Law and Morals', *Harvard Law Review* 71: 593–629.

Hart, H. L. A. (1961) *The Concept of Law*, Oxford: Oxford University Press.

Hart, H. L. A. (1982) *Essays on Bentham*, Oxford: Oxford University Press.

Hartney, M. (1991) 'Some Confusions Concerning Collective Rights', *Canadian Journal of Law and Jurisprudence* 4: 293.

Held, D. (1996) *Models of Democracy*, 2nd edn, Cambridge: Polity.

Hirschman, A. O. (1997) *The Passions and Interests*, New Haven: Princeton University Press.

Hobbes, T. (1957) *Leviathon*, London: Dent.

Hobbes, T. (1996) *Leviathan*, Cambridge: Cambridge University Press.

Hohfeld, W. N. (1919) *Fundamental Legal Conceptions as Applied in Legal Reasoning*, New Haven: Yale University Press.

Holmes, S. (1995) *Passions and Certainty: On the Theory of Liberal Democracy*, Chicago: Chicago University Press.

Holmes, S. and Sunstein, C. R. (2000) *The Cost of Rights: Why Liberty Depends on Taxes*, New York: Norton.

Horowitz, M. J. (1988) 'Rights', *Harvard Civil Rights–Civil Liberties Law Review* 23: 393–406.

Hunt, P. (1996) *Reclaiming Social Rights*, Aldershot: Dartmouth.

Hutchinson, A. L. (1995) *Waiting for Coraf: a Critique of Law and Rights*, Toronto: University of Toronto Press.

Hutton, W. and Giddens, A. (eds) (2000) *On the Edge: Living in Global Capitalism*, London: Jonathan Cape.

Ignatieff, M. (2001) *Human Rights as Politics and Idolatry*, Princeton: Princeton University Press.

Jain, M. (2001) 'Judicial Protection of Human Rights in India', in Leiser, B. and Campbell, T. (eds) *Human Rights in Philosophy and Practice*, Aldershot: Dartmouth, 197–211.

Jamieson, D. (2004) *Morality's Progress: Essays on Humans and Other Animals, and the Rest of Nature*, Oxford: Oxford University Press.

Johnson, B. (ed.) (1993) *Freedom and Interpretation: the Oxford Amnesty Lectures 1992*, New York: Basic Books.

Jones, P. (1994) *Rights*, London: Macmillan.

Kamenka, E. and Tay, A. E. (eds) (1978), *Human Rights*, London: Edward Arnold.

Kamm, F. (2002) 'Rights', in *Oxford Handbook of Jurisprudences and Philosophy of Law*, Oxford: Oxford University Press, 476–513.

Kant, I. (1948) *Groundwork of the Metaphysic of Morals*, in Paton, H. (ed.) *The Moral Law*, London: Hutchinson.

Kennedy, D. (2002) 'The International Human Rights Movement: Part of the Problem?', *European Human Rights Law Review* 3: 245–267.

Kingdom, Elizabeth (1991) *What's Wrong with Rights?* Edinburgh: Edinburgh University Press.

Knowles, D. (2002) *Hegel and the Philosophy of Right*, London: Routledge.

Kramer, M. H. (ed.) (2001) *Rights, Wrongs and Responsibilities*, London: Macmillan.

Kramer, M. H., Simmonds, N. E. and Steiner, H. (1998) *A Debate Over Rights*, Oxford: Oxford University Press.

Kymlica, W. (1995) *Multicultural Citizenship: A Liberal Theory of Minority Rights*, Oxford: Clarendon.

Langton, R. (1994) 'Speech Acts and Unspeakable Acts' in Campbell, T. and Sadurski, W. (eds) *Freedom of Communication*, Aldershot: Dartmouth.

Lessnoff, M. (1986) *Social Contract*, London: Macmillan.

Levy, N. (2002) *Moral Relativism: A Short Introduction*, Oxford: Oneworld Press.

Lochner v. New York (1905) 198 U.S. 45.

Locke, J. (1988) *Two Treatises on Government*, Laslett, P. (ed.) Cambridge: Cambridge University Press.

Louglin, M. (2000) *Sword and Scales: An Examination of the Relationship Between Law and Politics*, Oxford: Hart.

Lyons, D. (1969) 'Rights, Claimants and Beneficiaries', *American Philosophical Quarterly* 6: 173–1185.

Lyons, D. (1970) 'Correlative Rights and Duties', *Nous* 4: 45–57.

Lyons, D. (1994) *Rights, Welfare and Mill's Moral Theory*, Oxford: Oxford University Press.

McBarnet, D. (2004) *Crime, Compliance and Control*, Aldershot: Ashgate.

MacCormick, D.N. (1977) 'Rights in Legislation' in Hacker, P. M. S. and Raz, J. (eds) *Law, Morality and Society*, Oxford: Clarendon Press.

MacCormick, D. N. (1982) *Legal Right and Social Democracy*, Oxford: Clarendon.

McCorquodale, R. (1994) 'Self-Determination: A Human Rights Approach', *International and Comparative Law Quarterly* 43: 857–85.

McDonald, L. (1998) 'Can Collective and Individual Rights Coexist?', *Melbourne University Law Review* 22: 310–36.

McDonald, M. (1991) 'Should Communities Have Rights? Reflections on Liberal Individualism', *Canadian Journal of Law and Jurisprudence* 4: 217.

Macfarlane, L. J. (1985) *The Theory and Practice of Human Rights*, Hounslow: Temple Smith.

MacIntyre, A. (1981) *After Virtue*, London: Duckworth.

Mackie, J. (1977) *Ethics: Inventing Right and Wrong*, Harmondsworth: Penguin.

MacKinnon, C. (1989) *Towards a Feminist Theory of State*. Cambridge MA: Harvard University Press.

Macpherson, C. B. (1962) *The Political Theory of Possessive Individualism*, Oxford: Oxford University Press.

Mandel, D. (1989) *The Charter of Rights and the Legalisation of Politics in Canada*, Toronto: Wall and Thompson.

Martin, R. (1993) *A System of Rights*, Oxford: Clarendon.

Marx, K. (1977) *Selected Writings*, McLellan, D. (ed.), Oxford: Oxford University Press.

Meiklejohn, A. (1948) *Free Speech and its Relation to Self-Government*, New York: Harper.

Mill, J. S. (1910) *Utilitarianism, Liberty and Representative Government*, London: Everyman.

Miller, S. (2001) *Social Action: A Teleological Account*, Cambridge: Cambridge University Press.

Moore, G. E (1903) *Principia Ethica*. Cambridge: Cambridge University Press.

Moore, J. (ed.) (1997) *Hard Choices: Moral Dilemmas in Humanitarian Intervention*, Lanham MD: Rowan and Littlefield.

Mulhall P. and Swift, A. (1996) *Liberals and Communitarians*, Oxford: Blackwell.

Nagel, T. (2002) *Concealment and Exposure*, Oxford: Oxford University Press.

Nino, C. (1996) *The Constitution of Deliberative Democracy*, New Haven: Yale Univerisity Press.

Noddings, N. (1984) *Caring: A Feminist Approach to Ethics and Moral Education*, Berkeley: University of California Press.

Nozick, R. (1974) *Anarchy, State and Utopia*, Oxford: Blackwell.

Nussbaum, M. (2000) *Women and Human Development: The Capabilities Approach*, Cambridge: Cambridge University Press.

Okin, S. M. (1999) *Is Multiculturalism Good for Women?*, Princeton: Princeton University Press.

O'Neill, O. (1996) *Towards Justice and Virtue*, Cambridge: Cambridge University Press.

Organisation of African Unity (1981) 'African Charter of Human Rights and Peoples' Rights, O. A. U. Doc. CAB/ LEG/ 67/3 Rev. 5.

Paine, T. (1969) *Rights of Man*, Harmondsworth: Penguin.

Parfit, D. (1986) *Reasons and Persons*, Oxford: Oxford University Press.

Pateman, C. (1988) *The Sexual Contract*, Palo Alto: Stanford University Press.

Paul, E. F., Miller F. D. and Paul, J. (eds) (1984) *Human Rights*, Oxford: Blackwell.

Perelman, C. (1963) *The Idea of Justice and the Problem of Argument*, London: Routledge and Kegan Paul.

Pettit, P. (1997) *Republicanism: A Theory of Freedom and Government*, Oxford: Oxford University Press.

Plant, R., Lesser, H. and Taylor-Gooby, P (1980) *Political Philosophy and Social Welfare*, London: Routledge and Kegan and Paul.

Pogge, T. (1989) *Realizing Rawls*, Ithaca: Cornell University Press.

Pogge, T. (2002) *World Poverty and Human Rights*, Cambridge: Polity.

Pogge, T. (2003) 'The Right to Global Justice: Poverty as a Violation of Human Rights', UNESCO.

Pogge T. (forthcoming 2006) 'Severe poverty as a Human Rights Violation' in Pogge, T. (ed) *Freedom from Poverty as a Human Right: Who Owes What to the Very Poor?*, Oxford: Oxford University Press and Paris: UNESCO.

Posner, R. A. (1977) *Economic Analysis of Law*, Boston: Little Brown.

Post, R. C. (1991) 'Racist Speech, Democracy and the First Amendment', *William and Mary Law Review* 3: 267.

Rawls, J. (1972) *A Theory of Justice*, Oxford: Oxford University Press.

Rawls, J. (1980) 'Kantian Constructivism in Moral Theory', *Journal of Philosophy* 77.

Rawls, J. (1993) *Political Liberalism*, New York: Columbia University Press.

Rawls, J. (1993) 'The Law of Peoples' in Shute, S. and Hurley, S. (eds) *On Human Rights*, New York: Basic Books.

Rawls, J, (1995) 'Reply to Habermas', *Journal of Philosophy* 92: 132–80.

Rawls, J. (2001) *The Law of Peoples*, Cambridge MA: Harvard University Press.

Raz, J. (1975) *Practical Reason and Norms*, London: Hutchinson.

Raz, J. (1979) *The Authority of Law: Essays on Law and Philosophy*, Oxford: Oxford University Press.

Raz, J. (1984) 'Legal Rights', *Oxford Journal of Legal Studies* 4: 1–21.

Raz, J. (1986) *The Morality of Freedom*, Oxford: Oxford University Press.

Raz, J. (1994) *Ethics and the Public Domain*, Oxford: Oxford University Press.

Richards, D. A. J. (1986) *Toleration and the Constitution*, New York: Oxford University Press.

Risse, T., Ropp S. C. and Sikkink, K. (eds) (1999) *The Power of Human Rights*, Cambridge: Cambridge University Press.

Ritchie, D. G. (1895) *Natural Rights*, London: Swan Sonnenschein.

Ross, W. D. (1930) *The Right and the Good*, Oxford: Clarendon.

Rousseau, J. J. (1968) *The Social Contract*, Harmonsworth: Penguin.

Russell, P. H. (1991) 'Standing Up for Notwithstanding', *Alberta Law Review* 29: 293–309.

Sadurski, W. (1985) *Giving Desert its Due: Social Justice and Legal Theory*. Dordrecht: Reidel.

Sadurski, W. (1999) *Freedom of Speech and its Limits*, Dordrecht: Kluwer.

Sandel, M. (1982) *Liberalism and the Limits of Justice*, Cambridge: Cambridge University Press.

Sane, P. (2003) 'Abolishing Poverty Through the International Human Rights Framework: An Integrated Strategy', unpublished UNESCO working paper.

Sassen, S. (1996) *Losing Control? Sovereignty in an Age of Globalization*, New York: Columbia University Press.

Scanlon, T. (1972) 'A Theory of Freedom of Expression', *Philosophy and Public Affairs*, 1: 204–226.

Scanlon, T. (2003) *The Difficulty of Tolerance*, Cambridge: Cambridge University Press.

Schauer, F. (1982) *Free Speech: A Philosophical Enquiry*, Cambridge: Cambridge University Press.

Schauer, F. (1991) *Playing by the Rules: A Philosophical Examination of Rule-Based Decision-Making*, Oxford: Clarendon.

Schauer, F. (1994), Free Speech in a World of Private Power' in Campbell, T. and Sadurski, W. (eds) *Freedom of Communication*, Aldershot: Dartmouth.

Schumpeter, J. A. (1950) *Capitalism, Socialism and Democracy*, New York: Harper and Row.

Searle, J. (1969) *Speech Acts: An Essay in the Philosophy of Language*, Cambridge: Cambridge University Press.

Sen, A. (1999) *Development as Freedom*, New York: Knopf.

Shapiro I. and Kymlica, W. (eds) (1997) *Ethnicity and Group Rights*, New York: New York University Press.

Shklar, J. (1986) *Legalism*, Cambridge, MA: Harvard University Press.

Shue, H. (1996) *Basic Rights: Subsistence, Affluence and US Foreign Policy*, 2nd edition, Princeton: Princeton University Press.

Shute, S. and Hurley S. (eds) (1993) *On Human Rights*, New York: Basic Books.

Simma, B. and Alston, P. (1992) 'The Sources of Human Rights: Custom, Jus Cogens and General Principles', *Australian Yearbook of International Law* 12: 82–108.

Simpson, G. J.(ed) (2004) *International Criminal Courts*, Aldershot: Ashgate.

Singer, P. (1975) *Animal Liberation*, London: Jonathan Cape.

Singer, P. (1993) *Practical Ethics*, Cambridge: Cambridge University Press.

Smith, A. (1976) *The Wealth of Nations*, Oxford: Clarendon.

Steiner, H. J. and Alston, P. (1996) *International Human Rights in Context*, Oxford: Oxford University Press.

Steiner, P. (1994) *An Essay on Rights*, Oxford: Blackwell.

Stiglitz, J. (2002) *Civilization and its Discontents*, Harmondsworth: Penguin.

Sumner, L. W. (1987) *The Moral Foundation of Rights*, Oxford: Clarendon.

Swift, A. (2001) *Political Philosophy*, Cambridge: Polity.

Taylor, C.(1985) *Philosophical Papers*, Cambridge: Cambridge University Press.

Taylor, C. (1997) 'Nationalism and Modernity' in McKim, R. and McMahan, J. (eds) *The Morality of Nationalism*, New York: Oxford University Press, 31–55.

Teson, F. R. (1985) 'International Human Rights and Cultural Relativism', *Virginia Journal of International Law* 25: 869–98.

Thomson, J. J. (1990) *The Realm of Rights*, Cambridge MA, Harvard University Press.

Tierney, B. (1997) *The Idea of Natural Rights*, Atlanta: Scholars Press.

Tobin, J, (1978) 'A Proposal for International Monetary Reform' *Eastern Economic Journal* 4:153–59.
Tribe, L. (1990) *Abortion: The Clash of Absolutes*, New York: Nelson.
Tushnet, M. (1984) 'An Essay on Rights', *Texas Law Journal* 62: 1363–1409.
Tuck, R. (1979) *Natural Rights Theories: Their Origin and Development*, Cambridge: Cambridge University Press.
Unger, P. (1999), *Living High and Letting Die: Our Illusion of Innocence*, Oxford: Oxford University Press.
Unger, R. M. (1996) *What Should Legal Analysis Become?* New York: Verso.
United Nations (1948) Universal Declaration of Human Rights, GA Res 217A (III).
United Nations (1965) Convention on the Elimination of All Forms of Racial Discrimination, 660 UNTS 195.
United Nations (1996a) International Convenant on Civil and Political Rights, 999 UNTS 171.
United Nations (1996b) International Covenant on Social, Economic and Cultural Rights, 999 UNTS 3.
United Nations (1979) Convention on the Elimination of All Forms of Discrimination Against Women, 1249 UNTS 13.
United Nations (1989) Convention of the Rights of the Child, GA Res 44/25.
Vlastos, G. (1962) 'Justice and Equity' in Brandt, R. B. (ed.) *Social Justice*, Englewood Cliff: Prentice Hall, pp. 31–72.
Waldron, J. (1981) 'A Right to Do Wrong', *Ethics* 92: 21–39.
Waldron, J. (ed.) (1984) *Theories of Rights*, Oxford: Oxford University Press.
Waldron, J. (1987) *Nonsense Upon Stilts: Bentham, Burke and Marx on the Rights of Man*, London: Methuen
Waldron, J. (1989) 'The Rule of Law in Contemporary Legal Theory, *Ratio Juris* 2: 79–96.
Waldron, J. (1990) *The Law*, London: Routledge.
Waldron, J. (1993) *Liberal Rights*, Cambridge: Cambridge University Press.
Waldron, J. (1999) *Law and Disagreement*. Oxford: Oxford University Press.
Weber, M. (1964) *Social and Economic Organization*, Glencoe: Free Press.
Weinrib, E. (1989) 'Understanding Tort Law', *Valparaiso Law Review* 23: 486–526.
Wellman, C. (1975) 'Upholding Legal Rights', *Ethics* 86: 49–60.
Wellman, C. (1985) A *Theory of Rights*, Totowa: Rowman and Allanheld.
Wellman, C. (1995) *Real Rights*, Oxford: Oxford University Press.
Wellman, C. (1998) *The Proliferation of Rights: Moral Progress or Empty Rhetoric?* Boulder: Westview Press.
West, R. L. (2003) *Re-Imagining Justice*, Aldershot: Ashgate.
White, A. R. (1984) *Rights*, Oxford: Clarendon.
Williams, M. (2000) *Voice, Trust and Memory*, New Haven: Princeton University Press.
Wolff, J. (1996) *Introduction to Political Philosophy*, Oxford: Oxford University Press.
Wollstonecraft, M. (1975) A *Vindication of the Rights of Women*, Harmondsworth: Penguin.
Young, I. M. (1990) *Justice and the Politics of Difference*, Princeton: Princeton University Press.

Index